IT'S MORE THAN A JOURNAL, IT'S A JOURNEY
DON'T SKIP THIS IMPORTANT STUFF!!

Welcome to the most helpful journal you will ever own! This is the ONLY journal on the planet that not only gives you space to jot your thoughts, but it provides daily tips on topics including mental and physical health, happy hacks, managing stress, college and life success tips, myths, manners and even links to some of the best TED Talks ever! Our goal is to get inside your head (in a good way!). The stuff in here can literally rewire your brain for more positivity. Let's do this!

Want to be the best student you can be? It starts with positivity. Practicing positivity and creating new happiness habits gets us into a fresh optimistic frame of mind, which shifts the way we think and see others and the world around us. Findings from neuroscience show that positivity turns on all the learning centers in the brain. That's right, improvements all around, from energy and accuracy to creativity and productivity. Not to mention happiness leads to more success at work, school, health, friendship, sociability and happier people are even viewed as more attractive! Sheesh! This journal is life-changing!! (Pssst! Only if you use it consistently).

What's up with happiness? Happiness isn't just a current craze—it's a way of being. The Greeks defined happiness as the joy we feel as we move toward our potential. It's possible to experience so much joy in your college journey (along with struggles, stress, and all kinds of other emotions we'll tackle) as you pursue the path of your potential!

Dr. Martin Seligman, a pioneer in the field of positive psychology, laid out three types of happiness that are important to know, right from the get-go.

The first type, called "the pleasant life," is all about enjoying the little things. It's about spending time with loved ones, doing things you enjoy, and taking time to appreciate the simple joys in life like your favorite dessert or celebrating your team's big win. These things bring happiness in bursts, like little sparks of joy.

The second type, "the good life," goes deeper. It's about using your strengths and talents to do things that really matter to you. It's about setting goals that you care about and working towards them, which gives you a sense of purpose and satisfaction.

The third type of happiness, "the meaningful life," is about connecting to something bigger than yourself. It's about making a difference in the world, whether through helping others or expressing yourself creatively. This path brings a lasting sense of fulfillment and meaning, like you're part of something bigger.

Seligman believes that the happiest people on the planet find ways to blend all three of these types of happiness together. As you enjoy your college journey, remember it's about enjoying life's simple pleasures, using your gifts and talents in meaningful ways, and making a difference in the world. When you can do all three, you're on the path to real happiness and meaning.

How is this journal different?

For starters, it's technically a 2-year journal. Every page has a space at the top for the current date and journal entry. The bottom half of the page is to write in the following year on the same date. So, you'll go through the journal twice. One year of writing just on the top half of each page and the next year writing (and reviewing what you wrote last year) on the bottom half of each page.

Each day of the week you'll have some type of tip or prompt at the top. This is where the manners, stress busters, myths, happy hacks and TED Talk QR codes (and more) are found.

Next is the main journaling space. You're going to have some pretty awesome days ahead, and, let's be honest, some dark and difficult days as well. Remember, both are important to write about. And we included some bonus blank lined pages in the back if you have more to write on some days!

That's why we created two different writing sections—one for Memories Made and another for Tough Times and Lessons Learned. For Memories Made, in addition to writing down what you did that day, make a list of the good things that happened that day. Jot down what made you feel happy or peaceful. Maybe you learned a new idea in class or enjoyed a great chat with a friend. Take good notes about your feelings as well as events.

The Tough Times and Lessons Learned section is also important! But here's the caution: Emotions related to anger, sadness, stress, and fear are powerful. We can easily be consumed by them, and they can feel suffocating, drowning out any sight of light, hope or happiness. So, go ahead and write about the dark and difficult days AND also write down Lessons Learned from those Tough Times. Are you more resilient? More grateful? More humble? Did you learn patience? Have a new perspective? Hey, maybe the sting and pain of the experience is too raw to write about right now. That's okay. You can come back later and write about your lessons learned and how you've grown from them.

We hope you will also use the space in Lessons Learned to capture everyday lessons you learn in life. Maybe you learned that packing an umbrella around on stormy days is important ;) or that cramming the night before a test isn't the best. Or washing something red in with your white clothes is not a good idea, but removing your chapstick from your jeans before washing them is a great idea. Or maybe you learned that hot fudge with vanilla ice cream and Oreos is a game changer! This is the space to write down all kinds of lessons learned.

So, we have a suggestion for you. Knowing you are going to have some awesome epic days ahead, we recommend that you fold down (dog ear) the top corner of what you would consider your absolute best days of the year. That way you can find them more easily. Then come back frequently and reread and relive them!

Likewise, when you have one of your most difficult days we talked about earlier, fold the bottom corner of the page. That way you can come back to the difficult days later on and easily find them and write about your lessons learned, perhaps later on when you're feeling up to it. Make sense? Below the space for journaling you'll find a line for you to <u>write down something you are grateful for that day</u>. Did you know you can only be grateful in four areas? People, places, experiences, and things. So, fill in that blank, but be specific! Think about it and make it different each day.

Why is gratitude on every page such a big deal? Gratitude is closely linked to optimism (and a bazillion other things) and you'll need that when life and school gets stressful. Plus, what you focus on grows—literally the part of the brain that processes thoughts and memories linked to positivity is strengthened when you focus on gratitude. Here's the main point: We believe you will only be as happy as you are grateful.

Gratitude has been called the parent of all other virtues. Really think about what you are grateful for. Soak it in for a few seconds. Having a built-in gratitude prompt every day trains your brain to scan for positives around you and writing them down helps cement them in your brain.

> *"We know from studies that gratitude helps us recover from loss and trauma. It helps us deal with the slow drip of everyday stress, as well as the massive personal upheavals in the face of suffering and pain and loss and trials and tribulations. Gratitude is absolutely essential. It's part of our psychological immune system."* - Dr. Robert Emmons

However, the same thing is true with negativity, anxiety, stress and worry. When we are consumed with those emotions then we are more likely to notice things that irritate and stress us out, and our negativity bias grows.

The primary principle? We remember what we rehearse and review in our heads. This journal is about remembering, rehearsing, and reviewing the good (and the tough learning experiences) in your life and creating new neural networks that lead to flourishing in your personal life, school, and relationships.

Why is journaling regularly such a big deal?

I'm glad you asked! The research on the benefits of journaling has exploded in recent years. But here's the kicker—consistency and sincerity are key!

Take your time and don't rush it (we get it, some days are crazy busy and you won't have time or you'll forget, but come back to it!). The research crammed in this journal is like a toothbrush, it will only work if you use it regularly!

Remember, journaling isn't just about penning your day; it's a powerful tool for boosting your mental, emotional, and even physical well-being. Here's how research paints just a few of the numerous advantages:

Emotional and mental benefits:
- Reduced stress and anxiety: Writing down worries and negative thoughts can help to process them and release their emotional hold. Studies have shown journaling can

lead to lower levels of cortisol, a stress hormone.
- Improved mood and well-being: Expressing gratitude, reflecting on positive experiences, and setting goals can boost mood and cultivate a more optimistic outlook.
- Enhanced self-awareness: Journaling provides a space for introspection and reflection, helping you understand your thoughts, feelings, and motivations better.
- Increased resilience: By processing challenges and setbacks through journaling, you can develop coping mechanisms and build emotional resilience.
- Sharper memory and cognitive function: Regularly writing down thoughts and experiences can strengthen memory and cognitive skills.

Physical health benefits:
- Improved sleep quality: Journaling before bed can help to clear your mind and promote relaxation, leading to better sleep.
- Reduced blood pressure: Studies suggest that journaling can lower blood pressure, potentially due to its stress-reducing effects.
- Enhanced immune function: Research indicates that journaling might boost the immune system, possibly by reducing stress and promoting positive emotions.
- Pain management: Writing about chronic pain can help individuals cope with pain and improve their quality of life.

Additional benefits:
- Increased creativity: Journaling can be a springboard for creative expression and exploration of ideas.
- Improved communication skills: The practice of writing regularly can enhance your ability to express yourself clearly and concisely.
- Greater self-motivation: Reflecting on goals and progress through journaling can boost motivation and commitment to achieving them.

These are just a few of the dozens of benefits that research continues to reveal that stem from journaling. And we've made it as simple as we could: give you some daily inspiration, space to jot your thoughts, write what you are grateful for, and rate your day!

Who created this awesome journal anyway?

Big-Time Books and this journal specifically was created by "Dr. Dave" and two of his college-age daughters—Mallory and Aubrey. Dr. Dave Schramm is a family life professor and Extension Specialist at Utah State University. Drawing on his own research and decades of research on positivity, happiness, and meaning, he created and compiled many of the tips related to happiness and managing stress. Two of his three daughters attended Utah State and together they have all kinds of experience and tips to help you flourish in your college journey. This journal is just like taking a class in positivity—great research-backed facts and tips with some reading, reflecting, writing, and practicing.

We're in the business of helping people create a flourishing life. It starts with a more positive mindset, including happier thoughts. One of the traditions we started as a family with four children more than 20 years ago is sharing what we call "happy thoughts" at nighttime, right before we tucked our kids in bed. Nearly every night we said a family prayer together and then we each took turns thinking about and sharing something that happened that day that made us happy. Why? Because I knew about the research on positivity and happiness. When our brains review the day for happy times, we share them, and listen to other family members share happy thoughts, we all benefit (and sleep better).

Shawn Achor wrote about it this way, "an avalanche of studies had shown that happy thoughts, no matter the source, lead people to be more productive, more likable, more active, more healthy, more friendly, more helpful, more resilient, and more creative." (p. 265, The Happiness Advantage). And who doesn't want that!?

Our hope is that you will commit to going "all in" and try some of the suggestions and tips. You may find some of them very helpful. Others, not so much. And that's okay. Not all of the ideas will "stick." Find the ones that do. Commit to doing more of the things that work. Remember, information doesn't lead to transformation until there is installation and activation!

Enjoy this college journey while it lasts. The years go fast!

>Let's get started!

DATE: _____   (S) (M) (T) (W) (T) (F) (S)

MONDAY MANNERS:

> *Respect what others love. You don't have to like everything, but avoid putting down their interests, even as a joke. Mocking what someone enjoys creates disconnection. If someone loves baseball, no need to call it stupid. If a friend enjoys a place you didn't prefer, don't rattle off its flaws. If a roommate likes a restaurant, don't say it's gross. Those kinds of comments turn people off immediately. Instead, stay quiet or ask what they love about it. Differing opinions are okay, but expressing disgust for others' loves hurts feelings. Approach their interests with curiosity, not judgment.*

(Callout: Dog-ear the top corner of your BEST days to find them easier!)

(Callout: Each day has a different tip at the top to improve your life!)

MEMORIES MADE: _____
_____
_____
_____
_____
_____

TOUGH TIMES & LESSONS LEARNED: _____
_____
_____

(Callout: Make this specific and different every day!)

What are you grateful for today?
_____

(Callout: Don't forget your daily mood tracker!)

😫 😠 😴 🙁 🙂 😆

REMEMBER! WAIT TO WRITE BELOW UNTIL THIS DAY NEXT YEAR!

DATE: _____   (S) (M) (T) (W) (T) (F) (S)

MEMORIES MADE: Journal in this space one year from the date above!
Be sure to review how things were going one year ago today!
_____
_____
_____
_____

TOUGH TIMES & LESSONS LEARNED: _____
_____
_____

What are you grateful for today?

(Callout: Dog-ear the bottom corners of your most challenging days to find them easier!)

😫 😠 😴 🙁 🙂 😆

Did you know that the brain's synapses change at a rapid pace and can reflect new experiences and learning, especially prominent during college years due to exposure to diverse new ideas and knowledge?

DATE: _____

These first few pages are here for you to write down some things you don't want to forget, like roommates' names, classes, and instructors, as well as your GPS to guide you in your college journey (Goals for Personal Success!).

WHERE DO YOU LIVE? HOW MUCH IS IT PER MONTH? _____

ROOMMATES? NAMES AND INFO YOU DON'T WANT TO FORGET:

_____
_____
_____
_____
_____
_____
_____
_____
_____
_____

CLASSES: (Circle or highlight your favorite classes and instructors!)

COURSE TITLE	SEMESTER	INSTRUCTOR	GRADE

DATE: _____

Goals for Personal Success (G.P.S.)

Deciding to do something actually changes how your brain sees the world. To make your life better, first decide what you want to do, then make a plan to get it done.

WHAT ARE YOUR CAREER GOALS AS OF RIGHT NOW? _____
_____
_____
_____

WHAT ARE YOU GOING TO DO MORE OR LESS OF TO BECOME BETTER THIS YEAR?
_____
_____
_____

WHAT CLUBS OR STUDENT ORGANIZATIONS ARE YOU INTERESTED IN JOINING, AND WHY?
_____
_____
_____

DESCRIBE YOUR CURRENT HEALTH/WELLNESS HABITS. WHAT CHANGES ARE YOU MAKING?
_____
_____
_____

WHAT SPECIFIC FINANCIAL GOALS DO YOU HAVE FOR THIS YEAR? (SAVING / SPENDING)
_____
_____
_____

IDENTIFY ONE OR TWO SKILLS YOU WANT TO DEVELOP OR IMPROVE UPON THIS YEAR
_____
_____
_____

ENVISION YOURSELF FIVE YEARS FROM NOW. DESCRIBE YOUR IDEAL PERSONAL AND PROFESSIONAL LIFE. WHAT STEPS CAN YOU TAKE NOW TO MOVE CLOSER TO THIS VISION?
_____
_____
_____
_____
_____

DATE: _____   (S) (M) (T) (W) (T) (F) (S)

MONDAY MANNERS:

> " Respect what others love. You don't have to like everything, but avoid putting down their interests, even as a joke. Criticizing someone's passion creates disconnection. If someone loves baseball, no need to call it stupid. If a friend is from a place you didn't enjoy, don't rattle off its flaws. If a roommate likes a restaurant, don't say it's gross. Those kinds of comments turn people off immediately. Instead, stay quiet or ask what they love about it. Differing opinions are okay, but expressing disgust for others' loves hurts feelings. Approach their interests with curiosity, not judgment. "

MEMORIES MADE: _____
_____
_____
_____
_____
_____

TOUGH TIMES & LESSONS LEARNED: _____
_____
_____
_____
_____

What are you grateful for today?   Stressed Angry Tired Sad Happy Excited
_____

> REMEMBER! WAIT TO WRITE BELOW UNTIL THIS DAY NEXT YEAR!

DATE: _____   (S) (M) (T) (W) (T) (F) (S)

MEMORIES MADE: _____
_____
_____
_____
_____
_____

TOUGH TIMES & LESSONS LEARNED: _____
_____
_____
_____
_____

What are you grateful for today?   Stressed Angry Tired Sad Happy Excited
_____

Did you know that the phrase "tie the knot" is commonly believed to come from ancient customs where couples' hands were bound together as a symbol of their union. It now means to get married!

DATE: _____ S M T W T F S

TUESDAY TIPS:

> "Attend orientation to get acquainted with the campus and resources. In fact, attend as many of the meetings as you can to learn about different majors, programs, clubs and opportunities. Knowing the lay of the land is a critical first step for success. Get up, get out, and get to know all you can!"

MEMORIES MADE: _____
_____
_____
_____
_____
_____

TOUGH TIMES & LESSONS LEARNED: _____
_____
_____
_____
_____

What are you grateful for today?   Stressed Angry Tired Sad Happy Excited
_____

REMEMBER! WAIT TO WRITE BELOW UNTIL THIS DAY NEXT YEAR!

DATE: _____ S M T W T F S

MEMORIES MADE: _____
_____
_____
_____
_____
_____

TOUGH TIMES & LESSONS LEARNED: _____
_____
_____
_____
_____

What are you grateful for today?   Stressed Angry Tired Sad Happy Excited
_____

Did you know that frequent multitasking, like switching between study materials and social media, can reduce productivity and impair cognitive control, a crucial skill for effective studying?

DATE: _____ (S) (M) (T) (W) (T) (F) (S)

WEDNESDAY (HUMP DAY!) HAPPY HACKS

> It's time to discover your signature strengths. We're not talking about things like singing and dancing. Scan the QR code and take the time (it's free) to complete the assessment and then jot down your 5 signature strengths!
>
> 1.   4.
> 2.   5.
> 3.

MEMORIES MADE: _____
_____
_____
_____
_____
_____

TOUGH TIMES & LESSONS LEARNED: _____
_____
_____
_____
_____

What are you grateful for today?
_____

Stressed   Angry   Tired   Sad   Happy   Excited

REMEMBER! WAIT TO WRITE BELOW UNTIL THIS DAY NEXT YEAR!

DATE: _____ (S) (M) (T) (W) (T) (F) (S)

MEMORIES MADE: _____
_____
_____
_____
_____
_____

TOUGH TIMES & LESSONS LEARNED: _____
_____
_____
_____
_____

What are you grateful for today?
_____

Stressed   Angry   Tired   Sad   Happy   Excited

Did you know? How you choose to start your day can have a profound impact on the rest of your day? One study showed those watching just 3 minutes of negative news in the morning were more likely to rate their entire day as a bad day some 6-8 hours later.

DATE: _____ (S) (M) (T) (W) (T) (F) (S)

THURSDAY MYTHS:

> " Myth: "I must choose a major immediately and stick to it."
>
> Reality: Many students change their major. College is a journey of discovery. It's okay to start with an undeclared major and explore different classes. Think of your first year as a buffet – try different things before filling up your plate. "

MEMORIES MADE: _____
_____
_____
_____
_____
_____

TOUGH TIMES & LESSONS LEARNED: _____
_____
_____
_____
_____

What are you grateful for today?   Stressed Angry Tired Sad Happy Excited
_____

↳ REMEMBER! WAIT TO WRITE BELOW UNTIL THIS DAY NEXT YEAR!

DATE: _____ (S) (M) (T) (W) (T) (F) (S)

MEMORIES MADE: _____
_____
_____
_____
_____
_____

TOUGH TIMES & LESSONS LEARNED: _____
_____
_____
_____
_____

What are you grateful for today?   Stressed Angry Tired Sad Happy Excited
_____

Did you know? Establishing a regular sleep schedule, even on weekends, helps regulate your circadian rhythm and promotes deeper, more restful sleep. Be consistent for better sleep!

DATE:_____ S M T W T F S

FRIDAY FILL IN THE BLANKS:

> What do you miss about living at home?_____
> _____
> _____
>
> What do you enjoy most about living away from home?_____
> _____

MEMORIES MADE:_____
_____
_____
_____
_____

TOUGH TIMES & LESSONS LEARNED:_____
_____
_____
_____

What are you grateful for today?   Stressed   Angry   Tired   Sad   Happy   Excited
_____

REMEMBER! WAIT TO WRITE BELOW UNTIL THIS DAY NEXT YEAR!

DATE:_____ S M T W T F S

MEMORIES MADE:_____
_____
_____
_____
_____

TOUGH TIMES & LESSONS LEARNED:_____
_____
_____
_____

What are you grateful for today?   Stressed   Angry   Tired   Sad   Happy   Excited
_____

Did you know? Playing music, even at a basic level, can boost cognitive function and delay age-related decline! Pick up an instrument, keep your neurons dancing!

DATE: _____ (S) (M) (T) (W) (T) (F) (S)

SATURDAY TED TALKS:

> The TED talk "What Makes a Good Life?" by Robert Waldinger discusses the longest study on happiness and emphasizes that strong personal relationships are the most significant predictor of a person's happiness and longevity, surpassing wealth and fame. The 75-year study finds that close connections with family, friends, and community offer better mental and physical health and longer lifespans. Quality relationships protect against life's discontents, help to delay mental and physical decline, and are better indicators of happy and fulfilled lives than social status or wealth. Investing in relationships is key to a good life. Get to know some new friends and stay in touch with your former friends!

MEMORIES MADE: _____
_____
_____
_____
_____
_____

TOUGH TIMES & LESSONS LEARNED: _____
_____
_____
_____
_____

What are you grateful for today?   Stressed Angry Tired Sad Happy Excited
_____

> REMEMBER! WAIT TO WRITE BELOW UNTIL THIS DAY NEXT YEAR!

DATE: _____ (S) (M) (T) (W) (T) (F) (S)

MEMORIES MADE: _____
_____
_____
_____
_____
_____

TOUGH TIMES & LESSONS LEARNED: _____
_____
_____
_____
_____

What are you grateful for today?   Stressed Angry Tired Sad Happy Excited
_____

Did you know? The most common undergraduate major in the United States is Business Administration, reflecting trends in the job market and student interests.

DATE: _____ (S) (M) (T) (W) (T) (F) (S)

SUNDAY STRESS BUSTERS:

> Stress. To share or not to share? Is complaining or sharing your stress with others helpful? It depends! Some research suggests when we complain to just "get it off our chests" then it may not be helpful. Like a scab, when we continue to dig and poke at a wound, it tends to make things worse when we complain about stress, causing more stress and worry. However, sharing your stress and complaints with others may be helpful in some situations if the person is helpful in processing the situation, helps you see different perspectives, helps you find the positive and/or helps you think about what you can do about it moving forward. The goal is to move past the complaint to processing what to do next or how to respond.

MEMORIES MADE: _____
_____
_____
_____
_____
_____

TOUGH TIMES & LESSONS LEARNED: _____
_____
_____
_____
_____

What are you grateful for today?   Stressed Angry Tired Sad Happy Excited
_____

REMEMBER! WAIT TO WRITE BELOW UNTIL THIS DAY NEXT YEAR!

DATE: _____ (S) (M) (T) (W) (T) (F) (S)

MEMORIES MADE: _____
_____
_____
_____
_____
_____

TOUGH TIMES & LESSONS LEARNED: _____
_____
_____
_____
_____

What are you grateful for today?   Stressed Angry Tired Sad Happy Excited
_____

Did you know? Watching inspirational or motivational content can boost positivity and provide a helpful perspective shift during challenging times in college.

DATE: _____ (S) (M) (T) (W) (T) (F) (S)

MONDAY MANNERS:

> Watch for the "one." Leaving out just one person is unkind. Be the one who makes room and includes others. If you have an issue with someone, talk to them instead of avoiding them. Imagine being in their shoes; someday, you might be left out too. Remember, there's space for one more. You can't always invite everyone, but leaving out one person is hurtful. Don't exclude someone from group messages or plans. You wouldn't want to be remembered as the person who made others feel small or unwanted. It's much better to be remembered for your kindness than your greatness.

MEMORIES MADE: _____
_____
_____
_____
_____

TOUGH TIMES & LESSONS LEARNED: _____
_____
_____
_____
_____

What are you grateful for today?
_____

Stressed | Angry | Tired | Sad | Happy | Excited

REMEMBER! WAIT TO WRITE BELOW UNTIL THIS DAY NEXT YEAR!

DATE: _____ (S) (M) (T) (W) (T) (F) (S)

MEMORIES MADE: _____
_____
_____
_____
_____

TOUGH TIMES & LESSONS LEARNED: _____
_____
_____
_____
_____

What are you grateful for today?
_____

Stressed | Angry | Tired | Sad | Happy | Excited

Did you know? Spending time in nature, even just 20 minutes in a park, can significantly lower stress hormones and boost mood. Immerse yourself in the healing power of green spaces!

DATE: _____   S M T W T F S

TUESDAY TIPS:

> Give yourself grace – mistakes are normal! Many incoming college students put immense pressure on themselves, feeling like they need to be perfect. However, research shows that college freshmen who were told it's normal to forget some assignments and fail some tests were actually less likely to do so than a control group. Knowing that mistakes and setbacks are a natural part of the learning process can prevent students from falling into a downward spiral of anxiety and self-doubt. Embrace the fact that you don't have to be perfect – mistakes are normal, and they're an important part of growth and learning. Give yourself the grace to stumble occasionally, and focus on progress, not perfection.

MEMORIES MADE: _____
_____
_____
_____
_____
_____

TOUGH TIMES & LESSONS LEARNED: _____
_____
_____
_____
_____

What are you grateful for today?   Stressed Angry Tired Sad Happy Excited
_____

REMEMBER! WAIT TO WRITE BELOW UNTIL THIS DAY NEXT YEAR!

DATE: _____   S M T W T F S

MEMORIES MADE: _____
_____
_____
_____
_____
_____

TOUGH TIMES & LESSONS LEARNED: _____
_____
_____
_____
_____

What are you grateful for today?   Stressed Angry Tired Sad Happy Excited
_____

Did you know? Teaching someone else is the ultimate study hack! Explaining concepts verbally strengthens your own understanding and identifies areas needing clarity. Bonus points for forming study groups - shared knowledge is doubled power!

DATE: _____ (S) (M) (T) (W) (T) (F) (S)

WEDNESDAY (HUMP DAY!) HAPPY HACKS:

> Gratitude. This one is HUGE. So huge that there are going to be different types of happy hacks that focus on gratitude. Let's start with this one. Write down and reflect on 3 good things that happened today and why they happened. Try it every day for a week or two. The key is to be specific and jot down something different each time. Don't rush through it. Positivity is boosted in the process not in just going through the motions.
> 1.
> 2.
> 3.

MEMORIES MADE: _____
_____
_____
_____
_____
_____
_____

TOUGH TIMES & LESSONS LEARNED: _____
_____
_____
_____
_____

What are you grateful for today?   Stressed Angry Tired Sad Happy Excited
_____

REMEMBER! WAIT TO WRITE BELOW UNTIL THIS DAY NEXT YEAR!

DATE: _____ (S) (M) (T) (W) (T) (F) (S)

MEMORIES MADE: _____
_____
_____
_____
_____
_____
_____

TOUGH TIMES & LESSONS LEARNED: _____
_____
_____
_____
_____

What are you grateful for today?   Stressed Angry Tired Sad Happy Excited
_____

Did you know? Humans make approximately 35,000 conscious decisions every day, ranging from simple choices like what to eat for breakfast to more complex decisions like how to manage tasks at work or school. No wonder you're so tired!

DATE: _____ (S) (M) (T) (W) (T) (F) (S)

THURSDAY MYTHS:

> Myth: "I'll make lifelong friends in the first week."
>
> Reality: Building deep friendships takes time. While you might meet a lot of people quickly, finding your close circle can be a gradual process. Be patient, and keep smiling. It's like making sour dough bread – it can't be rushed.

MEMORIES MADE: _____
_____
_____
_____
_____
_____

TOUGH TIMES & LESSONS LEARNED: _____
_____
_____
_____
_____

What are you grateful for today?   Stressed Angry Tired Sad Happy Excited
_____

👉 REMEMBER! WAIT TO WRITE BELOW UNTIL THIS DAY NEXT YEAR!

DATE: _____ (S) (M) (T) (W) (T) (F) (S)

MEMORIES MADE: _____
_____
_____
_____
_____
_____

TOUGH TIMES & LESSONS LEARNED: _____
_____
_____
_____
_____

What are you grateful for today?   Stressed Angry Tired Sad Happy Excited
_____

Did you know? Skipping meals can lead to overeating later in the day, making regular meal consumption important for managing hunger and maintaining a healthy diet.

DATE: _____ (S) (M) (T) (W) (T) (F) (S)

FRIDAY FILL IN THE BLANKS:

> Time to discover Your. Core. Four. We're talking about your values! Not things you value. It's more character traits of the person you want to be. Think about what you want people at your funeral to think and say about you. Those are your values! Want to be happier? Align your thoughts, words, and behaviors with your values. Here are a few examples of values, but look up other values or think about the person you truly want to be. Write down Your. Core. Four. Values below. Then strive to live true to these at all times and in all places! Examples: Compassion, humility, positivity, appreciation, loyalty, forgiving, generosity, kindness, honesty, hard worker, loving, selfless, integrity, trustworthy, friendly...
>
> 1.   3.
> 2.   4.

MEMORIES MADE: _____
_____
_____
_____
_____
_____

TOUGH TIMES & LESSONS LEARNED: _____
_____
_____
_____
_____

What are you grateful for today?

Stressed Angry Tired Sad Happy Excited

▼ REMEMBER! WAIT TO WRITE BELOW UNTIL THIS DAY NEXT YEAR!

DATE: _____ (S) (M) (T) (W) (T) (F) (S)

MEMORIES MADE: _____
_____
_____
_____
_____
_____

TOUGH TIMES & LESSONS LEARNED: _____
_____
_____
_____
_____

What are you grateful for today?

Stressed Angry Tired Sad Happy Excited

Did you know? Your brain's memory capacity is considered nearly limitless;
it doesn't get 'used up' like the memory on your computer or phone.

DATE: _____ (S) (M) (T) (W) (T) (F) (S)

SATURDAY TED TALKS:

> Forget chasing happiness, says Brother David Steindl-Rast in his TED Talk "Want to be happy? Be grateful." He reveals a powerful secret: gratitude is the seed of happiness. Slow down, appreciate the present, savor small joys, and cultivate an "attitude of gratitude." This mindful awareness shifts your focus from what's lacking to what's abundant, nurturing genuine joy from within. Ditch the happiness hunt, practice gratitude daily, and watch your inner garden of happiness bloom!

MEMORIES MADE: _____
_____
_____
_____
_____

TOUGH TIMES & LESSONS LEARNED: _____
_____
_____
_____
_____

What are you grateful for today?

Stressed | Angry | Tired | Sad | Happy | Excited

REMEMBER! WAIT TO WRITE BELOW UNTIL THIS DAY NEXT YEAR!

DATE: _____ (S) (M) (T) (W) (T) (F) (S)

MEMORIES MADE: _____
_____
_____
_____
_____

TOUGH TIMES & LESSONS LEARNED: _____
_____
_____
_____
_____

What are you grateful for today?

Stressed | Angry | Tired | Sad | Happy | Excited

Did you know? The only muscle that never tires is the heart, which beats around 2.5 billion times over the average lifetime. Take care of your ticker!

DATE: _____ (S) (M) (T) (W) (T) (F) (S)

SUNDAY STRESS BUSTERS:

> Research suggests that when you label an emotion ("I'm frustrated" or "I'm worried") it helps reduce the brain's automatic reactivity. So the next time you are feeling stressed, anxious, annoyed, etc., put your feelings into words. Just pause and describe them, without judging, and it will reduce the emotional intensity! It will help prevent an emotional downward spiral. It's important NOT to criticize yourself for the emotions you're experiencing. The more you practice it, the more you'll rewire your brain and the more automatic it will become. Give it a try.

MEMORIES MADE: _____
_____
_____
_____
_____

TOUGH TIMES & LESSONS LEARNED: _____
_____
_____
_____
_____

What are you grateful for today?   Stressed Angry Tired Sad Happy Excited
_____

REMEMBER! WAIT TO WRITE BELOW UNTIL THIS DAY NEXT YEAR!

DATE: _____ (S) (M) (T) (W) (T) (F) (S)

MEMORIES MADE: _____
_____
_____
_____
_____

TOUGH TIMES & LESSONS LEARNED: _____
_____
_____
_____
_____

What are you grateful for today?   Stressed Angry Tired Sad Happy Excited
_____

Did you know? Humans are the only animals with chins; no other species exhibits this distinct facial feature.

DATE: _____ (S) (M) (T) (W) (T) (F) (S)

MONDAY MANNERS:

> Don't "ghost" people! If you can't make it to something or don't want to go, learn to politely decline instead of ignoring their text or calls—the sooner the better. Use one of these options or create your own: "Thanks for the invite. Super bummed I can't make it" or "Shoot! I'm busy that night, what about next weekend?" Saying "no" can be tough, but honesty is kinder than ignoring or avoiding others. Having a few go-to phrases helps. When you flip it around and you're inviting, it's better to know if someone can't come than feeling "ghosted," right?

MEMORIES MADE: _____
_____
_____
_____
_____

TOUGH TIMES & LESSONS LEARNED: _____
_____
_____
_____

What are you grateful for today?   Stressed Angry Tired Sad Happy Excited
_____

REMEMBER! WAIT TO WRITE BELOW UNTIL THIS DAY NEXT YEAR!

DATE: _____ (S) (M) (T) (W) (T) (F) (S)

MEMORIES MADE: _____
_____
_____
_____
_____

TOUGH TIMES & LESSONS LEARNED: _____
_____
_____
_____

What are you grateful for today?   Stressed Angry Tired Sad Happy Excited
_____

Did you know? Learning to say "no" to things that drain your energy is not selfish, but an act of self-care that protects your mental and emotional health. Set boundaries for a happier you!

DATE: _____ Ⓢ Ⓜ Ⓣ Ⓦ Ⓣ Ⓕ Ⓢ

TUESDAY TIPS:

> " As a professor, I HIGHLY encourage you to sit up near the front in your classes. It can be so hard to pay attention with countless distractions. Sit up front where you don't see as many people's laptops and all the distractions and websites they're looking at. And silence your phone and other sounds on tablets and laptops while you're at it. I once paused in the middle of class when a student's phone rang out loud. I went over and answered it and told the person on the other line that she was busy and I was the professor and to call her back later⋯no I didn't really, but I should have! "

MEMORIES MADE: _____
_____
_____
_____
_____
_____

TOUGH TIMES & LESSONS LEARNED: _____
_____
_____
_____
_____

What are you grateful for today?   Stressed Angry Tired Sad Happy Excited
_____

➤ REMEMBER! WAIT TO WRITE BELOW UNTIL THIS DAY NEXT YEAR!

DATE: _____ Ⓢ Ⓜ Ⓣ Ⓦ Ⓣ Ⓕ Ⓢ

MEMORIES MADE: _____
_____
_____
_____
_____
_____

TOUGH TIMES & LESSONS LEARNED: _____
_____
_____
_____
_____

What are you grateful for today?   Stressed Angry Tired Sad Happy Excited
_____

Did you know? Studying in short, focused bursts of 25-30 minutes with 5-minute breaks in between improves concentration, retention, and recall compared to long, uninterrupted sessions.
Work smart...and hard!

DATE: _____ (S) (M) (T) (W) (T) (F) (S)

WEDNESDAY (HUMP DAY!) HAPPY HACKS

> These science-backed happy hacks really do work! But every single one might not work for YOU. Think of them as a buffet meal. All kinds of options. Try one and see if it works. Stick with the ones that you love. Try some more. The key is finding what works for you and staying consistent. Remember the acronym S.C.A.R.E.D. It stands for Small Changes Are Really Effective Daily. Today's Wednesday happy hack is choosing to go "all-in" on this journal and staying consistent. Decide to thrive by writing, thinking, and doing. You've got this. Stick with it. Consistency is key!

MEMORIES MADE: _____
_____
_____
_____
_____

TOUGH TIMES & LESSONS LEARNED: _____
_____
_____
_____

What are you grateful for today?
_____

Stressed Angry Tired Sad Happy Excited

REMEMBER! WAIT TO WRITE BELOW UNTIL THIS DAY NEXT YEAR!

DATE: _____ (S) (M) (T) (W) (T) (F) (S)

MEMORIES MADE: _____
_____
_____
_____
_____

TOUGH TIMES & LESSONS LEARNED: _____
_____
_____
_____

What are you grateful for today?
_____

Stressed Angry Tired Sad Happy Excited

Did you know that the brain's synapses change at a rapid pace and can reflect new experiences and learning, especially prominent during college years due to exposure to diverse new ideas and knowledge?

DATE: _____ (S) (M) (T) (W) (T) (F) (S)

THURSDAY MYTHS:

> Myth: "College life is non-stop fun and parties."
>
> Reality: While college offers social opportunities, it's also a place of academic challenge and personal growth. Balancing social life with studies is crucial. It's like a dance where you sometimes step on your own toes figuring out the rhythm between responsibility and fun.

MEMORIES MADE: _____
_____
_____
_____
_____
_____

TOUGH TIMES & LESSONS LEARNED: _____
_____
_____
_____
_____
_____

What are you grateful for today?
_____

Stressed | Angry | Tired | Sad | Happy | Excited

REMEMBER! WAIT TO WRITE BELOW UNTIL THIS DAY NEXT YEAR!

DATE: _____ (S) (M) (T) (W) (T) (F) (S)

MEMORIES MADE: _____
_____
_____
_____
_____
_____

TOUGH TIMES & LESSONS LEARNED: _____
_____
_____
_____
_____
_____

What are you grateful for today?
_____

Stressed | Angry | Tired | Sad | Happy | Excited

Did you know? Babies are born with 300 bones, but by adulthood, they fuse together to form 206! Your skeleton goes through quite the remodel in your lifetime.

DATE: _____ (S) (M) (T) (W) (T) (F) (S)

FRIDAY FILL IN THE BLANKS:

> When you think about what brings you joy, what are the 4 "gainers" (brings you joy) and 4 "drainers" (drains your joy)?
>
> | Gainers | Drainers |
> |---------|----------|
> | _____ | _____ |
> | _____ | _____ |
> | _____ | _____ |
> | _____ | _____ |

MEMORIES MADE: _____
_____
_____
_____
_____

TOUGH TIMES & LESSONS LEARNED: _____
_____
_____
_____

What are you grateful for today?   Stressed Angry Tired Sad Happy Excited
_____

REMEMBER! WAIT TO WRITE BELOW UNTIL THIS DAY NEXT YEAR!

DATE: _____ (S) (M) (T) (W) (T) (F) (S)

MEMORIES MADE: _____
_____
_____
_____
_____

TOUGH TIMES & LESSONS LEARNED: _____
_____
_____
_____

What are you grateful for today?   Stressed Angry Tired Sad Happy Excited
_____

Did you know? Studies show that doodling during lectures can help with concentration and memory retention, as it keeps the brain active without causing distraction.

DATE: _____ (S) (M) (T) (W) (T) (F) (S)

SATURDAY TED TALKS:

> Dan Gilbert, in his TED Talk "The surprising science of happiness," challenges our expectations. Our minds, he argues, have a "psychological immune system" that buffers emotional blows. Lottery winners and paraplegics often end up equally happy! He emphasizes that true happiness stems not from achieving goals, but from finding meaning and appreciating the journey. Let go of rigid expectations, embrace the unexpected, and watch your happiness blossom!

MEMORIES MADE: _____
_____
_____
_____
_____
_____

TOUGH TIMES & LESSONS LEARNED: _____
_____
_____
_____
_____

What are you grateful for today?
_____

Stressed | Angry | Tired | Sad | Happy | Excited

REMEMBER! WAIT TO WRITE BELOW UNTIL THIS DAY NEXT YEAR!

DATE: _____ (S) (M) (T) (W) (T) (F) (S)

MEMORIES MADE: _____
_____
_____
_____
_____
_____

TOUGH TIMES & LESSONS LEARNED: _____
_____
_____
_____
_____

What are you grateful for today?
_____

Stressed | Angry | Tired | Sad | Happy | Excited

Did you know? Respectful space is essential! Be mindful of noise levels, personal belongings, and privacy needs. Give each other breathing room for individual recharge time.

DATE: _____ (S) (M) (T) (W) (T) (F) (S)

SUNDAY STRESS BUSTERS:

> Be a friend to yourself. Don't expect yourself to be perfect. Stop doing things that tear you down. Notice the good things you do, and dwell on those things. Don't try to force yourself to be perfect or always kind. Treat your feelings with respect. Other people may sound smarter and stronger and more sure of themselves. But your feelings are important. Listen to them. Instead of dwelling on a mistake, learn what you can from it and then let the mistake go. Examine the expectations you have for yourself. Check to be sure they are reasonable.

MEMORIES MADE: _____
_____
_____
_____
_____

TOUGH TIMES & LESSONS LEARNED: _____
_____
_____
_____

What are you grateful for today?   Stressed Angry Tired Sad Happy Excited
_____

REMEMBER! WAIT TO WRITE BELOW UNTIL THIS DAY NEXT YEAR!

DATE: _____ (S) (M) (T) (W) (T) (F) (S)

MEMORIES MADE: _____
_____
_____
_____
_____

TOUGH TIMES & LESSONS LEARNED: _____
_____
_____
_____

What are you grateful for today?   Stressed Angry Tired Sad Happy Excited
_____

Did you know? The human body's cells die and are replaced so frequently that over a period of seven years, nearly all the cells in your body will have been replaced.

DATE: _____ (S) (M) (T) (W) (T) (F) (S)

MONDAY MANNERS:

> Keep your phone on silent in public. If you're watching something with sound, find a private spot, use air pods, or wait until later. This applies to TikTok, Instagram, YouTube, Netflix, games, and anything noisy. Keep it quiet. It's tempting to do what's easy, but others don't want to hear your phone noises in public. If you forget headphones, watch without sound, wait, or turn it off. Kindly remind your roommates and friends about this important manner too!

MEMORIES MADE: _____
_____
_____
_____
_____
_____

TOUGH TIMES & LESSONS LEARNED: _____
_____
_____
_____
_____

What are you grateful for today?   Stressed Angry Tired Sad Happy Excited
_____

REMEMBER! WAIT TO WRITE BELOW UNTIL THIS DAY NEXT YEAR!

DATE: _____ (S) (M) (T) (W) (T) (F) (S)

MEMORIES MADE: _____
_____
_____
_____
_____
_____

TOUGH TIMES & LESSONS LEARNED: _____
_____
_____
_____
_____

What are you grateful for today?   Stressed Angry Tired Sad Happy Excited
_____

Did you know? Your brain generates electricity, about enough to power a small light bulb! No wonder some ideas feel so bright!

DATE: _____ (S) (M) (T) (W) (T) (F) (S)

TUESDAY TIPS:

> Keep copies of your syllabi and refer to them throughout the semester. A syllabus is kind of like a map and contract. It has everything you need to succeed and professors get bugged if you have a question about a project or due date and the answer is in the syllabus. Yep, it's a bunch of boring reading but you need to understand the big picture, policies, and procedures. All of the assignments, tests, due dates, and grading should be in there. Don't irritate a professor – read the syllabus dang it!

MEMORIES MADE: _____
_____
_____
_____
_____

TOUGH TIMES & LESSONS LEARNED: _____
_____
_____
_____
_____

What are you grateful for today?   Stressed Angry Tired Sad Happy Excited
_____

REMEMBER! WAIT TO WRITE BELOW UNTIL THIS DAY NEXT YEAR!

DATE: _____ (S) (M) (T) (W) (T) (F) (S)

MEMORIES MADE: _____
_____
_____
_____
_____

TOUGH TIMES & LESSONS LEARNED: _____
_____
_____
_____
_____

What are you grateful for today?   Stressed Angry Tired Sad Happy Excited
_____

Did you know? Listening to your favorite music can instantly boost your mood, providing a simple and effective way to increase happiness during stressful study sessions.

DATE: _____ (S) (M) (T) (W) (T) (F) (S)

WEDNESDAY (HUMP DAY!) HAPPY HACKS:

> Today's happy hack is to experiment with what we call Text 2 before 10. Try texting two people every day (or even just one or two days per week — put it in your calendar as a reoccurring reminder!) a simple text of kindness or gratitude. Think to yourself, "Who needs a text from me right now…" Then notice the nudges and follow the feelings. A name or a face will appear in your mind. Send that person a text! Be specific. Think parents, siblings, friends, grandparents, former teachers, coaches. Check in with people and thank them! Or check in and set up a time to go to lunch with someone. Have a relative who is ill? Send them an uplifting text message! This hack will change your life! (and the lives of those you text) TEXT 2 B4 10!

MEMORIES MADE: _____
_____
_____
_____
_____
_____

TOUGH TIMES & LESSONS LEARNED: _____
_____
_____
_____
_____

What are you grateful for today? _____

Stressed | Angry | Tired | Sad | Happy | Excited

REMEMBER! WAIT TO WRITE BELOW UNTIL THIS DAY NEXT YEAR!

DATE: _____ (S) (M) (T) (W) (T) (F) (S)

MEMORIES MADE: _____
_____
_____
_____
_____
_____

TOUGH TIMES & LESSONS LEARNED: _____
_____
_____
_____
_____

What are you grateful for today? _____

Stressed | Angry | Tired | Sad | Happy | Excited

Did you know? Creating and sticking to a routine can reduce anxiety and increase feelings of control and happiness, especially important during the unpredictable college years.

DATE: _____ S M T W T F S

THURSDAY MYTHS:

> Myth: "I don't need to attend every lecture; I'll just study the slides."
>
> Reality: Attending lectures is crucial for understanding the material in depth. Professors often share insights that aren't in the slides. Think of it as a live podcast where you can't hit pause — if you're not there, you miss out.

MEMORIES MADE: _____
_____
_____
_____
_____

TOUGH TIMES & LESSONS LEARNED: _____
_____
_____
_____

What are you grateful for today?   Stressed Angry Tired Sad Happy Excited
_____

REMEMBER! WAIT TO WRITE BELOW UNTIL THIS DAY NEXT YEAR!

DATE: _____ S M T W T F S

MEMORIES MADE: _____
_____
_____
_____
_____

TOUGH TIMES & LESSONS LEARNED: _____
_____
_____
_____

What are you grateful for today?   Stressed Angry Tired Sad Happy Excited
_____

Did you know that the term "Give the cold shoulder" stems from medieval England and was common way to politely tell guests it was time to leave was to serve them a cold cut of meat from the shoulder. It now means to deliberately act unfriendly or indifferent.

DATE: _____ (S) (M) (T) (W) (T) (F) (S)

FRIDAY FILL IN THE BLANKS:

> "
> To me, life is all about _____
> _____
>
> If I died tomorrow, what I would miss the very most is _____
> _____
> "

MEMORIES MADE: _____
_____
_____
_____
_____

TOUGH TIMES & LESSONS LEARNED: _____
_____
_____
_____
_____

What are you grateful for today?
_____   Stressed Angry Tired Sad Happy Excited

↳ **REMEMBER! WAIT TO WRITE BELOW UNTIL THIS DAY NEXT YEAR!**

DATE: _____ (S) (M) (T) (W) (T) (F) (S)

MEMORIES MADE: _____
_____
_____
_____
_____

TOUGH TIMES & LESSONS LEARNED: _____
_____
_____
_____
_____

What are you grateful for today?
_____   Stressed Angry Tired Sad Happy Excited

Did you know? Research suggests that chewing gum while studying and then chewing the same flavor during an exam can help recall information, thanks to context-dependent memory.

DATE: _____ (S) (M) (T) (W) (T) (F) (S)

SATURDAY TED TALKS:

> In his dynamic TED Talk, Matt Killingsworth makes a compelling case that the secret to happiness lies in living in the now! Through his innovative "Track Your Happiness" app, he uncovers startling insights: our minds love to wander, but this very wandering is a happiness hijacker. He passionately argues that by anchoring ourselves in the present moment, we unlock a more vibrant, joyful existence. It's a powerful reminder: embrace the now, and transform your life into a happier journey!

MEMORIES MADE: _____
_____
_____
_____
_____
_____

TOUGH TIMES & LESSONS LEARNED: _____
_____
_____
_____
_____

What are you grateful for today?
_____

Stressed | Angry | Tired | Sad | Happy | Excited

REMEMBER! WAIT TO WRITE BELOW UNTIL THIS DAY NEXT YEAR!

DATE: _____ (S) (M) (T) (W) (T) (F) (S)

MEMORIES MADE: _____
_____
_____
_____
_____
_____

TOUGH TIMES & LESSONS LEARNED: _____
_____
_____
_____
_____

What are you grateful for today?
_____

Stressed | Angry | Tired | Sad | Happy | Excited

Did you know? The phrase "bless you!" after a sneeze is often traced back to the time of Pope Gregory I in the 6th century during a bubonic plague epidemic. Sneezing was one of the plague's symptoms, and saying "bless you" was a way to offer a prayer for good health.

DATE: _____   (S) (M) (T) (W) (T) (F) (S)

SUNDAY STRESS BUSTERS:

> **"** Cold shock to the system! After your usual warm shower, try switching the water to as cold a temperature as you can tolerate. Try to endure the cold water for 15 to 30 seconds, challenging yourself to breathe through it. Embrace the discomfort. The natural reaction to cold water – tightening, gasping, resisting – mirrors our response to sudden stress. Recognize that physical stress doesn't have to trigger psychological stress. In the cold shower, choose between just enduring or using the moment to enhance stress resilience. Aim to keep a relaxed mind amid the shock. Remind yourself that your body is built to adapt and benefit from this. (Just give it a try! Google the benefits!) **"**

MEMORIES MADE: _____
_____
_____
_____
_____
_____

TOUGH TIMES & LESSONS LEARNED: _____
_____
_____
_____
_____

What are you grateful for today?
_____

Stressed   Angry   Tired   Sad   Happy   Excited

> REMEMBER! WAIT TO WRITE BELOW UNTIL THIS DAY NEXT YEAR!

DATE: _____   (S) (M) (T) (W) (T) (F) (S)

MEMORIES MADE: _____
_____
_____
_____
_____
_____

TOUGH TIMES & LESSONS LEARNED: _____
_____
_____
_____
_____

What are you grateful for today?
_____

Stressed   Angry   Tired   Sad   Happy   Excited

Did you know? You are about 1 centimeter taller in the morning than in the evening, due to the compression of spinal discs throughout the day.

PUZZLE TIME! LET'S GET YOUR BRAIN FIRED UP!

FIND ALL THE FOUR-LETTER WORDS IN THE BOXES BELOW AS FAST AS YOU CAN

A E	I B	S E	L D	U D	S A	A L
C K	D R	R U	O L	C K	S B	C M
I N	S S	F E	L O	H R	A L	R E
D M	I K	A K	D R	I C	B L	D I
A F	I T	S L	A Y	A I	S P	T E
E M	F G	I K	L P	T L	S A	C U
L E	H T	A Y	S E	P E	E D	G E
I K	P A	G O	T R	C I	E S	U H
A S	T E	L E	E R	A E	T U	I E
L I	E R	L W	S I	L F	I S	X T
N O	A E	A Y	O G	I E	I E	K E
M O	L H	L D	W L	C V	C P	B A
R U	W I	A E	F I	A I	A T	A T
G U	I K	S Y	G T	N G	S F	Y S
N G	O E	A E	A E	R E	A E	E E
I K	M H	C R	R D	F E	P K	P K
T O	G P	V T	M S	P L	L E	P T
S A	S A	S A	I T	I A	B U	E Y
X I	R P	Y P	A Y	W L	T P	F L
N J	W A	O N	S E	O G	T U	O G
E I	N O	X A	A M	W L	R E	F G
T P	L I	L E	X E	O F	B A	R O

DATE: _____ (S) (M) (T) (W) (T) (F) (S)

MONDAY MANNERS:

> Observe then serve. When you're at another person's place, be quick to help out. Ask what they need help with, or just jump up and pitch in! This manner is important in your own apartment and in other people's places. If you're eating at a friend's house or a guest at someone's home for dinner, you can ask to set the table or fill glasses with water. And always clean up after yourself. Don't be the one relaxing while others are working. A little help goes a long way.

MEMORIES MADE: _____
_____
_____
_____
_____

TOUGH TIMES & LESSONS LEARNED: _____
_____
_____
_____

What are you grateful for today?   Stressed Angry Tired Sad Happy Excited
_____

REMEMBER! WAIT TO WRITE BELOW UNTIL THIS DAY NEXT YEAR!

DATE: _____ (S) (M) (T) (W) (T) (F) (S)

MEMORIES MADE: _____
_____
_____
_____
_____

TOUGH TIMES & LESSONS LEARNED: _____
_____
_____
_____

What are you grateful for today?   Stressed Angry Tired Sad Happy Excited
_____

Did you know? Active recall, a study method involving testing oneself rather than passive review, is shown to significantly improve memory retention and academic performance.

DATE: _____ (S) (M) (T) (W) (T) (F) (S)

TUESDAY TIPS:

> Instead of writing down every word on a professor's slides, try to understand the main points and summarize it in your own words. WAY too many students get frustrated because they are typing furiously and trying to get every word from my slides—and they aren't paying attention to what I'm saying. Summarize what you are hearing, then review your notes later that day or night and fill in the blanks and refresh your brain soon after you took the notes. It will stick longer.

MEMORIES MADE: _____
_____
_____
_____
_____

TOUGH TIMES & LESSONS LEARNED: _____
_____
_____
_____
_____

What are you grateful for today?   Stressed Angry Tired Sad Happy Excited
_____

REMEMBER! WAIT TO WRITE BELOW UNTIL THIS DAY NEXT YEAR!

DATE: _____ (S) (M) (T) (W) (T) (F) (S)

MEMORIES MADE: _____
_____
_____
_____
_____

TOUGH TIMES & LESSONS LEARNED: _____
_____
_____
_____
_____

What are you grateful for today?   Stressed Angry Tired Sad Happy Excited
_____

Did you know? The human brain is sometimes more active when we sleep than when we are awake, especially during dreams.

DATE: _____ (S) (M) (T) (W) (T) (F) (S)

WEDNESDAY (HUMP DAY!) HAPPY HACKS:

> "Mindfulness seems to be getting quite a bit of buzz in recent years. It's because this age-old practice is powerful. Mindfulness is the practice of being aware of and paying attention to your thoughts, emotions, body sensations, and environment moment by moment, with a gentle and caring approach. It's about noticing but not judging what's happening right now, in the present, without getting caught up in past memories or future worries. This skill helps us stay focused on the present, making us more aware of our actions and surroundings. It also teaches us not to react too strongly or feel overwhelmed by what's happening around us, leading to a calmer and more centered state of mind. Give it a try!"

MEMORIES MADE: _____
_____
_____
_____
_____
_____

TOUGH TIMES & LESSONS LEARNED: _____
_____
_____
_____
_____

What are you grateful for today?
_____

Stressed | Angry | Tired | Sad | Happy | Excited

REMEMBER! WAIT TO WRITE BELOW UNTIL THIS DAY NEXT YEAR!

DATE: _____ (S) (M) (T) (W) (T) (F) (S)

MEMORIES MADE: _____
_____
_____
_____
_____
_____

TOUGH TIMES & LESSONS LEARNED: _____
_____
_____
_____
_____

What are you grateful for today?
_____

Stressed | Angry | Tired | Sad | Happy | Excited

Did you know? "Phantom vibration syndrome" is a phenomenon where people think their phone is vibrating, when it is not. This reflects the high level of phone dependency and constant anticipation of communication.

DATE: _____ Ⓢ Ⓜ Ⓣ Ⓦ Ⓣ Ⓕ Ⓢ

THURSDAY MYTHS:

> "
> Myth: "I can leave assignments until the last minute."
>
> Reality: Procrastination is a common trap. Time management is a critical skill to develop early. It's like cooking – start too late, and you might end up with something half-baked.
> "

MEMORIES MADE: _____
_____
_____
_____
_____

TOUGH TIMES & LESSONS LEARNED: _____
_____
_____
_____
_____

What are you grateful for today?   Stressed Angry Tired Sad Happy Excited
_____

↙ **REMEMBER! WAIT TO WRITE BELOW UNTIL THIS DAY NEXT YEAR!**

DATE: _____ Ⓢ Ⓜ Ⓣ Ⓦ Ⓣ Ⓕ Ⓢ

MEMORIES MADE: _____
_____
_____
_____
_____

TOUGH TIMES & LESSONS LEARNED: _____
_____
_____
_____
_____

What are you grateful for today?   Stressed Angry Tired Sad Happy Excited
_____

Did you know? Juggling for just 10 minutes a day can significantly improve hand-eye coordination, cognitive flexibility, and even problem-solving skills. Time to grab some juggling balls!

DATE: _____ (S) (M) (T) (W) (T) (F) (S)

FRIDAY FILL IN THE BLANKS:

> " To avoid future regrets, what are one or two things you can do, starting today, to bring more balance in your life?
> _____
> _____
> _____ "

MEMORIES MADE: _____
_____
_____
_____
_____
_____

TOUGH TIMES & LESSONS LEARNED: _____
_____
_____
_____
_____

What are you grateful for today?   Stressed Angry Tired Sad Happy Excited
_____

REMEMBER! WAIT TO WRITE BELOW UNTIL THIS DAY NEXT YEAR!

DATE: _____ (S) (M) (T) (W) (T) (F) (S)

MEMORIES MADE: _____
_____
_____
_____
_____
_____

TOUGH TIMES & LESSONS LEARNED: _____
_____
_____
_____
_____

What are you grateful for today?   Stressed Angry Tired Sad Happy Excited
_____

Did you know? Yawning isn't just contagious, it actually helps cool down your brain!
Open wide and share the refreshing effect (just not in front of others or during class!)

DATE: _____ (S) (M) (T) (W) (T) (F) (S)

SATURDAY TED TALKS:

> In her TED talk "How to Make Stress Your Friend," Kelly McGonigal suggests a new way to view stress: as a positive. She explains that changing our attitude towards stress can alter our body's response to it. Instead of seeing stress as harmful, recognizing it as a helpful response can make us stronger, more social, and healthier. Stress can encourage the release of the hormone oxytocin, known as the "cuddle hormone," which enhances empathy and social support, and even protects our cardiovascular system. McGonigal's key message is that embracing stress rather than fearing it can lead to better health and resilience.

MEMORIES MADE: _____
_____
_____
_____
_____

TOUGH TIMES & LESSONS LEARNED: _____
_____
_____
_____
_____

What are you grateful for today?   Stressed Angry Tired Sad Happy Excited

REMEMBER! WAIT TO WRITE BELOW UNTIL THIS DAY NEXT YEAR!

DATE: _____ (S) (M) (T) (W) (T) (F) (S)

MEMORIES MADE: _____
_____
_____
_____
_____
_____

TOUGH TIMES & LESSONS LEARNED: _____
_____
_____
_____
_____

What are you grateful for today?   Stressed Angry Tired Sad Happy Excited

Did you know? Staying hydrated with water throughout the day not only quenches thirst but also aids in digestion, regulates body temperature, and improves cognitive function.
Hydrate for optimal health!

DATE: _____ (S) (M) (T) (W) (T) (F) (S)

SUNDAY STRESS BUSTERS:

> "
> Experiment with a seven-minute high-intensity interval training (HIIT) session. It's simpler than it sounds. Select a few exercises like jumping jacks, planks, push-ups, squats, or lunges, aiming to push yourself to your limits for short bursts. Use a timer, setting it for seven minutes, and alternate between 30 seconds of exercise and 10 seconds of rest. Add your favorite music for motivation. The key is to embrace the challenge and discomfort as you rotate through the exercises. This customizable workout is about stressing your body positively, regardless of fitness level. Focus on each 30-second interval, using this time to metabolically burn through stress. Remember, your body thrives on this kind of effort and it's a great stress reliever!
> "

MEMORIES MADE: _____
_____
_____
_____
_____
_____

TOUGH TIMES & LESSONS LEARNED: _____
_____
_____
_____
_____

What are you grateful for today?   Stressed Angry Tired Sad Happy Excited
_____

REMEMBER! WAIT TO WRITE BELOW UNTIL THIS DAY NEXT YEAR!

DATE: _____ (S) (M) (T) (W) (T) (F) (S)

MEMORIES MADE: _____
_____
_____
_____
_____
_____

TOUGH TIMES & LESSONS LEARNED: _____
_____
_____
_____
_____

What are you grateful for today?   Stressed Angry Tired Sad Happy Excited
_____

Did you know? Your femur is stronger than concrete and can support 30 times the weight of your body.

DATE: _____ (S) (M) (T) (W) (T) (F) (S)

MONDAY MANNERS:

> "Introduce yourself and say hi to new people, even if it feels weird. Practice makes it easier. Not sure how? Try, "I'm Taylor. What's your name?" This skill helps you in life. Being new or not, knowing anyone is tough. Saying hi confidently is a big plus. Lots of people feel like outsiders, so connecting others and connecting with others is a gift. Be the one who brings people together. It makes social situations better for everyone."

MEMORIES MADE: _____
_____
_____
_____
_____
_____

TOUGH TIMES & LESSONS LEARNED: _____
_____
_____
_____
_____

What are you grateful for today?
_____

Stressed | Angry | Tired | Sad | Happy | Excited

REMEMBER! WAIT TO WRITE BELOW UNTIL THIS DAY NEXT YEAR!

DATE: _____ (S) (M) (T) (W) (T) (F) (S)

MEMORIES MADE: _____
_____
_____
_____
_____
_____

TOUGH TIMES & LESSONS LEARNED: _____
_____
_____
_____
_____

What are you grateful for today?
_____

Stressed | Angry | Tired | Sad | Happy | Excited

Did you know? Learning a new skill at any age, from coding to playing an instrument, keeps your brain active and helps stave off cognitive decline. Challenge yourself, stay sharp!

DATE: _____ (S) (M) (T) (W) (T) (F) (S)

TUESDAY TIPS:

> Take responsibility, don't have your parents call or email a professor about issues you should take care of, which is nearly everything. The best way to approach a professor is to set up a time through email. Avoid language that blames or is critical. When I get an email like this, it doesn't help your cause: "Dr. Dave, the test you gave was super hard and had questions that weren't on the study guide. I don't think that's fair and I want two questions dropped." Instead, try something like this: "Hey Dr. Dave, I love the things I'm learning in your class. The test was harder than I thought. Could I set up a time to come to your office and talk about a couple questions on the test I didn't understand? Thanks so much!" See the difference?

MEMORIES MADE: _____
_____
_____
_____
_____
_____

TOUGH TIMES & LESSONS LEARNED: _____
_____
_____
_____
_____

What are you grateful for today?   Stressed Angry Tired Sad Happy Excited
_____

REMEMBER! WAIT TO WRITE BELOW UNTIL THIS DAY NEXT YEAR!

DATE: _____ (S) (M) (T) (W) (T) (F) (S)

MEMORIES MADE: _____
_____
_____
_____
_____
_____

TOUGH TIMES & LESSONS LEARNED: _____
_____
_____
_____
_____

What are you grateful for today?   Stressed Angry Tired Sad Happy Excited
_____

Did you know? The term "oopsie daisy" is a variation of "ups-a-daisy," which dates back to the 17th century. It was initially "up-a-daisy" and used as an encouragement for someone to get up after a fall, later evolving into an expression for a minor mistake. Oops!

DATE: _____ (S) (M) (T) (W) (T) (F) (S)

WEDNESDAY (HUMP DAY!) HAPPY HACKS

> "Cherish your friends. Friends bring happiness. Research shows that the opposite of connection is rejection and loneliness and how this can be harmful to our physical and mental health. Social connection is as essential to our long-term survival as food and water. Japan and leaders in the United Kingdom have even appointed Ministers of Loneliness (not kidding, look it up!) to combat the epidemic of loneliness and the devastating effects it is having on the people in their lands. It starts with being a kind and grateful person. Make time to hang out and do things with a good group of friends. These can be your roommates or even other new friends you meet."

MEMORIES MADE: _____
_____
_____
_____
_____

TOUGH TIMES & LESSONS LEARNED: _____
_____
_____
_____
_____

What are you grateful for today?   Stressed   Angry   Tired   Sad   Happy   Excited
_____

REMEMBER! WAIT TO WRITE BELOW UNTIL THIS DAY NEXT YEAR!

DATE: _____ (S) (M) (T) (W) (T) (F) (S)

MEMORIES MADE: _____
_____
_____
_____
_____

TOUGH TIMES & LESSONS LEARNED: _____
_____
_____
_____
_____

What are you grateful for today?   Stressed   Angry   Tired   Sad   Happy   Excited
_____

Did you know? The brain's prefrontal cortex, responsible for decision-making and self-control, is not fully developed until the mid-20s, affecting college students' decision-making processes.

DATE: _____ (S) (M) (T) (W) (T) (F) (S)

THURSDAY MYTHS:

> Myth: "College professors are distant and unapproachable."
>
> Reality: Most professors are eager to help and engage with students. Attending office hours and participating in class can enrich your learning experience. They're more like guides in a museum – approach them, and you'll learn a lot.

MEMORIES MADE: _____
_____
_____
_____
_____
_____

TOUGH TIMES & LESSONS LEARNED: _____
_____
_____
_____
_____

What are you grateful for today?
_____

Stressed | Angry | Tired | Sad | Happy | Excited

REMEMBER! WAIT TO WRITE BELOW UNTIL THIS DAY NEXT YEAR!

DATE: _____ (S) (M) (T) (W) (T) (F) (S)

MEMORIES MADE: _____
_____
_____
_____
_____
_____

TOUGH TIMES & LESSONS LEARNED: _____
_____
_____
_____
_____

What are you grateful for today?
_____

Stressed | Angry | Tired | Sad | Happy | Excited

Did you know? Setting and achieving small, manageable goals can boost confidence and happiness, helping to maintain motivation and a positive outlook in college.

DATE: _____ (S) (M) (T) (W) (T) (F) (S)

FRIDAY FILL IN THE BLANKS:

> "All of us are in the process of creating our own life story. Who are the top 10 people in your life that helped you get where you are today? (bonus points if you reach out to some of them and let them know they cracked your top 10!)
> 1. 6.
> 2. 7.
> 3. 8.
> 4. 9.
> 5. 10."

MEMORIES MADE: _____
_____
_____
_____
_____
_____

TOUGH TIMES & LESSONS LEARNED: _____
_____
_____
_____
_____

What are you grateful for today?   Stressed Angry Tired Sad Happy Excited
_____

REMEMBER! WAIT TO WRITE BELOW UNTIL THIS DAY NEXT YEAR!

DATE: _____ (S) (M) (T) (W) (T) (F) (S)

MEMORIES MADE: _____
_____
_____
_____
_____
_____

TOUGH TIMES & LESSONS LEARNED: _____
_____
_____
_____
_____

What are you grateful for today?   Stressed Angry Tired Sad Happy Excited
_____

Did you know? Regularly reading books not only expands your knowledge but also strengthens brain connectivity and stimulates cognitive function. Get lost in a good book!

DATE: _____ S M T W T F S

SATURDAY TED TALKS:

> Forget chasing happiness through external factors! Wendy Suzuki, in her TED Talk "The brain-changing benefits of exercise," reveals a powerful secret: exercise is your brain's best friend. It doesn't just boost mood, it boosts memory, focus, and even protects against neurodegenerative diseases like Alzheimer's. Think of your brain like a muscle; the more you work it out, the stronger and sharper it gets. So, lace up your shoes, hit the gym, or take a walk – your brain will thank you for it!

MEMORIES MADE: _____
_____
_____
_____
_____

TOUGH TIMES & LESSONS LEARNED: _____
_____
_____
_____
_____

What are you grateful for today?

Stressed | Angry | Tired | Sad | Happy | Excited

REMEMBER! WAIT TO WRITE BELOW UNTIL THIS DAY NEXT YEAR!

DATE: _____ S M T W T F S

MEMORIES MADE: _____
_____
_____
_____
_____

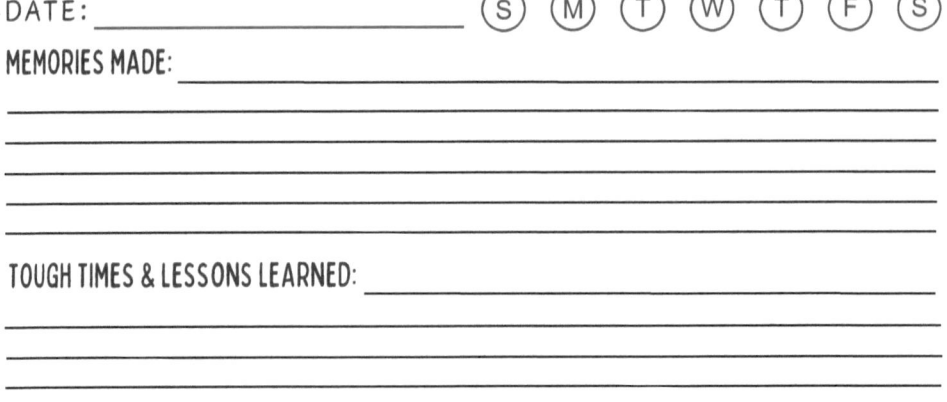

TOUGH TIMES & LESSONS LEARNED: _____
_____
_____
_____
_____

What are you grateful for today?

Stressed | Angry | Tired | Sad | Happy | Excited

Did you know? The tradition of 'Spring Break' originated in the 1930s when a swim coach in Maine took his team to Florida to train, eventually evolving into the phenomenon it is today (thanks coach!).

DATE: _____ (S) (M) (T) (W) (T) (F) (S)

SUNDAY STRESS BUSTERS:

> The BIG 3. Research suggests whether a stressor results in a crisis or not depends on these 3: resources, relationships, and prior experiences with that stressor. Many of the stress tips we'll share revolve around the resources you have to lean on and the relationships you have with others. And if you have managed bombing a test or surviving a break up, then you tend to manage stresses better because you know what to do and you know you have survived. Focus on these BIG 3 throughout your college years and throughout life! You've got this!

MEMORIES MADE: _____

_____
_____
_____
_____
_____

TOUGH TIMES & LESSONS LEARNED: _____

_____
_____
_____
_____

What are you grateful for today?

_____

Stressed | Angry | Tired | Sad | Happy | Excited

REMEMBER! WAIT TO WRITE BELOW UNTIL THIS DAY NEXT YEAR!

DATE: _____ (S) (M) (T) (W) (T) (F) (S)

MEMORIES MADE: _____

_____
_____
_____
_____
_____

TOUGH TIMES & LESSONS LEARNED: _____

_____
_____
_____
_____

What are you grateful for today?

_____

Stressed | Angry | Tired | Sad | Happy | Excited

Did you know? The strongest material in your body is the enamel covering your teeth, which is designed to withstand the force of biting and chewing.

DATE: _____   (S) (M) (T) (W) (T) (F) (S)

MONDAY MANNERS:

> "Discover new friends if your current ones exclude or make you feel bad. It's tough but seek those who appreciate you for who you are. Your new pals might not be the coolest, and that's okay. Spend time with those who treat you well and value your friendship. Don't try to fit in where you're not appreciated. Many would love your personality and light. Finding new friends takes effort—put yourself out there, invite, and be open. Look for those who might be lonely or new. Differences don't matter if they're good people who enjoy and include you. The effort is worthwhile."

MEMORIES MADE: _____
_____
_____
_____
_____

TOUGH TIMES & LESSONS LEARNED: _____
_____
_____
_____

What are you grateful for today?   Stressed · Angry · Tired · Sad · Happy · Excited
_____

> REMEMBER! WAIT TO WRITE BELOW UNTIL THIS DAY NEXT YEAR!

DATE: _____   (S) (M) (T) (W) (T) (F) (S)

MEMORIES MADE: _____
_____
_____
_____
_____

TOUGH TIMES & LESSONS LEARNED: _____
_____
_____
_____

What are you grateful for today?   Stressed · Angry · Tired · Sad · Happy · Excited
_____

Did you know? Surprisingly, your body houses a 'second brain' within your gut, significantly influencing your mood and overall well-being through intricate connections.

DATE: _____ (S) (M) (T) (W) (T) (F) (S)

TUESDAY TIPS:

> Have fun and enjoy this unique phase of life! Most people only experience college for a few years and that's it! Life goes fast. Your college years will go super fast. It may not seem like it in the moment. While it's important to take school seriously, don't take yourself too seriously. When it's time to have fun, let yourself have fun! College students' favorite acronymn is YOLO You Only Live Once. Just be safe and remember your parents' favorite acronymn is DDDT – Don't Do Dumb Things. :)

MEMORIES MADE: _____
_____
_____
_____
_____
_____

TOUGH TIMES & LESSONS LEARNED: _____
_____
_____
_____
_____

What are you grateful for today?   Stressed Angry Tired Sad Happy Excited
_____

REMEMBER! WAIT TO WRITE BELOW UNTIL THIS DAY NEXT YEAR!

DATE: _____ (S) (M) (T) (W) (T) (F) (S)

MEMORIES MADE: _____
_____
_____
_____
_____
_____

TOUGH TIMES & LESSONS LEARNED: _____
_____
_____
_____
_____

What are you grateful for today?   Stressed Angry Tired Sad Happy Excited
_____

Did you know? The human heart creates enough pressure when it pumps blood out to the body to squirt blood 30 feet. Yikes!

DATE: _____ (S) (M) (T) (W) (T) (F) (S)

WEDNESDAY (HUMP DAY!) HAPPY HACKS:

> Experience flow. A flow state in positive psychology is when you're totally absorbed in and focused on an activity that matches your skills. You don't think about yourself much or your performance. Athletes call this being "in the zone." The brain behaves differently during flow. Flow brings joy, deep focus, and a sense of timelessness. Discovered by Mihaly Csikszentmihalyi, it happens when the challenge of what you're doing is just right for your abilities. This state enhances well-being, boosts creativity, and improves performance by creating a perfect balance between challenge and skill in an enjoyable task. Examples include playing sports, games, reading, creative hobbies, making things with your hands, gardening, and solving puzzles. What is it that brings you flow? What can you do to make more time for it in your life?

MEMORIES MADE: _____
_____
_____
_____
_____
_____

TOUGH TIMES & LESSONS LEARNED: _____
_____
_____
_____
_____

What are you grateful for today?   Stressed Angry Tired Sad Happy Excited
_____

REMEMBER! WAIT TO WRITE BELOW UNTIL THIS DAY NEXT YEAR!

DATE: _____ (S) (M) (T) (W) (T) (F) (S)

MEMORIES MADE: _____
_____
_____
_____
_____
_____

TOUGH TIMES & LESSONS LEARNED: _____
_____
_____
_____
_____

What are you grateful for today?   Stressed Angry Tired Sad Happy Excited
_____

Did you know? If all the DNA in your body were uncoiled, it would stretch out to about 10 billion miles, from Earth to Pluto and back.

DATE: _____ (S) (M) (T) (W) (T) (F) (S)

THURSDAY MYTHS:

> Myth: "I'll eat healthy and exercise regularly."
>
> Reality: Maintaining a healthy lifestyle requires effort and planning. The convenience of fast food and the demands of coursework can make it challenging. It's like juggling – keeping all balls in the air is harder than it looks.

MEMORIES MADE: _____
_____
_____
_____
_____
_____

TOUGH TIMES & LESSONS LEARNED: _____
_____
_____
_____
_____

What are you grateful for today?
_____

Stressed | Angry | Tired | Sad | Happy | Excited

REMEMBER! WAIT TO WRITE BELOW UNTIL THIS DAY NEXT YEAR!

DATE: _____ (S) (M) (T) (W) (T) (F) (S)

MEMORIES MADE: _____
_____
_____
_____
_____
_____

TOUGH TIMES & LESSONS LEARNED: _____
_____
_____
_____
_____

What are you grateful for today?
_____

Stressed | Angry | Tired | Sad | Happy | Excited

Did you know? The phenomenon of 'imposter syndrome', where individuals doubt their accomplishments, is particularly common among high-achieving college students.

DATE: _____ (S) (M) (T) (W) (T) (F) (S)

FRIDAY FILL IN THE BLANKS:

> ❝ Life check! Your future self (and your kids!) may be interested in what the price of different things are right now. Fill in the blank for the average price of the following:
>
> Gallon of milk: _____   Movie tickets: _____
>
> Gallon of gasoline: _____   Candy bar: _____
>
> Tuition for one semester: _____   Your most expensive textbook: _____ ❞

MEMORIES MADE: _____
_____
_____
_____
_____

TOUGH TIMES & LESSONS LEARNED: _____
_____
_____
_____

What are you grateful for today?   Stressed Angry Tired Sad Happy Excited
_____

REMEMBER! WAIT TO WRITE BELOW UNTIL THIS DAY NEXT YEAR!

DATE: _____ (S) (M) (T) (W) (T) (F) (S)

MEMORIES MADE: _____
_____
_____
_____
_____

TOUGH TIMES & LESSONS LEARNED: _____
_____
_____
_____

What are you grateful for today?   Stressed Angry Tired Sad Happy Excited
_____

Did you know? The average person walks the equivalent of five times around the equator in a lifetime.

DATE: _____ (S) (M) (T) (W) (T) (F) (S)

SATURDAY TED TALKS:

> In his TED talk "How to Stay Calm When You Know You'll Be Stressed," Daniel Levitin talks about planning ahead to handle stress better. He recommends thinking about what might go wrong in advance and preparing for it. This method is called "prospective hindsight" or "pre-mortem." Levitin points out that stress can make it hard to think clearly and make good decisions. By having a plan ready before stress hits, we can stay calm and make smarter choices. His main message is that preparing for stressful situations in advance can help us deal with them more effectively when they happen.

MEMORIES MADE: _____
_____
_____
_____
_____
_____

TOUGH TIMES & LESSONS LEARNED: _____
_____
_____
_____
_____

What are you grateful for today?

Stressed | Angry | Tired | Sad | Happy | Excited

REMEMBER! WAIT TO WRITE BELOW UNTIL THIS DAY NEXT YEAR!

DATE: _____ (S) (M) (T) (W) (T) (F) (S)

MEMORIES MADE: _____
_____
_____
_____
_____
_____

TOUGH TIMES & LESSONS LEARNED: _____
_____
_____
_____
_____

What are you grateful for today?

Stressed | Angry | Tired | Sad | Happy | Excited

Did you know? The average college student spends around 10 hours per week on social media. Scholars suggest 30 min/day is better. Time to unplug and explore the world beyond your screen!

DATE: _____ (S) (M) (T) (W) (T) (F) (S)

SUNDAY STRESS BUSTERS:

> "Humor is a great way to relieve stress. When we laugh, our body releases chemicals that make us feel good and reduce stress. Laughing also lowers the stress hormones in our body, helping us relax. Humor helps us see things in a lighter way, breaking the cycle of stress and worry. It makes us feel more positive and hopeful, even when things are tough. Laughing with others also strengthens our connections with them. Overall, humor not only makes us feel better in the moment, but it can also improve our health and help us deal with stress better."

MEMORIES MADE: _____
_____
_____
_____
_____

TOUGH TIMES & LESSONS LEARNED: _____
_____
_____
_____
_____

What are you grateful for today?
_____

Stressed | Angry | Tired | Sad | Happy | Excited

REMEMBER! WAIT TO WRITE BELOW UNTIL THIS DAY NEXT YEAR!

DATE: _____ (S) (M) (T) (W) (T) (F) (S)

MEMORIES MADE: _____
_____
_____
_____
_____

TOUGH TIMES & LESSONS LEARNED: _____
_____
_____
_____
_____

What are you grateful for today?
_____

Stressed | Angry | Tired | Sad | Happy | Excited

Did you know? Collaborating with classmates on projects not only strengthens understanding but also hones communication and teamwork skills, valuable assets for any career path.

DATE: _____ (S) (M) (T) (W) (T) (F) (S)

MONDAY MANNERS:

> Be a grateful and friendly passenger. When someone gives you a ride, say hello and chat a bit. Be kind to everyone in the car—no whispering or going silent while staring at your phone. Always say thank you when you leave. It's important to appreciate those helping you get where you need to be. Using your phone to avoid talking might seem easy, but it's not polite. Make sure to be a friendly and thankful passenger.

MEMORIES MADE: _____
_____
_____
_____
_____
_____

TOUGH TIMES & LESSONS LEARNED: _____
_____
_____
_____
_____

What are you grateful for today?

Stressed Angry Tired Sad Happy Excited

REMEMBER! WAIT TO WRITE BELOW UNTIL THIS DAY NEXT YEAR!

DATE: _____ (S) (M) (T) (W) (T) (F) (S)

MEMORIES MADE: _____
_____
_____
_____
_____
_____

TOUGH TIMES & LESSONS LEARNED: _____
_____
_____
_____
_____

What are you grateful for today?

Stressed Angry Tired Sad Happy Excited

Did you know? A single human brain generates more electrical impulses in one day than all the telephones of the world combined.

DATE: _____ S M T W T F S

TUESDAY TIPS:

> Embrace Carol Dweck's concept of a "growth mindset" by viewing challenges as opportunities for development. Recognize that intelligence and talents can be cultivated through effort, learning, and persistence. Shift from thinking "I can't do this" to "I can't do this yet." Cultivate a love for learning and resilience in the face of setbacks. This approach fosters continuous growth and improvement in all aspects of life.

MEMORIES MADE: _____
_____
_____
_____
_____
_____

TOUGH TIMES & LESSONS LEARNED: _____
_____
_____
_____
_____

What are you grateful for today?   Stressed Angry Tired Sad Happy Excited
_____

REMEMBER! WAIT TO WRITE BELOW UNTIL THIS DAY NEXT YEAR!

DATE: _____ S M T W T F S

MEMORIES MADE: _____
_____
_____
_____
_____
_____

TOUGH TIMES & LESSONS LEARNED: _____
_____
_____
_____
_____

What are you grateful for today?   Stressed Angry Tired Sad Happy Excited
_____

Did you know? Your body's longest nerve, the sciatic nerve, runs from the lower back down to the feet, and is as thick as your thumb.

DATE: _____ (S) (M) (T) (W) (T) (F) (S)

WEDNESDAY (HUMP DAY!) HAPPY HACKS

> Helping others who hurt brings happiness. When people are hurting, our job is to be healers, not preachers. What may be needed most in relationships with others is not a set of magical skills, but simple awareness, sensitivity, and a heavy helping of compassion. Emotional wounds require emotional first aid. When someone you care about is hurting, hit the pause button, offer the gift of your all-in attention, and listen for understanding. The greatest gift you can give another person is not your time. It's your attention and compassion.

MEMORIES MADE: _____
_____
_____
_____
_____
_____

TOUGH TIMES & LESSONS LEARNED: _____
_____
_____
_____
_____

What are you grateful for today?   Stressed Angry Tired Sad Happy Excited
_____

REMEMBER! WAIT TO WRITE BELOW UNTIL THIS DAY NEXT YEAR!

DATE: _____ (S) (M) (T) (W) (T) (F) (S)

MEMORIES MADE: _____
_____
_____
_____
_____
_____

TOUGH TIMES & LESSONS LEARNED: _____
_____
_____
_____
_____

What are you grateful for today?   Stressed Angry Tired Sad Happy Excited
_____

Did you know? Highlighting isn't the memory hero we thought it was! Studies show it can lead to passive reading and hinder information processing. Underline key points or rewrite notes in your own words instead.

DATE: _____ (S) (M) (T) (W) (T) (F) (S)

THURSDAY MYTHS:

> Myth: "Online classes are a breeze."
>
> Reality: Online courses demand self-discipline and time management. Without the structure of a physical classroom, it's easy to fall behind. It's like being your own boss – sounds great, but there's no one to remind you of deadlines.

MEMORIES MADE: _____
_____
_____
_____
_____

TOUGH TIMES & LESSONS LEARNED: _____
_____
_____
_____

What are you grateful for today?
_____

Stressed | Angry | Tired | Sad | Happy | Excited

REMEMBER! WAIT TO WRITE BELOW UNTIL THIS DAY NEXT YEAR!

DATE: _____ (S) (M) (T) (W) (T) (F) (S)

MEMORIES MADE: _____
_____
_____
_____
_____

TOUGH TIMES & LESSONS LEARNED: _____
_____
_____
_____

What are you grateful for today?
_____

Stressed | Angry | Tired | Sad | Happy | Excited

Did you know? The Guinness World Record for the longest lecture was set by Errol Muzawazi in 2009, lasting 121 hours - a test of endurance for any student!

DATE: _____ (S) (M) (T) (W) (T) (F) (S)

FRIDAY FILL IN THE BLANKS:

> Looking back at your years in high school and living at home, ask yourself, "I just didn't spend enough time _____
> _____
>
> And "I spent too much time _____
> _____

MEMORIES MADE: _____
_____
_____
_____
_____
_____

TOUGH TIMES & LESSONS LEARNED: _____
_____
_____
_____
_____

What are you grateful for today?   Stressed   Angry   Tired   Sad   Happy   Excited
_____

REMEMBER! WAIT TO WRITE BELOW UNTIL THIS DAY NEXT YEAR!

DATE: _____ (S) (M) (T) (W) (T) (F) (S)

MEMORIES MADE: _____
_____
_____
_____
_____
_____

TOUGH TIMES & LESSONS LEARNED: _____
_____
_____
_____
_____

What are you grateful for today?   Stressed   Angry   Tired   Sad   Happy   Excited
_____

Did you know? You produce enough earwax in a year to make a peanut-sized ball!
Don't worry, it naturally cleans and protects your ears.

DATE: _____ S M T W T F S

SATURDAY TED TALKS:

> In her powerful TED Talk, Brené Brown challenges the notion of perfection and vulnerability as weakness. Forget hiding flaws and fears! She argues that true connection and courage come from embracing vulnerability. Sharing authentically, despite fear, leads to deeper relationships, increased creativity, and a more fulfilling life. Vulnerability isn't about seeking discomfort, but about showing your true self and allowing yourself to be seen, flaws and all. So, open yourself up, be brave enough to be imperfect, and watch your connections and sense of belonging improve!

MEMORIES MADE: _____
_____
_____
_____
_____
_____

TOUGH TIMES & LESSONS LEARNED: _____
_____
_____
_____
_____

What are you grateful for today?
_____

Stressed | Angry | Tired | Sad | Happy | Excited

REMEMBER! WAIT TO WRITE BELOW UNTIL THIS DAY NEXT YEAR!

DATE: _____ S M T W T F S

MEMORIES MADE: _____
_____
_____
_____
_____
_____

TOUGH TIMES & LESSONS LEARNED: _____
_____
_____
_____
_____

What are you grateful for today?
_____

Stressed | Angry | Tired | Sad | Happy | Excited

Did you know? Listening to music can actually get you high! It releases dopamine, the "reward" chemical, in the brain, making you feel happy and energized. Turn up the tunes and feel the good vibes flow!

DATE: _____ (S) (M) (T) (W) (T) (F) (S)

SUNDAY STRESS BUSTERS:

> Allow yourself to have vacations from stress. Sometimes we feel so worn-out or frustrated that we want to cry or scream. That's a good time for a mental vacation. Find a place where you can be alone. Lie down, close your eyes, and imagine that you are lying on a beautiful, peaceful beach. Imagine the sun on your face. Listen to the sounds of waves. Feel the warm sand. Breathe deeply and slowly. Enjoy relaxing for several minutes. When you're feeling better, open your eyes. Think of some small thing you can do to make things run more smoothly.

MEMORIES MADE: _____
_____
_____
_____
_____
_____

TOUGH TIMES & LESSONS LEARNED: _____
_____
_____
_____
_____

What are you grateful for today?
_____

Stressed | Angry | Tired | Sad | Happy | Excited

REMEMBER! WAIT TO WRITE BELOW UNTIL THIS DAY NEXT YEAR!

DATE: _____ (S) (M) (T) (W) (T) (F) (S)

MEMORIES MADE: _____
_____
_____
_____
_____
_____

TOUGH TIMES & LESSONS LEARNED: _____
_____
_____
_____
_____

What are you grateful for today?
_____

Stressed | Angry | Tired | Sad | Happy | Excited

Did you know? Reflecting on and appreciating small daily achievements can boost happiness and self-esteem, an important practice for maintaining positivity in college. Celebrate those small wins!

DATE: _____ (S) (M) (T) (W) (T) (F) (S)

MONDAY MANNERS:

> "Use good manners at restaurants – both fast food and sit-down. Smile and make eye contact with your server. Clearly say your order, and if you're unsure, ask questions politely. Order quickly or ask for more time, but don't keep the server waiting. Know how you like your food cooked. When served, say "thank you." Keep noise down to not disturb others. Put away your phones. Don't make a big mess and don't forget to leave a tip. Always treat those serving you with kindness and respect."

MEMORIES MADE: _____
_____
_____
_____
_____
_____

TOUGH TIMES & LESSONS LEARNED: _____
_____
_____
_____
_____

What are you grateful for today?   Stressed Angry Tired Sad Happy Excited
_____

REMEMBER! WAIT TO WRITE BELOW UNTIL THIS DAY NEXT YEAR!

DATE: _____ (S) (M) (T) (W) (T) (F) (S)

MEMORIES MADE: _____
_____
_____
_____
_____
_____

TOUGH TIMES & LESSONS LEARNED: _____
_____
_____
_____
_____

What are you grateful for today?   Stressed Angry Tired Sad Happy Excited
_____

Did you know? Having plants in a dorm room or study space can reduce stress, improve air quality, and enhance concentration and memory.

DATE: _____ (S) (M) (T) (W) (T) (F) (S)

TUESDAY TIPS:

> Martin Seligman's concept of "Learned Optimism" suggests that being positive isn't just something you're born with; you can actually learn to be more optimistic. We can train our brain to see challenges as temporary setbacks, not permanent defeats. It's like building mental muscles through techniques like identifying unhelpful thought patterns, reframing events, and celebrating small wins. This helps you handle tough times better and makes you feel happier overall. It's all about training your brain to focus on the good side of things instead of the bad.

MEMORIES MADE: _____
_____
_____
_____
_____

TOUGH TIMES & LESSONS LEARNED: _____
_____
_____
_____
_____

What are you grateful for today?   Stressed Angry Tired Sad Happy Excited
_____

REMEMBER! WAIT TO WRITE BELOW UNTIL THIS DAY NEXT YEAR!

DATE: _____ (S) (M) (T) (W) (T) (F) (S)

MEMORIES MADE: _____
_____
_____
_____
_____

TOUGH TIMES & LESSONS LEARNED: _____
_____
_____
_____
_____

What are you grateful for today?   Stressed Angry Tired Sad Happy Excited
_____

Did you know? Babies can taste sweet and sour right after birth, but bitterness and umami (savory taste) only develop later! Sensory experiences unfold like a blooming flower.

DATE: _____ (S) (M) (T) (W) (T) (F) (S)

WEDNESDAY (HUMP DAY!) HAPPY HACKS:

> Ready for another happy hack on gratitude? Start by jotting down 3 people, places, experiences, and things you are grateful for below. Then keep adding to the list, journal or make a note in your phone. When you are waiting in a long line somewhere, pull out your phone and add to the list in these four categories. Keep growing the list and you will be more grateful and happy. Trust me.

MEMORIES MADE: _____
_____
_____
_____
_____
_____

TOUGH TIMES & LESSONS LEARNED: _____
_____
_____
_____
_____

What are you grateful for today?   Stressed   Angry   Tired   Sad   Happy   Excited
_____

REMEMBER! WAIT TO WRITE BELOW UNTIL THIS DAY NEXT YEAR!

DATE: _____ (S) (M) (T) (W) (T) (F) (S)

MEMORIES MADE: _____
_____
_____
_____
_____
_____

TOUGH TIMES & LESSONS LEARNED: _____
_____
_____
_____
_____

What are you grateful for today?   Stressed   Angry   Tired   Sad   Happy   Excited
_____

Did you know? The human eye can process 36,000 bits of information every hour, contributing to a significant portion of the sensory information we receive.

DATE:_____ (S) (M) (T) (W) (T) (F) (S)

THURSDAY MYTHS:

> Myth: "I won't change much as a person."
>
> Reality: College is a transformative experience. You'll be exposed to new ideas, people, and cultures that will shape your perspectives. Imagine yourself as a smartphone; college is the series of updates that make you faster, better, and more efficient.

MEMORIES MADE: _____
_____
_____
_____
_____
_____

TOUGH TIMES & LESSONS LEARNED: _____
_____
_____
_____
_____

What are you grateful for today?   Stressed Angry Tired Sad Happy Excited
_____

REMEMBER! WAIT TO WRITE BELOW UNTIL THIS DAY NEXT YEAR!

DATE:_____ (S) (M) (T) (W) (T) (F) (S)

MEMORIES MADE: _____
_____
_____
_____
_____
_____

TOUGH TIMES & LESSONS LEARNED: _____
_____
_____
_____
_____

What are you grateful for today?   Stressed Angry Tired Sad Happy Excited
_____

Did you know? Eating dark chocolate in moderation can not only boost mood, but also improve focus and concentration, beneficial for long study sessions. But go easy my friends!

DATE: _____ (S) (M) (T) (W) (T) (F) (S)

FRIDAY FILL IN THE BLANKS:

> What would you say are the qualities of a true friend? How can you improve these qualities in your own life?
> _____
> _____
> _____
> _____

MEMORIES MADE: _____
_____
_____
_____
_____
_____

TOUGH TIMES & LESSONS LEARNED: _____
_____
_____
_____
_____

What are you grateful for today?   Stressed Angry Tired Sad Happy Excited
_____

REMEMBER! WAIT TO WRITE BELOW UNTIL THIS DAY NEXT YEAR!

DATE: _____ (S) (M) (T) (W) (T) (F) (S)

MEMORIES MADE: _____
_____
_____
_____
_____
_____

TOUGH TIMES & LESSONS LEARNED: _____
_____
_____
_____
_____

What are you grateful for today?   Stressed Angry Tired Sad Happy Excited
_____

Did you know? Standing on one leg for 10 seconds each day can improve balance, strengthen core muscles, and even boost cognitive function. Stand tall and balance for better health!

DATE: _____ (S) (M) (T) (W) (T) (F) (S)

SATURDAY TED TALKS:

> In his TED talk "The surprising habits of original thinkers," Adam Grant reveals the unexpected traits of originality. Embrace failure, it's the fertile ground for new ideas. Question assumptions, challenge the status quo. Embrace curiosity, explore diverse perspectives. Collaborate with unexpected partners, cross-pollinate ideas. Be a good listener, diverse voices spark innovation. Remember, originality isn't about being different, it's about thinking differently.

MEMORIES MADE: _____
_____
_____
_____
_____

TOUGH TIMES & LESSONS LEARNED: _____
_____
_____
_____
_____

What are you grateful for today?

Stressed | Angry | Tired | Sad | Happy | Excited

REMEMBER! WAIT TO WRITE BELOW UNTIL THIS DAY NEXT YEAR!

DATE: _____ (S) (M) (T) (W) (T) (F) (S)

MEMORIES MADE: _____
_____
_____
_____
_____

TOUGH TIMES & LESSONS LEARNED: _____
_____
_____
_____
_____

What are you grateful for today?

Stressed | Angry | Tired | Sad | Happy | Excited

Did you know? Studies have found that students who handwrite their notes, as opposed to typing, have better comprehension and retention of the material.

DATE: _____ (S) (M) (T) (W) (T) (F) (S)

SUNDAY STRESS BUSTERS:

> **"** Draw strength from friends and family members. You may have some friends who help you make decisions, feel loved, and feel hopeful. Call them. Ask them if they will listen to you. Talk to them. Tell them how you feel. You may have some friends or family members who make you angrier or upsetter (haha). It might be good not to talk to them when you feel stressed. Anger makes stress worse. When stress starts to pile up, phone a friend! **"**

MEMORIES MADE: _____
_____
_____
_____
_____
_____

TOUGH TIMES & LESSONS LEARNED: _____
_____
_____
_____
_____

What are you grateful for today?   Stressed Angry Tired Sad Happy Excited
_____

REMEMBER! WAIT TO WRITE BELOW UNTIL THIS DAY NEXT YEAR!

DATE: _____ (S) (M) (T) (W) (T) (F) (S)

MEMORIES MADE: _____
_____
_____
_____
_____
_____

TOUGH TIMES & LESSONS LEARNED: _____
_____
_____
_____
_____

What are you grateful for today?   Stressed Angry Tired Sad Happy Excited
_____

Did you know? Taking a 20-minute power nap in the afternoon can improve alertness, memory, and cognitive function, boosting your afternoon performance. Recharge and refocus!

DATE: _____ (S) (M) (T) (W) (T) (F) (S)

MONDAY MANNERS:

> "Don't spread mean stuff. Sharing a screenshot of a mean text or telling rude stories isn't being a good friend. Even if you mean well, it hurts everyone and creates unnecessary drama. If it's even potentially hurtful, don't say it and don't share it. You might think you're helping by letting someone know, but it usually just backfires and makes things worse. People make mistakes, and sharing it makes it worse. Don't be part of it. Instead, be supportive and kind in your words and texts. Encourage others to do the same."

MEMORIES MADE: _____
_____
_____
_____
_____
_____

TOUGH TIMES & LESSONS LEARNED: _____
_____
_____
_____
_____

What are you grateful for today?   Stressed Angry Tired Sad Happy Excited
_____

REMEMBER! WAIT TO WRITE BELOW UNTIL THIS DAY NEXT YEAR!

DATE: _____ (S) (M) (T) (W) (T) (F) (S)

MEMORIES MADE: _____
_____
_____
_____
_____
_____

TOUGH TIMES & LESSONS LEARNED: _____
_____
_____
_____
_____

What are you grateful for today?   Stressed Angry Tired Sad Happy Excited
_____

Did you know? Your body can regenerate its liver! Take care of this vital organ, and it will take care of you.

DATE: _____ S M T W T F S

TUESDAY TIPS:

> Explore the college town or city beyond the campus. Make time to do this. It's even better exploring with your peeps. Most college towns are pretty darn cool. Talk with some locals. Learn about the history. Try eating at some fan favorites. Be adventurous. Google the good stuff. Then BAM! Be sure to write about it all in this journal!!

MEMORIES MADE: _____
_____
_____
_____
_____

TOUGH TIMES & LESSONS LEARNED: _____
_____
_____
_____
_____

What are you grateful for today?   Stressed Angry Tired Sad Happy Excited
_____

REMEMBER! WAIT TO WRITE BELOW UNTIL THIS DAY NEXT YEAR!

DATE: _____ S M T W T F S

MEMORIES MADE: _____
_____
_____
_____
_____

TOUGH TIMES & LESSONS LEARNED: _____
_____
_____
_____
_____

What are you grateful for today?   Stressed Angry Tired Sad Happy Excited
_____

Did you know? Snack attack, memory hack! Healthy snacks like nuts and fruits provide brain-boosting nutrients during study sessions. Ditch the junk food and fuel your focus naturally.

DATE: _____ (S) (M) (T) (W) (T) (F) (S)

WEDNESDAY (HUMP DAY!) HAPPY HACKS

> Compassion is king! One of our favorite words in the English language is the word "compassion." It is different, but related to empathy, sympathy and altruism. It is an emotional response to empathy. Compassion is not just feeling sympathy for pain, hardship or discomfort. It also includes a deep longing to help relieve the suffering. It literally means "to suffer with." It is a pure desire to live with love. In all of your striving, strive for compassion. Our closest relationships can't survive without compassion and they can't flourish without kindness.

MEMORIES MADE: _____
_____
_____
_____
_____
_____

TOUGH TIMES & LESSONS LEARNED: _____
_____
_____
_____
_____

What are you grateful for today?   Stressed Angry Tired Sad Happy Excited
_____

REMEMBER! WAIT TO WRITE BELOW UNTIL THIS DAY NEXT YEAR!

DATE: _____ (S) (M) (T) (W) (T) (F) (S)

MEMORIES MADE: _____
_____
_____
_____
_____
_____

TOUGH TIMES & LESSONS LEARNED: _____
_____
_____
_____
_____

What are you grateful for today?   Stressed Angry Tired Sad Happy Excited
_____

Did you know? Your stomach produces enough acid in a year to dissolve a car!
Luckily, your stomach lining protects you from this inner bath of acid.

DATE: _____ (S) (M) (T) (W) (T) (F) (S)

THURSDAY MYTHS:

> "
> Myth: "I'll never feel homesick."
>
> Reality: Most students experience homesickness, especially in the first year. It's a natural part of adjusting to a new environment. Think of it as a sign that you have people and places worth missing.
> "

MEMORIES MADE: _____

TOUGH TIMES & LESSONS LEARNED: _____

What are you grateful for today?

Stressed Angry Tired Sad Happy Excited

_____

REMEMBER! WAIT TO WRITE BELOW UNTIL THIS DAY NEXT YEAR!

DATE: _____ (S) (M) (T) (W) (T) (F) (S)

MEMORIES MADE: _____

TOUGH TIMES & LESSONS LEARNED: _____

What are you grateful for today?

Stressed Angry Tired Sad Happy Excited

_____

Did you know? Human bones are about 31% water, emphasizing the importance of hydration for bone health.

DATE: _____ (S) (M) (T) (W) (T) (F) (S)

FRIDAY FILL IN THE BLANKS:

> " What are you looking forward to most in the next 30 days? And why?
> _____
> _____
> _____
> "

MEMORIES MADE: _____
_____
_____
_____
_____

TOUGH TIMES & LESSONS LEARNED: _____
_____
_____
_____
_____

What are you grateful for today?
_____

Stressed | Angry | Tired | Sad | Happy | Excited

↩ REMEMBER! WAIT TO WRITE BELOW UNTIL THIS DAY NEXT YEAR!

DATE: _____ (S) (M) (T) (W) (T) (F) (S)

MEMORIES MADE: _____
_____
_____
_____
_____

TOUGH TIMES & LESSONS LEARNED: _____
_____
_____
_____
_____

What are you grateful for today?
_____

Stressed | Angry | Tired | Sad | Happy | Excited

Did you know? Your hair grows about 6 inches per year, meaning most heads of hair have strands of varying ages! A rainbow of growth phases.

DATE: _____ S M T W T F S

SATURDAY TED TALKS:

> In her TED talk "Your Body Language Shapes Who You Are," Amy Cuddy explains how our body language not only affects how others see us but also how we see ourselves. She discusses "power poses" - standing in confident postures, even when we don't feel confident. These poses can boost feelings of confidence and impact our chances of success. Cuddy shares research showing that just two minutes in a power pose can significantly increase testosterone (a hormone linked to confidence) and decrease cortisol (a stress hormone). Her message is that changing our body posture can change our confidence and our life outcomes.

MEMORIES MADE: _____
_____
_____
_____
_____
_____

TOUGH TIMES & LESSONS LEARNED: _____
_____
_____
_____
_____

What are you grateful for today?   Stressed Angry Tired Sad Happy Excited
_____

REMEMBER! WAIT TO WRITE BELOW UNTIL THIS DAY NEXT YEAR!

DATE: _____ S M T W T F S

MEMORIES MADE: _____
_____
_____
_____
_____
_____

TOUGH TIMES & LESSONS LEARNED: _____
_____
_____
_____
_____

What are you grateful for today?   Stressed Angry Tired Sad Happy Excited
_____

Did you know? Bees can smell fear! So, stay calm during your next encounter with these buzzing friends.

DATE:_____ S M T W T F S

SUNDAY STRESS BUSTERS:

> When you are feeling tired and discouraged and don't want to do anything, look for a little job. Maybe you could wipe off the cabinets. Maybe you could take out the trash. Look for a little job to get started. Once you finish the little job, give yourself credit for it. Don't beat yourself up with a long list of all the things you still need to do. Once you get started with a little job, you may feel like tackling bigger jobs.

MEMORIES MADE: _____
_____
_____
_____
_____

TOUGH TIMES & LESSONS LEARNED: _____
_____
_____
_____
_____

What are you grateful for today?

Stressed | Angry | Tired | Sad | Happy | Excited

REMEMBER! WAIT TO WRITE BELOW UNTIL THIS DAY NEXT YEAR!

DATE:_____ S M T W T F S

MEMORIES MADE: _____
_____
_____
_____
_____

TOUGH TIMES & LESSONS LEARNED: _____
_____
_____
_____
_____

What are you grateful for today?

Stressed | Angry | Tired | Sad | Happy | Excited

Did you know? The average person breathes in the equivalent of 13 pints (about 6.2 liters) of air every minute.

DATE: _____ (S) (M) (T) (W) (T) (F) (S)

MONDAY MANNERS:

> "Pay attention to how you smell! Do all the little, but important things such as showering daily, using deodorant, brush your teeth morning and night, use floss and mouthwash. Keep gum or mints handy. Wash your hair regularly—it can get smelly quick! Perfume, cologne, or body spray is okay but go easy! Taking care of your hygiene should be near the top of your priorities."

MEMORIES MADE: _____
_____
_____
_____
_____

TOUGH TIMES & LESSONS LEARNED: _____
_____
_____
_____
_____

What are you grateful for today?   Stressed Angry Tired Sad Happy Excited
_____

REMEMBER! WAIT TO WRITE BELOW UNTIL THIS DAY NEXT YEAR!

DATE: _____ (S) (M) (T) (W) (T) (F) (S)

MEMORIES MADE: _____
_____
_____
_____
_____
_____

TOUGH TIMES & LESSONS LEARNED: _____
_____
_____
_____
_____

What are you grateful for today?   Stressed Angry Tired Sad Happy Excited
_____

Did you know? The average human could swim through the blood vessels of a blue whale's heart, illustrating the vast difference in size between species.

DATE: _____ (S) (M) (T) (W) (T) (F) (S)

TUESDAY TIPS:

> " Be open to and accept constructive feedback. Keep in mind that when a professor critiques your work, he or she is doing you a favor. It's not personal; any work can be improved. The more "red ink" you see on a paper, the more time that the professor took to point out ways for you to improve. Welcome the input! Humility is key in college! "

MEMORIES MADE: _____
_____
_____
_____
_____

TOUGH TIMES & LESSONS LEARNED: _____
_____
_____
_____
_____

What are you grateful for today?
_____

Stressed | Angry | Tired | Sad | Happy | Excited

REMEMBER! WAIT TO WRITE BELOW UNTIL THIS DAY NEXT YEAR!

DATE: _____ (S) (M) (T) (W) (T) (F) (S)

MEMORIES MADE: _____
_____
_____
_____
_____

TOUGH TIMES & LESSONS LEARNED: _____
_____
_____
_____
_____

What are you grateful for today?
_____

Stressed | Angry | Tired | Sad | Happy | Excited

Did you know? Celebrating differences sparks joy! Embrace your roommates' quirks, explore their interests, and appreciate the unique flavors they bring to the friendship. Diversity is the spice of life!

DATE: _____ (S) (M) (T) (W) (T) (F) (S)

WEDNESDAY (HUMP DAY!) HAPPY HACKS:

> "More moving means more happiness. Yep, moving your body moves your brain, which improves your mood, reduces stress, and helps you sleep better. Why? Exercise releases chemicals like serotonin and dopamine, making you feel good. It also boosts self-esteem and brain health, making you more focused and creative. Get your friends or roommates to join in, which makes it even more fun! Plus, slaying your fitness goals builds confidence. Of course, long-term benefits include a healthier and happier life. Commit to hitting the rec center, joining a gym, or moving more in your apartment! Get those steps in and both your body and brain will benefit!"

MEMORIES MADE: _____
_____
_____
_____
_____

TOUGH TIMES & LESSONS LEARNED: _____
_____
_____
_____

What are you grateful for today?   Stressed Angry Tired Sad Happy Excited
_____

⬅ REMEMBER! WAIT TO WRITE BELOW UNTIL THIS DAY NEXT YEAR!

DATE: _____ (S) (M) (T) (W) (T) (F) (S)

MEMORIES MADE: _____
_____
_____
_____
_____

TOUGH TIMES & LESSONS LEARNED: _____
_____
_____
_____

What are you grateful for today?   Stressed Angry Tired Sad Happy Excited
_____

Did you know? Taking a break from technology and spending time in silence can boost creativity, improve focus, and reduce mental fatigue. Disconnect to reconnect with yourself.

DATE: _____ (S) (M) (T) (W) (T) (F) (S)

THURSDAY MYTHS:

> Myth: "I'll be partying every weekend."
>
> Reality: While college offers social opportunities, there's also studying, extracurricular activities, and maybe a part-time job. Your weekends might look more like a jigsaw puzzle of responsibilities than a non-stop party scene...and that's okay!

MEMORIES MADE: _____
_____
_____
_____
_____
_____

TOUGH TIMES & LESSONS LEARNED: _____
_____
_____
_____
_____

What are you grateful for today?   Stressed Angry Tired Sad Happy Excited
_____

REMEMBER! WAIT TO WRITE BELOW UNTIL THIS DAY NEXT YEAR!

DATE: _____ (S) (M) (T) (W) (T) (F) (S)

MEMORIES MADE: _____
_____
_____
_____
_____
_____

TOUGH TIMES & LESSONS LEARNED: _____
_____
_____
_____
_____

What are you grateful for today?   Stressed Angry Tired Sad Happy Excited
_____

Did you know? The phrase "bite the bullet" is believed to have originated from the practice of having a patient clench a bullet between their teeth as a way to endure pain during surgical procedures without anesthesia in the past.

DATE: _____ (S) (M) (T) (W) (T) (F) (S)

FRIDAY FILL IN THE BLANKS:

" My favorite food is _____ because _____

The best concert I ever attended was _____

My all-time favorite movie is _____

I enjoy listening to _____ my favorite song by them is _____ "

MEMORIES MADE: _____
_____
_____
_____
_____

TOUGH TIMES & LESSONS LEARNED: _____
_____
_____
_____

What are you grateful for today?
_____

Stressed | Angry | Tired | Sad | Happy | Excited

REMEMBER! WAIT TO WRITE BELOW UNTIL THIS DAY NEXT YEAR!

DATE: _____ (S) (M) (T) (W) (T) (F) (S)

MEMORIES MADE: _____
_____
_____
_____
_____

TOUGH TIMES & LESSONS LEARNED: _____
_____
_____
_____

What are you grateful for today?
_____

Stressed | Angry | Tired | Sad | Happy | Excited

Did you know? The phrase "break the ice" originally referred to the breaking of ice to allow ships to pass in cold regions, this phrase now means to initiate conversation or ease social tension, making it easier for people to communicate.

DATE: _____ (S) (M) (T) (W) (T) (F) (S)

SATURDAY TED TALKS:

> In "The Power of Appreciation" TED talk, Mike Robbins emphasizes the transformative impact of expressing genuine appreciation in personal and professional realms. He distinguishes appreciation from recognition, advocating for a culture that values emotional connection and acknowledges the inherent worth of individuals, beyond just their achievements. Robbins suggests that fostering an environment of gratitude and appreciation can lead to increased connection, productivity, and overall well-being.

MEMORIES MADE: _____
_____
_____
_____
_____
_____

TOUGH TIMES & LESSONS LEARNED: _____
_____
_____
_____
_____

What are you grateful for today?   Stressed Angry Tired Sad Happy Excited
_____

REMEMBER! WAIT TO WRITE BELOW UNTIL THIS DAY NEXT YEAR!

DATE: _____ (S) (M) (T) (W) (T) (F) (S)

MEMORIES MADE: _____
_____
_____
_____
_____
_____

TOUGH TIMES & LESSONS LEARNED: _____
_____
_____
_____
_____

What are you grateful for today?   Stressed Angry Tired Sad Happy Excited
_____

Did you know? Your tears have different chemical compositions depending on whether you're crying from sadness, pain, or irritation. They're emotional messengers!

DATE: _____ Ⓢ Ⓜ Ⓣ Ⓦ Ⓣ Ⓕ Ⓢ

SUNDAY STRESS BUSTERS:

> Deal with rejection in healthy ways. One powerful stressor for most people is the feeling that no one cares. Maybe when you talk to your mother she only preaches to you. Maybe your boyfriend or girlfriend doesn't understand you or show respect for your feelings. Some researchers now tell us that the healthiest people are not necessarily those who had perfect childhoods but those who have made peace with their childhoods. Maybe Mom was not nice and maybe Dad deserted the family. But healthy people don't stay angry and upset with the past. They accept what has happened, and they live in the present. They accept what their parents have done and can do for them. They build good friendships.

MEMORIES MADE: _____
_____
_____
_____
_____
_____

TOUGH TIMES & LESSONS LEARNED: _____
_____
_____
_____
_____

What are you grateful for today?   Stressed Angry Tired Sad Happy Excited
_____

REMEMBER! WAIT TO WRITE BELOW UNTIL THIS DAY NEXT YEAR!

DATE: _____ Ⓢ Ⓜ Ⓣ Ⓦ Ⓣ Ⓕ Ⓢ

MEMORIES MADE: _____
_____
_____
_____
_____
_____

TOUGH TIMES & LESSONS LEARNED: _____
_____
_____
_____
_____

What are you grateful for today?   Stressed Angry Tired Sad Happy Excited
_____

Did you know? Taking just 15 minutes to color in an adult coloring book can activate relaxation pathways in the brain, similar to meditation, reducing stress and anxiety. Unleash your inner child and find your zen! Heck, here's one for you to try!

DRAWING AND DOODLING WHILE TAKING SOME DEEP BREATHS CAN HELP YOU RELAX AND FEEL LESS STRESSED!

PLUS, WHO DOESN'T LOVE A CUTE YORKIE!?

DATE: _____   (S) (M) (T) (W) (T) (F) (S)

MONDAY MANNERS:

> "Phone manners matter. Most people communicate with others by texting but it's important to know and use basic phone manners. Answer with a "hello" and end the conversation with a "good-bye." Speak clearly and minimize distractions around you while you're listening so you can pay attention to what the person is saying. It's annoying when you are talking with someone on the phone, and you know they are distracted and not paying attention. The greatest gift you can give the person you are talking with is your all-in attention."

MEMORIES MADE: _____
_____
_____
_____
_____
_____

TOUGH TIMES & LESSONS LEARNED: _____
_____
_____
_____
_____

What are you grateful for today?   Stressed Angry Tired Sad Happy Excited
_____

REMEMBER! WAIT TO WRITE BELOW UNTIL THIS DAY NEXT YEAR!

DATE: _____   (S) (M) (T) (W) (T) (F) (S)

MEMORIES MADE: _____
_____
_____
_____
_____
_____

TOUGH TIMES & LESSONS LEARNED: _____
_____
_____
_____
_____

What are you grateful for today?   Stressed Angry Tired Sad Happy Excited
_____

Did you know? The phrase "bury the hatchet" comes from a Native American custom of burying one's hatchet or tomahawk when peace was made between groups.

DATE: _____ (S) (M) (T) (W) (T) (F) (S)

TUESDAY TIPS:

> " Take advantage of the college library and its resources. And there's all kinds of resources to check out. You might be thinking "Who goes to the library these days?" You should! Just knowing the resources that are there to help you can be so helpful! Plus, you're paying fees for all kinds of resources on campus, you may as well use them! "

MEMORIES MADE: _____
_____
_____
_____
_____
_____

TOUGH TIMES & LESSONS LEARNED: _____
_____
_____
_____
_____
_____

What are you grateful for today?
_____

Stressed | Angry | Tired | Sad | Happy | Excited

REMEMBER! WAIT TO WRITE BELOW UNTIL THIS DAY NEXT YEAR!

DATE: _____ (S) (M) (T) (W) (T) (F) (S)

MEMORIES MADE: _____
_____
_____
_____
_____
_____

TOUGH TIMES & LESSONS LEARNED: _____
_____
_____
_____
_____
_____

What are you grateful for today?
_____

Stressed | Angry | Tired | Sad | Happy | Excited

Did you know? Mindful eating, which involves paying attention to hunger and fullness cues, can aid in weight management and improve your relationship with food. Slow down and enjoy it!

DATE: _____ Ⓢ Ⓜ Ⓣ Ⓦ Ⓣ Ⓕ Ⓢ

WEDNESDAY (HUMP DAY!) HAPPY HACKS:

> View the future with hope! There are at least three ways you can view your future. 1. You can think about all the things that could go wrong, which creates worry, anxiety and fear, and results in no positive forward movement. 2. You can fantasize about all the wonderful things that could be part of the future, with no grounding in reality. This can actually be fun to think about and it creates some positivity, but it doesn't last as you come back down to reality if there isn't any action to make it happen. Or 3. View the future with hope. Hope is what propels us to take action, to create positive forward momentum in life. It includes meaningful and realistic goals. Hope is exciting and it's balanced and grounded with reality of the work it will take to overcome challenges. This type of hope leads to positive forward action.

MEMORIES MADE: _____
_____
_____
_____
_____
_____

TOUGH TIMES & LESSONS LEARNED: _____
_____
_____
_____
_____

What are you grateful for today?   Stressed Angry Tired Sad Happy Excited
_____

REMEMBER! WAIT TO WRITE BELOW UNTIL THIS DAY NEXT YEAR!

DATE: _____ Ⓢ Ⓜ Ⓣ Ⓦ Ⓣ Ⓕ Ⓢ

MEMORIES MADE: _____
_____
_____
_____
_____
_____

TOUGH TIMES & LESSONS LEARNED: _____
_____
_____
_____
_____

What are you grateful for today?   Stressed Angry Tired Sad Happy Excited
_____

Did you know? Your body has a type of sweat gland called an apocrine gland, which is concentrated in the underarm and groin areas and becomes active at puberty.

DATE: _____ (S) (M) (T) (W) (T) (F) (S)

THURSDAY MYTHS:

> Myth: "I can rely on last-minute studying."
>
> Reality: Consistent studying is more effective than a last-minute cram session. It's like training for a marathon; you can't prepare the night before and expect to cross the finish line with ease.

MEMORIES MADE: _____
_____
_____
_____
_____

TOUGH TIMES & LESSONS LEARNED: _____
_____
_____
_____

What are you grateful for today?
_____

Stressed | Angry | Tired | Sad | Happy | Excited

REMEMBER! WAIT TO WRITE BELOW UNTIL THIS DAY NEXT YEAR!

DATE: _____ (S) (M) (T) (W) (T) (F) (S)

MEMORIES MADE: _____
_____
_____
_____
_____

TOUGH TIMES & LESSONS LEARNED: _____
_____
_____
_____

What are you grateful for today?
_____

Stressed | Angry | Tired | Sad | Happy | Excited

Did you know? Your gut bacteria can influence your mood, sleep, and even brain function! These tiny creatures have hidden powers. Down some yogurt occasionally and keep em' happy!

DATE: _____ (S) (M) (T) (W) (T) (F) (S)

FRIDAY FILL IN THE BLANKS:

> "
> When I feel overwhelmed with college work, I usually...
> _____
>
> and one strategy I want to try to manage stress better is...
> _____
> "

MEMORIES MADE: _____
_____
_____
_____
_____

TOUGH TIMES & LESSONS LEARNED: _____
_____
_____
_____
_____

What are you grateful for today?   Stressed Angry Tired Sad Happy Excited
_____

REMEMBER! WAIT TO WRITE BELOW UNTIL THIS DAY NEXT YEAR!

DATE: _____ (S) (M) (T) (W) (T) (F) (S)

MEMORIES MADE: _____
_____
_____
_____
_____

TOUGH TIMES & LESSONS LEARNED: _____
_____
_____
_____
_____

What are you grateful for today?   Stressed Angry Tired Sad Happy Excited
_____

Did you know? The human body has an internal clock known as the circadian rhythm, which regulates the timing of when we feel sleepy and when we feel alert.

DATE: _____ (S) (M) (T) (W) (T) (F) (S)

SATURDAY TED TALKS:

> Stressed? You may need more grit! In her TED talk "Grit: The Power of Passion and Perseverance," Angela Lee Duckworth talks about 'grit' as a key to success. Grit is the combination of passion and perseverance. She found that grittier people are more likely to succeed in various challenging settings, like education or careers. Duckworth explains that it's not intelligence or talent that leads to success, but the ability to stick with your future day in, day out, not just for a week or month, but for years. She emphasizes working hard and staying committed to long-term goals as the real secret to achieving objectives.

MEMORIES MADE: _____
_____
_____
_____
_____
_____

TOUGH TIMES & LESSONS LEARNED: _____
_____
_____
_____
_____

What are you grateful for today?   Stressed Angry Tired Sad Happy Excited

REMEMBER! WAIT TO WRITE BELOW UNTIL THIS DAY NEXT YEAR!

DATE: _____ (S) (M) (T) (W) (T) (F) (S)

MEMORIES MADE: _____
_____
_____
_____
_____
_____

TOUGH TIMES & LESSONS LEARNED: _____
_____
_____
_____
_____

What are you grateful for today?   Stressed Angry Tired Sad Happy Excited

Did you know? The Greek system (fraternities and sororities) in colleges started in the 1770s as literary societies and has evolved into the social organizations they are today.

DATE: _____ S M T W T F S

SUNDAY STRESS BUSTERS:

> Incorporate short breaks into your study sessions to give your mind a much-needed rest. Stepping away from your work and studies, even for just a few minutes, allows you to stretch, take a leisurely walk, or engage in a brief meditation. These pauses are essential for revitalizing your mind, improving focus, and ultimately boosting productivity when you resume studying. Remember, a refreshed mind is more effective than one that's been overworked.

MEMORIES MADE: _____
_____
_____
_____
_____

TOUGH TIMES & LESSONS LEARNED: _____
_____
_____
_____
_____

What are you grateful for today?
_____

Stressed | Angry | Tired | Sad | Happy | Excited

REMEMBER! WAIT TO WRITE BELOW UNTIL THIS DAY NEXT YEAR!

DATE: _____ S M T W T F S

MEMORIES MADE: _____
_____
_____
_____
_____

TOUGH TIMES & LESSONS LEARNED: _____
_____
_____
_____
_____

What are you grateful for today?
_____

Stressed | Angry | Tired | Sad | Happy | Excited

Did you know? Cooking with olive oil adds healthy fats and antioxidants to your meals, supporting heart health and brain function. Drizzle with goodness!

DATE: _____ (S) (M) (T) (W) (T) (F) (S)

MONDAY MANNERS:

> Secure a job successfully by following key steps. Not everyone chooses to work while at college. But if you do, here's some tips and manners! Have someone review your resume. Review application details for accuracy, including email and phone number. Be sure to check your voicemail regularly and answer calls, even if you don't recognize the number. Land an interview? Dress appropriately, be friendly, respectful and thankful. Speak up, maintain eye contact and put your phone away. Land the job? Be positive, honest and hardworking to make a good impression.

MEMORIES MADE: _____
_____
_____
_____
_____

TOUGH TIMES & LESSONS LEARNED: _____
_____
_____
_____

What are you grateful for today?

Stressed | Angry | Tired | Sad | Happy | Excited

REMEMBER! WAIT TO WRITE BELOW UNTIL THIS DAY NEXT YEAR!

DATE: _____ (S) (M) (T) (W) (T) (F) (S)

MEMORIES MADE: _____
_____
_____
_____
_____

TOUGH TIMES & LESSONS LEARNED: _____
_____
_____
_____

What are you grateful for today?

Stressed | Angry | Tired | Sad | Happy | Excited

Did you know? Humans share 50% of their DNA with bananas, showcasing the fundamental similarities across living organisms.

DATE: _____ (S) (M) (T) (W) (T) (F) (S)

TUESDAY TIPS:

> Explore diverse courses and majors before settling on one. Okay, here us out. You may already know exactly what you want to do and what you want to major in. But hey now, there are TONS of fun classes to explore. And there are really few other times in your life when you have so many opportunities to learn about crazy awesome topics! And who knows, the cool class you take may lead to a new direction in life!

MEMORIES MADE: _____
_____
_____
_____
_____

TOUGH TIMES & LESSONS LEARNED: _____
_____
_____
_____
_____

What are you grateful for today?   Stressed Angry Tired Sad Happy Excited
_____

REMEMBER! WAIT TO WRITE BELOW UNTIL THIS DAY NEXT YEAR!

DATE: _____ (S) (M) (T) (W) (T) (F) (S)

MEMORIES MADE: _____
_____
_____
_____
_____

TOUGH TIMES & LESSONS LEARNED: _____
_____
_____
_____
_____

What are you grateful for today?   Stressed Angry Tired Sad Happy Excited
_____

Did you know? Regularly consuming omega-3 fatty acids, found in fish like salmon, can improve heart health and reduce the risk of chronic diseases, highlighting the importance of diet in health.

DATE: _____ (S) (M) (T) (W) (T) (F) (S)

WEDNESDAY (HUMP DAY!) HAPPY HACKS

> More about hope! Last week's happy hack was about viewing the future with hope! There are at least three elements of hope. First, is the belief that our future can be better than our current reality. Whether things are currently awful or awesome, hope is believing that things can get better. Second, we believe we have the power to make it better. This could also include a belief that you can draw on a higher power or other resources to make it better. And third, there are many pathways to get to better places. What might you add about hope?

MEMORIES MADE: _____
_____
_____
_____
_____
_____

TOUGH TIMES & LESSONS LEARNED: _____
_____
_____
_____
_____

What are you grateful for today?   Stressed Angry Tired Sad Happy Excited
_____

REMEMBER! WAIT TO WRITE BELOW UNTIL THIS DAY NEXT YEAR!

DATE: _____ (S) (M) (T) (W) (T) (F) (S)

MEMORIES MADE: _____
_____
_____
_____
_____
_____

TOUGH TIMES & LESSONS LEARNED: _____
_____
_____
_____
_____

What are you grateful for today?   Stressed Angry Tired Sad Happy Excited
_____

Did you know? Berries, like blueberries and strawberries, are packed with antioxidants and flavonoids that protect brain cells and boost cognitive function. Berry your way to a healthier brain!

DATE: _____ S M T W T F S

THURSDAY MYTHS:

> Myth: "I must participate in Greek life to enjoy college."
>
> Reality: Greek life is just one aspect of the college experience. There are numerous clubs and organizations to explore. It's like a buffet – there are many options, and Greek life is just one dish.

MEMORIES MADE: _____
_____
_____
_____
_____

TOUGH TIMES & LESSONS LEARNED: _____
_____
_____
_____
_____

What are you grateful for today?

Stressed Angry Tired Sad Happy Excited

REMEMBER! WAIT TO WRITE BELOW UNTIL THIS DAY NEXT YEAR!

DATE: _____ S M T W T F S

MEMORIES MADE: _____
_____
_____
_____
_____

TOUGH TIMES & LESSONS LEARNED: _____
_____
_____
_____
_____

What are you grateful for today?

Stressed Angry Tired Sad Happy Excited

Did you know? Practice makes perfect! Test yourself with flashcards, practice problems, or past exams to identify weaknesses and solidify understanding. Turn test prep into a game, not a chore!

DATE: _____ (S) (M) (T) (W) (T) (F) (S)

FRIDAY FILL IN THE BLANKS:

> "
> If I could redo one thing this semester, it would be...
> _____
>
> because...
> _____
> "

MEMORIES MADE: _____
_____
_____
_____
_____

TOUGH TIMES & LESSONS LEARNED: _____
_____
_____
_____

What are you grateful for today?
_____

Stressed | Angry | Tired | Sad | Happy | Excited

REMEMBER! WAIT TO WRITE BELOW UNTIL THIS DAY NEXT YEAR!

DATE: _____ (S) (M) (T) (W) (T) (F) (S)

MEMORIES MADE: _____
_____
_____
_____
_____

TOUGH TIMES & LESSONS LEARNED: _____
_____
_____
_____

What are you grateful for today?
_____

Stressed | Angry | Tired | Sad | Happy | Excited

Did you know? Positive social interactions on a daily basis can significantly increase levels of happiness and overall life satisfaction among college students. Smile and say hello more!

DATE: _____ S M T W T F S

SATURDAY TED TALKS:

> Gretchen Rubin's TED talk, "Five Half-Truths About Happiness," challenges common beliefs about happiness. She argues that the ideas that happiness is purely internal, requires big life changes, comes from following your passion, is achieved by indulging yourself, and is a final destination, are oversimplified. True happiness, according to Rubin, involves a deeper understanding of these concepts, recognizing the importance of external influences, small joys, and the ongoing journey towards contentment, rather than viewing happiness as an absolute state to be reached.

MEMORIES MADE: _____

TOUGH TIMES & LESSONS LEARNED: _____

What are you grateful for today? _____

Stressed | Angry | Tired | Sad | Happy | Excited

REMEMBER! WAIT TO WRITE BELOW UNTIL THIS DAY NEXT YEAR!

DATE: _____ S M T W T F S

MEMORIES MADE: _____

TOUGH TIMES & LESSONS LEARNED: _____

What are you grateful for today? _____

Stressed | Angry | Tired | Sad | Happy | Excited

Did you know? The only part of the body that has no blood supply is the cornea of the eye. It receives oxygen directly from the air.

DATE: _____ (S) (M) (T) (W) (T) (F) (S)

SUNDAY STRESS BUSTERS:

> When stress weighs heavily, don't underestimate the power of seeking support from your social network. Whether it's confiding in friends, family members, or seeking guidance from counselors, sharing your burdens can alleviate the weight on your shoulders. Opening up about your experiences not only provides immediate relief but also invites fresh insights and strategies for effectively managing stress in the long run.

MEMORIES MADE: _____
_____
_____
_____
_____
_____

TOUGH TIMES & LESSONS LEARNED:
_____
_____
_____
_____

What are you grateful for today?
_____

Stressed Angry Tired Sad Happy Excited

REMEMBER! WAIT TO WRITE BELOW UNTIL THIS DAY NEXT YEAR!

DATE: _____ (S) (M) (T) (W) (T) (F) (S)

MEMORIES MADE: _____
_____
_____
_____
_____
_____

TOUGH TIMES & LESSONS LEARNED: _____
_____
_____
_____
_____

What are you grateful for today?
_____

Stressed Angry Tired Sad Happy Excited

Did you know? The human body contains about 0.2 milligrams of gold, most of which is in our blood. So don't go digging for it!!

SUDOKU CHALLENGE!

	4			2		8	6	5
7				6		8		
1					4	7		2
	1	8	7	4				
		5	2		9	6		
				8	6	1	5	
9		1	5					6
				8		2		7
8	7	3		6			2	

WORD SCRAMBLE! (COLLEGE EDITION)

1. PSCLHARSHIO _____
2. AANLFNIIC IDA _____
3. MRJAO _____
4. ENEDISRT ALHL _____
5. IBALYRR _____
6. EXBSKTOTO _____
7. PLAAITONCPI _____
8. DEEREG _____
9. ATPVRIE _____
10. AOBRCSLEH _____
11. MAESRTS _____
12. TACNPEEACC _____

DATE: _____ (S) (M) (T) (W) (T) (F) (S)

MONDAY MANNERS:

> *Take charge of your appointments. Whether it's a teeth cleaning at the dentist or a haircut, manage your appointments. If it's a visit to the dentist or doctor, speak up about your concerns and questions. Getting a haircut? Be prepared to share what you want—bring a picture and communicate what you want with both clarity and kindness. Put your phone away unless you're using it to take notes. If something comes up and you can't make it, cancel within 24 hours if possible. If you like someone, note their name for future requests.*

MEMORIES MADE: _____
_____
_____
_____
_____

TOUGH TIMES & LESSONS LEARNED: _____
_____
_____
_____

What are you grateful for today?   Stressed   Angry   Tired   Sad   Happy   Excited
_____

REMEMBER! WAIT TO WRITE BELOW UNTIL THIS DAY NEXT YEAR!

DATE: _____ (S) (M) (T) (W) (T) (F) (S)

MEMORIES MADE: _____
_____
_____
_____
_____

TOUGH TIMES & LESSONS LEARNED: _____
_____
_____
_____

What are you grateful for today?   Stressed   Angry   Tired   Sad   Happy   Excited
_____

Did you know? The human eye can detect color differences as small as one ten-millionth of a shade! We're masters of chromatic perception.

DATE: _____ S M T W T F S

TUESDAY TIPS:

> While it's important to engage in extracurricular activities for a well-rounded college experience, it's crucial to maintain a balance. It's tempting to dive into numerous clubs, sports, and social events, but overcommitting can lead to burnout. Remember, these activities should enhance your life, not overwhelm it. Late nights and time-consuming commitments can encroach on essential study time, potentially harming your academic performance. If you find your grades beginning to falter, the added stress can detract from both your enjoyment of extracurriculars and your overall well-being. Prioritize and choose activities that complement your academic goals, allowing you to enjoy the best of both worlds without compromising your education.

MEMORIES MADE: _____
_____
_____
_____
_____
_____

TOUGH TIMES & LESSONS LEARNED: _____
_____
_____
_____
_____

What are you grateful for today?

Stressed | Angry | Tired | Sad | Happy | Excited

_____

> REMEMBER! WAIT TO WRITE BELOW UNTIL THIS DAY NEXT YEAR!

DATE: _____ S M T W T F S

MEMORIES MADE: _____
_____
_____
_____
_____
_____

TOUGH TIMES & LESSONS LEARNED: _____
_____
_____
_____
_____

What are you grateful for today?

Stressed | Angry | Tired | Sad | Happy | Excited

_____

Did you know? The surface area of a human lung is equal to a tennis court, primarily due to the presence of thousands of tiny alveoli.

DATE: _____ S M T W T F S

WEDNESDAY (HUMP DAY!) HAPPY HACKS

> " If you ever struggle with getting along with another person here's 2 tips to help. First, notice what is important to them. Look for the good and find out what they like and enjoy in their life. The principles is seeking for understanding. Second, turn outward and serve them. Random acts of kindness, with no expectation of anything in return, will bring a spirit of friendship and gratitude and can soften hard hearts. "

MEMORIES MADE: _____
_____
_____
_____
_____

TOUGH TIMES & LESSONS LEARNED: _____
_____
_____
_____
_____

What are you grateful for today?
_____

Stressed Angry Tired Sad Happy Excited

REMEMBER! WAIT TO WRITE BELOW UNTIL THIS DAY NEXT YEAR!

DATE: _____ S M T W T F S

MEMORIES MADE: _____
_____
_____
_____
_____

TOUGH TIMES & LESSONS LEARNED: _____
_____
_____
_____
_____

What are you grateful for today?
_____

Stressed Angry Tired Sad Happy Excited

Did you know? Excessive screen time, especially before bed, can disrupt sleep patterns by suppressing the production of melatonin, the hormone responsible for regulating sleep-wake cycles.

DATE: _____ (S) (M) (T) (W) (T) (F) (S)

THURSDAY MYTHS:

> Myth: "I don't need to network in college."
>
> Reality: Building a network is crucial. Connections can lead to internships, jobs, and valuable opportunities. It's like planting seeds in a garden; nurture them, and they'll grow into something beneficial. Go make some connections!

MEMORIES MADE: _____
_____
_____
_____
_____

TOUGH TIMES & LESSONS LEARNED: _____
_____
_____
_____
_____

What are you grateful for today?
_____

Stressed | Angry | Tired | Sad | Happy | Excited

REMEMBER! WAIT TO WRITE BELOW UNTIL THIS DAY NEXT YEAR!

DATE: _____ (S) (M) (T) (W) (T) (F) (S)

MEMORIES MADE: _____
_____
_____
_____
_____

TOUGH TIMES & LESSONS LEARNED: _____
_____
_____
_____
_____

What are you grateful for today?
_____

Stressed | Angry | Tired | Sad | Happy | Excited

Did you know? Food can be a friendship builder! Cook meals together, share snacks, and have potlucks to celebrate diverse culinary treasures. Food connects hearts and stomachs!

DATE: _____ (S) (M) (T) (W) (T) (F) (S)

FRIDAY FILL IN THE BLANKS:

> "
> Write about a person you are so grateful you have met so far and describe why:
> _____
> _____
> _____
> _____
> "

MEMORIES MADE: _____
_____
_____
_____
_____

TOUGH TIMES & LESSONS LEARNED: _____
_____
_____
_____
_____

What are you grateful for today?
_____

Stressed | Angry | Tired | Sad | Happy | Excited

REMEMBER! WAIT TO WRITE BELOW UNTIL THIS DAY NEXT YEAR!

DATE: _____ (S) (M) (T) (W) (T) (F) (S)

MEMORIES MADE: _____
_____
_____
_____
_____

TOUGH TIMES & LESSONS LEARNED: _____
_____
_____
_____
_____

What are you grateful for today?
_____

Stressed | Angry | Tired | Sad | Happy | Excited

Did you know? Prioritizing sleep is crucial for college students. Aim for 7-8 hours of quality sleep each night to boost memory, focus, and overall well-being. Sleepy students are grumpy students!

DATE: _____ (S) (M) (T) (W) (T) (F) (S)

SATURDAY TED TALKS:

> Here's my own TEDx talk! (Dr. Dave) Haha! I argue that strong employee satisfaction is the "secret sauce" to business success. Forget traditional incentives; focus on the family fundamentals: safety, satisfaction, and connection. I compare workplaces to families, emphasizing the power of creating a supportive environment where employees feel valued and seen. Investing in employee well-being leads to increased engagement, productivity, and ultimately, a booming business. So, when you are looking for a job, pay attention to whether they treat employees like family!

MEMORIES MADE: _____
_____
_____
_____
_____

TOUGH TIMES & LESSONS LEARNED: _____
_____
_____
_____
_____

What are you grateful for today?
_____

Stressed | Angry | Tired | Sad | Happy | Excited

REMEMBER! WAIT TO WRITE BELOW UNTIL THIS DAY NEXT YEAR!

DATE: _____ (S) (M) (T) (W) (T) (F) (S)

MEMORIES MADE: _____
_____
_____
_____
_____

TOUGH TIMES & LESSONS LEARNED: _____
_____
_____
_____
_____

What are you grateful for today?
_____

Stressed | Angry | Tired | Sad | Happy | Excited

Did you know? The term 'alma mater' comes from Latin, meaning 'nourishing mother', originally used to describe a school, college, or university that one formerly attended.

DATE: _____ (S) (M) (T) (W) (T) (F) (S)

SUNDAY STRESS BUSTERS:

> "Get outside yourself. Sometimes we worry so much about our problems that we can't see anything else. It may help to take some cookies to some friends you've made or volunteer some time for a sorority, fraternity or community group. You don't need a lot of extra demands. But taking a little time to turn outward and help others can bring peace, meaning and satisfaction."

MEMORIES MADE: _____
_____
_____
_____
_____

TOUGH TIMES & LESSONS LEARNED: _____
_____
_____
_____

What are you grateful for today?   Stressed Angry Tired Sad Happy Excited
_____

REMEMBER! WAIT TO WRITE BELOW UNTIL THIS DAY NEXT YEAR!

DATE: _____ (S) (M) (T) (W) (T) (F) (S)

MEMORIES MADE: _____
_____
_____
_____
_____
_____

TOUGH TIMES & LESSONS LEARNED: _____
_____
_____
_____

What are you grateful for today?   Stressed Angry Tired Sad Happy Excited
_____

Did you know? The concept of 'sabbatical leave' for professors, typically every seven years, is based on the biblical practice of allowing land to rest every seventh year.

DATE: _____ (S) (M) (T) (W) (T) (F) (S)

MONDAY MANNERS:

> " Notice the good and seek out the positive. Instead of joining the trend of constant complaints and criticisms, actively look for, find, and express the good. Be generous in giving sincere compliments and expressing gratitude to others. Look for the silver lining in less-than-ideal situations. This positive attitude pleasantly surprises others and a positive person is more attractive anyway. Avoid being a constant complainer and drainer, as most people can't stand negativity. You'll always find what you're looking for so search for the good. "

MEMORIES MADE: _____
_____
_____
_____
_____

TOUGH TIMES & LESSONS LEARNED: _____
_____
_____
_____

What are you grateful for today?
_____

Stressed | Angry | Tired | Sad | Happy | Excited

REMEMBER! WAIT TO WRITE BELOW UNTIL THIS DAY NEXT YEAR!

DATE: _____ (S) (M) (T) (W) (T) (F) (S)

MEMORIES MADE: _____
_____
_____
_____
_____

TOUGH TIMES & LESSONS LEARNED: _____
_____
_____
_____

What are you grateful for today?
_____

Stressed | Angry | Tired | Sad | Happy | Excited

Did you know? Your tongue has over 8,000 taste buds, helping you savor all the culinary delights life offers!

DATE: _____ (S) (M) (T) (W) (T) (F) (S)

TUESDAY TIPS:

> " Take care of your physical and mental health. Read that again. Seriously, this is one of the most important investments you'll make. When you're running low on mental fuel, your entire life will be affected in negative ways. Take care of your body and brain — and there's all kinds of tips out there, including tons of them here in this journal!! Start with focusing on sleep, diet, and exercise. "

MEMORIES MADE: _____
_____
_____
_____
_____

TOUGH TIMES & LESSONS LEARNED: _____
_____
_____
_____
_____

What are you grateful for today?
_____

Stressed | Angry | Tired | Sad | Happy | Excited

REMEMBER! WAIT TO WRITE BELOW UNTIL THIS DAY NEXT YEAR!

DATE: _____ (S) (M) (T) (W) (T) (F) (S)

MEMORIES MADE: _____
_____
_____
_____
_____

TOUGH TIMES & LESSONS LEARNED: _____
_____
_____
_____
_____

What are you grateful for today?
_____

Stressed | Angry | Tired | Sad | Happy | Excited

Did you know? Your sense of smell is the last sense to activate in the morning and the first to diminish at night.

DATE: _____ Ⓢ Ⓜ Ⓣ Ⓦ Ⓣ Ⓕ Ⓢ

WEDNESDAY (HUMP DAY!) HAPPY HACKS:

> Absorb and stay with the good stuff that happens. It takes about 10-30 seconds to install a positive experience in the brain. To save and store it in the hippocampus, we need to focus on and hold on to the good stuff just a little longer than we do. Absorb the sights and sounds. Soak it in and live in the amazing moments. Don't move on too quickly. Even as you journal. Take time to pause and relive and rehearse the good in your mind. Emotional or negative events don't take nearly as long to store or recall them. So soak in the good times a bit longer.

MEMORIES MADE: _____
_____
_____
_____
_____

TOUGH TIMES & LESSONS LEARNED: _____
_____
_____
_____

What are you grateful for today?
_____

Stressed | Angry | Tired | Sad | Happy | Excited

REMEMBER! WAIT TO WRITE BELOW UNTIL THIS DAY NEXT YEAR!

DATE: _____ Ⓢ Ⓜ Ⓣ Ⓦ Ⓣ Ⓕ Ⓢ

MEMORIES MADE: _____
_____
_____
_____
_____

TOUGH TIMES & LESSONS LEARNED: _____
_____
_____
_____

What are you grateful for today?
_____

Stressed | Angry | Tired | Sad | Happy | Excited

Did you know? The population of the earth is about 8 billion people, but there are an estimated 10 quintillion ants, meaning for every human, there are about 1.25 million ants! This might be a good time to re-evaluate who the real rulers of the planet are.

DATE: _____ (S) (M) (T) (W) (T) (F) (S)

THURSDAY MYTHS:

> Myth: "I can easily work a full-time job and attend full-time classes."
>
> Reality: Balancing a full course load with a full-time job is extremely challenging. It's like trying to ride two bikes at once - possible, but requires exceptional balance and effort.

MEMORIES MADE: _____
_____
_____
_____
_____

TOUGH TIMES & LESSONS LEARNED: _____
_____
_____
_____

What are you grateful for today?
_____
Stressed Angry Tired Sad Happy Excited

REMEMBER! WAIT TO WRITE BELOW UNTIL THIS DAY NEXT YEAR!

DATE: _____ (S) (M) (T) (W) (T) (F) (S)

MEMORIES MADE: _____
_____
_____
_____
_____

TOUGH TIMES & LESSONS LEARNED: _____
_____
_____
_____

What are you grateful for today?
_____
Stressed Angry Tired Sad Happy Excited

Did you know? Daydreaming, contrary to popular belief, can boost creativity and problem-solving skills! Let your mind wander and watch the sparks fly.

DATE: _____ S M T W T F S

FRIDAY FILL IN THE BLANKS:

" If you could talk to your high school self, what advice would you give and why?
_____
_____
_____
_____
"

MEMORIES MADE: _____
_____
_____
_____
_____

TOUGH TIMES & LESSONS LEARNED: _____
_____
_____
_____

What are you grateful for today?   Stressed Angry Tired Sad Happy Excited
_____

REMEMBER! WAIT TO WRITE BELOW UNTIL THIS DAY NEXT YEAR!

DATE: _____ S M T W T F S

MEMORIES MADE: _____
_____
_____
_____
_____

TOUGH TIMES & LESSONS LEARNED: _____
_____
_____
_____

What are you grateful for today?   Stressed Angry Tired Sad Happy Excited
_____

Did you know? A balanced diet can impact mental health; deficiencies in certain nutrients like omega-3 fatty acids and vitamin D can increase the risk of mood disorders.

DATE: _____ (S) (M) (T) (W) (T) (F) (S)

SATURDAY TED TALKS:

> In her TED Talk "There's More to Life than Being Happy," Emily Esfahani Smith discusses the difference between being happy and having meaning in life. She explains that while happiness is about momentary pleasure, a meaningful life intertwines with contributing to others and being part of something bigger. Pursuing meaning, rather than temporary happiness, can lead to a more fulfilling and resilient life. She emphasizes that the quest for meaning, defined by connection, purpose, and transcendence, is what truly enriches our lives, even if it doesn't always make us "happy" in the conventional sense.

MEMORIES MADE: _____
_____
_____
_____
_____

TOUGH TIMES & LESSONS LEARNED: _____
_____
_____
_____
_____

What are you grateful for today?
_____

Stressed | Angry | Tired | Sad | Happy | Excited

REMEMBER! WAIT TO WRITE BELOW UNTIL THIS DAY NEXT YEAR!

DATE: _____ (S) (M) (T) (W) (T) (F) (S)

MEMORIES MADE: _____
_____
_____
_____
_____

TOUGH TIMES & LESSONS LEARNED: _____
_____
_____
_____
_____

What are you grateful for today?
_____

Stressed | Angry | Tired | Sad | Happy | Excited

Did you know? Human saliva contains a painkiller called opiorphin that is six times more powerful than morphine. Sore? Swallow your spit :)

DATE: _____ (S) (M) (T) (W) (T) (F) (S)

SUNDAY STRESS BUSTERS:

> " Be patient. Some struggles and stresses solve themselves with time. Eventually the semester ends, the big test comes and goes, you move on to another relationship, or you find a different place to live or change majors. The rain stops and the sun comes out. Work on the things you can change. Be patient with things that take time. "

MEMORIES MADE: _____
_____
_____
_____
_____

TOUGH TIMES & LESSONS LEARNED: _____
_____
_____
_____
_____

What are you grateful for today?   Stressed Angry Tired Sad Happy Excited
_____

REMEMBER! WAIT TO WRITE BELOW UNTIL THIS DAY NEXT YEAR!

DATE: _____ (S) (M) (T) (W) (T) (F) (S)

MEMORIES MADE: _____
_____
_____
_____
_____

TOUGH TIMES & LESSONS LEARNED: _____
_____
_____
_____
_____

What are you grateful for today?   Stressed Angry Tired Sad Happy Excited
_____

Did you know? The Earth is hurtling through space at 67,000 miles per hour!
Buckle up, Earthlings, and enjoy the cosmic ride.

DATE: _____ (S) (M) (T) (W) (T) (F) (S)

MONDAY MANNERS:

> Embrace "I don't know." If you're not sure about a topic, admit it instead of speculating. Saying, "I'm not sure" or "Let me get back to you" is okay. Rushed opinions can cause problems. You're not required to answer immediately, especially if you haven't looked into the issue or don't know the facts. Maturity lies in recognizing your knowledge limits. It's totally fine to admit you're not sure about something and then do some digging to boost your understanding before sharing your opinion on a topic. It's better to take time to learn it than fake it!

MEMORIES MADE: _____
_____
_____
_____
_____
_____

TOUGH TIMES & LESSONS LEARNED: _____
_____
_____
_____
_____

What are you grateful for today?
_____

Stressed | Angry | Tired | Sad | Happy | Excited

REMEMBER! WAIT TO WRITE BELOW UNTIL THIS DAY NEXT YEAR!

DATE: _____ (S) (M) (T) (W) (T) (F) (S)

MEMORIES MADE: _____
_____
_____
_____
_____
_____

TOUGH TIMES & LESSONS LEARNED: _____
_____
_____
_____
_____

What are you grateful for today?
_____

Stressed | Angry | Tired | Sad | Happy | Excited

Did you know? Adding a pinch of cinnamon to your meals can regulate blood sugar, aid digestion, and even fight cravings for unhealthy snacks. Sprinkle your way to better health!

DATE: _____ (S) (M) (T) (W) (T) (F) (S)

TUESDAY TIPS:

> Develop a healthy exercise routine. Most schools have great rec centers with all the equipment you need, and tons of stuff you'll never use. But even if you're not a big gym rat, go for a jog outside or do some simple yoga or other exercise where you live. The key to remember is moving your body moves your brain. Make it a priority. Schedule it and stick to it. Few things will improve your physical and mental health more than regular exercise. Remember the acronym PITT - Put In The Time.

MEMORIES MADE: _____
_____
_____
_____
_____
_____

TOUGH TIMES & LESSONS LEARNED: _____
_____
_____
_____
_____

What are you grateful for today?   Stressed   Angry   Tired   Sad   Happy   Excited
_____

REMEMBER! WAIT TO WRITE BELOW UNTIL THIS DAY NEXT YEAR!

DATE: _____ (S) (M) (T) (W) (T) (F) (S)

MEMORIES MADE: _____
_____
_____
_____
_____
_____

TOUGH TIMES & LESSONS LEARNED: _____
_____
_____
_____
_____

What are you grateful for today?   Stressed   Angry   Tired   Sad   Happy   Excited
_____

Did you know? Setting healthy boundaries in relationships protects your mental and emotional well-being, establishes respect, and allows for positive interactions. Know your limits, set your terms!

DATE: _____ S M T W T F S

WEDNESDAY (HUMP DAY!) HAPPY HACKS

> One of the best happy hacks is RAKs! Random Acts of Kindness. The top happiness scholars have said that doing something kind for someone else will temporarily boost your well-being more than any other exercise. It doesn't have to be big. Open a door for someone, do the dishes for a roommate, let someone check out before you at the grocery store. Get creative. For ideas, just YouTube random acts of kindness. Kindness is king!! Go for it! Make time to be kind.

MEMORIES MADE: _____
_____
_____
_____
_____

TOUGH TIMES & LESSONS LEARNED: _____
_____
_____
_____
_____

What are you grateful for today?

Stressed | Angry | Tired | Sad | Happy | Excited

REMEMBER! WAIT TO WRITE BELOW UNTIL THIS DAY NEXT YEAR!

DATE: _____ S M T W T F S

MEMORIES MADE: _____
_____
_____
_____
_____

TOUGH TIMES & LESSONS LEARNED: _____
_____
_____
_____
_____

What are you grateful for today?

Stressed | Angry | Tired | Sad | Happy | Excited

Did you know? You lose about 4kg of skin cells every year, with dead skin making up a significant portion of household dust....gross

DATE: _____ S M T W T F S

THURSDAY MYTHS:

> Myth: "I'll read every assigned book from cover to cover."
>
> Reality: While it's good to keep up with readings, sometimes you'll have to prioritize. Skimming, summaries, and focusing on key sections become necessary skills. It's like a reading buffet – sometimes, you just sample.

MEMORIES MADE: _____
_____
_____
_____
_____
_____

TOUGH TIMES & LESSONS LEARNED: _____
_____
_____
_____
_____

What are you grateful for today?
_____

Stressed Angry Tired Sad Happy Excited

REMEMBER! WAIT TO WRITE BELOW UNTIL THIS DAY NEXT YEAR!

DATE: _____ S M T W T F S

MEMORIES MADE: _____
_____
_____
_____
_____
_____

TOUGH TIMES & LESSONS LEARNED: _____
_____
_____
_____
_____

What are you grateful for today?
_____

Stressed Angry Tired Sad Happy Excited

Did you know? There are more atoms in one grain of sand than stars in the Milky Way galaxy! A humbling perspective on the vastness of existence.

DATE:_____ (S) (M) (T) (W) (T) (F) (S)

FRIDAY FILL IN THE BLANKS:

> Life check! Your future self (and your kids!) may be interested in what the price of different things are right now. Fill in the blank for the average prices of the following:
>
> Dozen eggs: New cell phone:
>
> Meal at a fast-food restaurant: Monthly gym pass:
>
> Your last haircut: Postage stamp:

MEMORIES MADE: _____
_____
_____
_____
_____

TOUGH TIMES & LESSONS LEARNED: _____
_____
_____
_____

What are you grateful for today?   Stressed Angry Tired Sad Happy Excited
_____

REMEMBER! WAIT TO WRITE BELOW UNTIL THIS DAY NEXT YEAR!

DATE:_____ (S) (M) (T) (W) (T) (F) (S)

MEMORIES MADE: _____
_____
_____
_____
_____

TOUGH TIMES & LESSONS LEARNED: _____
_____
_____
_____

What are you grateful for today?   Stressed Angry Tired Sad Happy Excited
_____

Did you know? Many famous inventions, like Facebook and Google, originated on college campuses, showcasing the innovative potential of college students.

DATE: _____   (S) (M) (T) (W) (T) (F) (S)

SATURDAY TED TALKS:

> Stressed? Be still. In his TED talk "The Art of Stillness," Pico Iyer discusses the importance of taking time to be still in our fast-paced, constantly connected world. He suggests that by slowing down and finding quiet moments, we can escape the noise and chaos of daily life. This stillness allows us to reflect, recharge, and have a clearer understanding of our surroundings and ourselves. Iyer emphasizes that in an age where everyone is always moving and doing, the real adventure may be found in stopping and being still. He encourages people to find moments of stillness to gain insight and peace.

MEMORIES MADE: _____
_____
_____
_____
_____
_____

TOUGH TIMES & LESSONS LEARNED: _____
_____
_____
_____
_____

What are you grateful for today?   Stressed Angry Tired Sad Happy Excited
_____

REMEMBER! WAIT TO WRITE BELOW UNTIL THIS DAY NEXT YEAR!

DATE: _____   (S) (M) (T) (W) (T) (F) (S)

MEMORIES MADE: _____
_____
_____
_____
_____
_____

TOUGH TIMES & LESSONS LEARNED: _____
_____
_____
_____
_____

What are you grateful for today?   Stressed Angry Tired Sad Happy Excited
_____

Did you know? Singing releases endorphins, natural painkillers, and can decrease stress hormones, improving mood and reducing pain. Belt out your worries!

DATE: _____ (S) (M) (T) (W) (T) (F) (S)

SUNDAY STRESS BUSTERS:

> "Don't fall into the trap of comparing yourself to everyone around you. For example, your roommate might be an amazing cook, and your friend might sing like a star, be super creative, ace math, or keep everything perfectly organized. But it's important to remember that no one is perfect at everything. Everyone has their own special skills. Take some time to find out what you're really good at. Enjoy those talents. Have fun with them and think about how you can use them to make a difference for other people. That's what really matters. And you'll stress less."

MEMORIES MADE: _____
_____
_____
_____
_____

TOUGH TIMES & LESSONS LEARNED:
_____
_____
_____
_____

What are you grateful for today?   Stressed Angry Tired Sad Happy Excited
_____

REMEMBER! WAIT TO WRITE BELOW UNTIL THIS DAY NEXT YEAR!

DATE: _____ (S) (M) (T) (W) (T) (F) (S)

MEMORIES MADE: _____
_____
_____
_____
_____
_____

TOUGH TIMES & LESSONS LEARNED: _____
_____
_____
_____
_____

What are you grateful for today?   Stressed Angry Tired Sad Happy Excited
_____

Did you know? Different genres of music activate different parts of the brain! Classical music might light up your analytical centers, while electronic music could get your motor cortex grooving. Explore the soundscapes and map your inner brain disco!

DATE: _____ S M T W T F S

MONDAY MANNERS:

> " Be careful what you post online! Remember if you post it online, it NEVER goes away. Writing and posting on social media from behind a screen might feel secure, but it's not! Be extra careful online because screenshots can capture anything, even things you thought would disappear. And don't forget your future employer, professors, roommates and parents may see it. If you're not comfortable with that, don't do it, don't post it! "

MEMORIES MADE: _____
_____
_____
_____
_____

TOUGH TIMES & LESSONS LEARNED: _____
_____
_____
_____
_____

What are you grateful for today?
_____

Stressed Angry Tired Sad Happy Excited

REMEMBER! WAIT TO WRITE BELOW UNTIL THIS DAY NEXT YEAR!

DATE: _____ S M T W T F S

MEMORIES MADE: _____
_____
_____
_____
_____

TOUGH TIMES & LESSONS LEARNED: _____
_____
_____
_____
_____

What are you grateful for today?
_____

Stressed Angry Tired Sad Happy Excited

Did you know? Eating spicy foods can temporarily increase metabolism and fat burning, offering a flavorful way to support weight loss efforts.

DATE: _____ (S) (M) (T) (W) (T) (F) (S)

TUESDAY TIPS:

> "Avoid requesting special favors from your professors, like extra credit or dropping your lowest assignment grade. It's unfair for a professor to offer something to one student and not to everyone. This can create an unequal playing field in the classroom. Instead, focus on doing your best with the opportunities provided to all students. It's important to maintain fairness and integrity in your academic journey."

MEMORIES MADE: _____
_____
_____
_____
_____

TOUGH TIMES & LESSONS LEARNED: _____
_____
_____
_____

What are you grateful for today?
_____

Stressed | Angry | Tired | Sad | Happy | Excited

REMEMBER! WAIT TO WRITE BELOW UNTIL THIS DAY NEXT YEAR!

DATE: _____ (S) (M) (T) (W) (T) (F) (S)

MEMORIES MADE: _____
_____
_____
_____
_____

TOUGH TIMES & LESSONS LEARNED: _____
_____
_____
_____

What are you grateful for today?
_____

Stressed | Angry | Tired | Sad | Happy | Excited

Did you know? Utilizing spaced repetition techniques while studying, revisiting information at increasing intervals, strengthens memory and long-term knowledge retention.
Remember for longer!

DATE: _____   (S) (M) (T) (W) (T) (F) (S)

WEDNESDAY (HUMP DAY!) HAPPY HACKS:

> Don't rehash the past. Some challenges and struggles in life are really difficult. Some even require some time to mourn and grieve. But most challenges don't require mourning, reviewing, and replaying in our minds. When we choose to rehash the past and hang on to memories of how we've been wronged and hurt, we can quickly become a prisoner in the dark dungeons of despair and discouragement. When opposition and crises arise, we get to decide whether we will become bitter or better, hardened or humbled. It's your choice.

MEMORIES MADE: _____
_____
_____
_____
_____
_____

TOUGH TIMES & LESSONS LEARNED: _____
_____
_____
_____
_____

What are you grateful for today?   Stressed Angry Tired Sad Happy Excited
_____

REMEMBER! WAIT TO WRITE BELOW UNTIL THIS DAY NEXT YEAR!

DATE: _____   (S) (M) (T) (W) (T) (F) (S)

MEMORIES MADE: _____
_____
_____
_____
_____
_____

TOUGH TIMES & LESSONS LEARNED: _____
_____
_____
_____
_____

What are you grateful for today?   Stressed Angry Tired Sad Happy Excited
_____

Did you know? There are more stars in the universe than grains of sand on all the beaches on Earth combined! So next time you feel insignificant, remember you're just a tiny speck amidst an unimaginably vast cosmos.

DATE: _____ (S) (M) (T) (W) (T) (F) (S)

THURSDAY MYTHS:

> Myth: "I'll decorate my dorm room like a Pinterest board."
>
> Reality: Budget, space, and time constraints often mean your dorm room will be more functional than a design masterpiece. It's like an episode of a home makeover show, but with a much smaller budget.

MEMORIES MADE: _____
_____
_____
_____
_____
_____

TOUGH TIMES & LESSONS LEARNED: _____
_____
_____
_____
_____

What are you grateful for today?
_____

Stressed | Angry | Tired | Sad | Happy | Excited

⬇ REMEMBER! WAIT TO WRITE BELOW UNTIL THIS DAY NEXT YEAR!

DATE: _____ (S) (M) (T) (W) (T) (F) (S)

MEMORIES MADE: _____
_____
_____
_____
_____
_____

TOUGH TIMES & LESSONS LEARNED: _____
_____
_____
_____
_____

What are you grateful for today?
_____

Stressed | Angry | Tired | Sad | Happy | Excited

Did you know? Everyone has a unique tongue print, just like a fingerprint!
Your mouth has its own special ID.

DATE: _____ (S) (M) (T) (W) (T) (F) (S)

FRIDAY FILL IN THE BLANKS:

> "
> Who would you like to spend an hour with (anyone in history!) and why?
> _____
> _____
> _____
> _____
> "

MEMORIES MADE: _____
_____
_____
_____
_____

TOUGH TIMES & LESSONS LEARNED: _____
_____
_____
_____
_____

What are you grateful for today?   😖   😠   😴   🙁   🙂   😆
_____   Stressed   Angry   Tired   Sad   Happy   Excited

↙ REMEMBER! WAIT TO WRITE BELOW UNTIL THIS DAY NEXT YEAR!

DATE: _____ (S) (M) (T) (W) (T) (F) (S)

MEMORIES MADE: _____
_____
_____
_____
_____

TOUGH TIMES & LESSONS LEARNED: _____
_____
_____
_____
_____

What are you grateful for today?   😖   😠   😴   🙁   🙂   😆
_____   Stressed   Angry   Tired   Sad   Happy   Excited

Did you know? The human body contains enough sulphur to kill all fleas on an average dog, enough carbon to make 900 pencils, and enough potassium to fire a toy cannon.

DATE: _____ (S) (M) (T) (W) (T) (F) (S)

SATURDAY TED TALKS:

> In his TED talk "All it Takes is 10 Mindful Minutes," Andy Puddicombe emphasizes the importance of taking a short break each day to be mindful. He suggests spending just 10 minutes doing nothing but experiencing the present moment. This means not checking social media, texts, emails, thinking about the past or future, or getting distracted. Instead, it's about focusing on the here and now, being aware of your thoughts and feelings without getting caught up in them. This practice can help clear your mind, reduce stress, and improve focus and creativity. He encourages everyone to make time for this daily mindfulness break.

MEMORIES MADE: _____
_____
_____
_____
_____
_____

TOUGH TIMES & LESSONS LEARNED: _____
_____
_____
_____
_____

What are you grateful for today?   Stressed Angry Tired Sad Happy Excited
_____

REMEMBER! WAIT TO WRITE BELOW UNTIL THIS DAY NEXT YEAR!

DATE: _____ (S) (M) (T) (W) (T) (F) (S)

MEMORIES MADE: _____
_____
_____
_____
_____
_____

TOUGH TIMES & LESSONS LEARNED: _____
_____
_____
_____
_____

What are you grateful for today?   Stressed Angry Tired Sad Happy Excited
_____

Did you know? Cognitive-behavioral therapy (CBT) is an effective treatment for various mental health issues, as it helps individuals change negative thought patterns and behaviors.

DATE: _____ (S) (M) (T) (W) (T) (F) (S)

SUNDAY STRESS BUSTERS:

> **"** Be patient and hold on through tough times. Many of life's challenges, like overwhelming semesters, daunting exams, or living situations that aren't ideal, often resolve over time. Whether it's the end of a difficult semester, the completion of a major test, or a significant change like finding a new home or switching your major, time can bring relief and new beginnings. Remember, after every storm, the sun eventually shines again. Focus your energy on what you can control and be patient with the processes that naturally need more time to unfold. This approach will help you navigate through the ups and downs with grace and resilience. **"**

MEMORIES MADE: _____
_____
_____
_____
_____

TOUGH TIMES & LESSONS LEARNED: _____
_____
_____
_____

What are you grateful for today?
_____

Stressed | Angry | Tired | Sad | Happy | Excited

⬅ **REMEMBER! WAIT TO WRITE BELOW UNTIL THIS DAY NEXT YEAR!**

DATE: _____ (S) (M) (T) (W) (T) (F) (S)

MEMORIES MADE: _____
_____
_____
_____
_____

TOUGH TIMES & LESSONS LEARNED: _____
_____
_____
_____

What are you grateful for today?
_____

Stressed | Angry | Tired | Sad | Happy | Excited

Did you know? Playing brain games like chess or Sudoku can sharpen critical thinking skills, increase problem-solving abilities, and improve memory retention. BAM! Put your brain to the test on this next page!

TIME FOR SOME WORD SEARCH FUN - COLLEGE STYLE!

```
G O O C M Y S H P B S R S F
L F Z R A A B D M Z S P K E
O H U S D G J S E K M D L E
A U S M U X R O S A Q S A S
N E R Z I U Q A R A N G B A
T O R T E S T D D T L A S E
D S E M C K R E A D R C E R
S C T L S T U T O R N X Z X
E E U U X D B J U B A G J S
M B T O D X Q A Z M P R V H
S K A O S Y E E D A R G Z K
U K C X N Z I W K C Y Q Y A
Y B M H Y P U O R G Y E A S
R S B P J O I S K O O B U L
```

Dean	Books
Dorm	Class
Exam	Clubs
Fees	Essay
Grad	Grade
Labs	Group
Loan	Major
Quiz	Notes
Read	Study
Test	Tutor

DATE: _____ (S) (M) (T) (W) (T) (F) (S)

MONDAY MANNERS:

> If you see something, say something! If your friend or roommate starts acting withdrawn, talks about suicide, sends troubling messages or other sudden changes in their mood or behavior, talk to a professional or professor immediately. There are even phone numbers and websites where you can share information about a situation anonymously. Your actions may alter a distressing path or save a life. Mental health matters; check on your friends and be aware. If you're worried, speak up!

MEMORIES MADE: _____
_____
_____
_____
_____
_____

TOUGH TIMES & LESSONS LEARNED: _____
_____
_____
_____
_____

What are you grateful for today? Stressed Angry Tired Sad Happy Excited
_____

REMEMBER! WAIT TO WRITE BELOW UNTIL THIS DAY NEXT YEAR!

DATE: _____ (S) (M) (T) (W) (T) (F) (S)

MEMORIES MADE: _____
_____
_____
_____
_____
_____

TOUGH TIMES & LESSONS LEARNED: _____
_____
_____
_____
_____

What are you grateful for today? Stressed Angry Tired Sad Happy Excited
_____

Did you know? Your sense of taste is the weakest in the morning due to the overnight accumulation of bacteria in your mouth. Gross...brush your teeth!

DATE: _____ (S) (M) (T) (W) (T) (F) (S)

TUESDAY TIPS:

> "Don't make skipping class a habit – showing up really counts. Think of it this way: you wouldn't buy a concert ticket and then not go to the show, right? The same goes for your education. You've already paid for your seat in the classroom, so you might as well get the full experience. Plus, you never know what pearls of wisdom you might miss out on by skipping. So, pull yourself out of bed, grab that cup of Perk, and get to class. It's an investment in your future, and let's face it, getting your money's worth always feels good, especially when it comes to your own growth and learning."

MEMORIES MADE: _____
_____
_____
_____
_____

TOUGH TIMES & LESSONS LEARNED: _____
_____
_____
_____
_____

What are you grateful for today?   Stressed Angry Tired Sad Happy Excited
_____

REMEMBER! WAIT TO WRITE BELOW UNTIL THIS DAY NEXT YEAR!

DATE: _____ (S) (M) (T) (W) (T) (F) (S)

MEMORIES MADE: _____
_____
_____
_____
_____

TOUGH TIMES & LESSONS LEARNED: _____
_____
_____
_____
_____

What are you grateful for today?   Stressed Angry Tired Sad Happy Excited
_____

Did you know? Your kidneys filter about 150 liters of blood every day!
Those filtration ninjas are hard at work keeping you clean.

DATE: _____ (S) (M) (T) (W) (T) (F) (S)

WEDNESDAY (HUMP DAY!) HAPPY HACKS:

> Faith matters. More than 100 years of research clearly shows numerous benefits for individuals and couples who not only believe in a higher power, but practice what they believe. For example, some scholars have examined hundreds of studies and find that attending religious services (any faith) and engaging in spiritual practices such as prayer and reading sacred texts, is related to better mental and physical health, better family relationships, higher levels of happiness, and less depression, anxiety, substance abuse and even suicide risk. Consider strengthening your faith and bringing along a friend as well.

MEMORIES MADE: _____
_____
_____
_____
_____
_____

TOUGH TIMES & LESSONS LEARNED: _____
_____
_____
_____
_____

What are you grateful for today?   Stressed Angry Tired Sad Happy Excited
_____

> REMEMBER! WAIT TO WRITE BELOW UNTIL THIS DAY NEXT YEAR!

DATE: _____ (S) (M) (T) (W) (T) (F) (S)

MEMORIES MADE: _____
_____
_____
_____
_____
_____

TOUGH TIMES & LESSONS LEARNED: _____
_____
_____
_____
_____

What are you grateful for today?   Stressed Angry Tired Sad Happy Excited
_____

Did you know? The average college student spends about 17 hours each week preparing for classes, which includes studying, reading, and writing assignments. Whew!

DATE: _____ (S) (M) (T) (W) (T) (F) (S)

THURSDAY MYTHS:

> Myth: "I must find my soulmate in college."
>
> Reality: College is a time to meet new people, but finding a lifelong partner isn't a prerequisite. It's a journey of self-discovery, not a matchmaking service. (Google a report I helped with called "The soulmate trap."

MEMORIES MADE: _____
_____
_____
_____
_____
_____

TOUGH TIMES & LESSONS LEARNED: _____
_____
_____
_____
_____

What are you grateful for today?   Stressed Angry Tired Sad Happy Excited
_____

REMEMBER! WAIT TO WRITE BELOW UNTIL THIS DAY NEXT YEAR!

DATE: _____ (S) (M) (T) (W) (T) (F) (S)

MEMORIES MADE: _____
_____
_____
_____
_____
_____

TOUGH TIMES & LESSONS LEARNED: _____
_____
_____
_____
_____

What are you grateful for today?   Stressed Angry Tired Sad Happy Excited
_____

Did you know? Music Makes Memories: Playing or listening to music you enjoy can activate memory centers in the brain and even improve cognitive function. Put on your favorite tunes and give your brain a boost! (with headphones of course)

DATE: _____ (S) (M) (T) (W) (T) (F) (S)

FRIDAY FILL IN THE BLANKS:

> "
> The most challenging obstacle I've faced in college so far is...
> _____
>
> And the way I overcame it was...
> _____
> "

MEMORIES MADE: _____
_____
_____
_____
_____

TOUGH TIMES & LESSONS LEARNED: _____
_____
_____
_____
_____

What are you grateful for today?   Stressed Angry Tired Sad Happy Excited
_____

↩ **REMEMBER! WAIT TO WRITE BELOW UNTIL THIS DAY NEXT YEAR!**

DATE: _____ (S) (M) (T) (W) (T) (F) (S)

MEMORIES MADE: _____
_____
_____
_____
_____

TOUGH TIMES & LESSONS LEARNED: _____
_____
_____
_____
_____

What are you grateful for today?   Stressed Angry Tired Sad Happy Excited
_____

Did you know? The invention of the microwave oven was inspired by a researcher who noticed chocolate melting in his pocket while standing in front of a radar transmitter. Deliciously unexpected!

DATE: _____ (S) (M) (T) (W) (T) (F) (S)

SATURDAY TED TALKS:

> In his TED talk "Why You Should Define Your Fears Instead of Your Goals," Tim Ferriss talks about focusing on our fears instead of just our goals. He suggests a technique called "fear-setting," similar to goal-setting, where we list our fears, imagine the worst-case scenarios, and then think about how we could prevent or fix these situations. By doing this, we can understand our fears better and realize that they often aren't as bad as we think. This method helps us take action, reduces anxiety, and can lead to a more fulfilled and less fearful life. Ferriss believes that understanding our fears can be more important than setting goals.

MEMORIES MADE: _____
_____
_____
_____
_____

TOUGH TIMES & LESSONS LEARNED: _____
_____
_____
_____
_____

What are you grateful for today?
_____

Stressed | Angry | Tired | Sad | Happy | Excited

REMEMBER! WAIT TO WRITE BELOW UNTIL THIS DAY NEXT YEAR!

DATE: _____ (S) (M) (T) (W) (T) (F) (S)

MEMORIES MADE: _____
_____
_____
_____
_____

TOUGH TIMES & LESSONS LEARNED: _____
_____
_____
_____
_____

What are you grateful for today?
_____

Stressed | Angry | Tired | Sad | Happy | Excited

Did you know? Studying in different environments can boost memory and comprehension.
Break free from the library rut and try a park, coffee shop, or even your own backyard!

DATE: _____   S M T W T F S

SUNDAY STRESS BUSTERS:

> Make mindfulness a part of your daily life. Taking time for meditation or yoga can really lower stress and clear your mind. Just spend a few quiet minutes each day focusing inward to calm your thoughts. This small practice can make a big difference, helping you feel more centered and at peace as you go about your day. It's a simple way to connect with yourself and improve your overall well-being.

MEMORIES MADE: _____
_____
_____
_____
_____
_____

TOUGH TIMES & LESSONS LEARNED: _____
_____
_____
_____
_____

What are you grateful for today?   Stressed Angry Tired Sad Happy Excited
_____

REMEMBER! WAIT TO WRITE BELOW UNTIL THIS DAY NEXT YEAR!

DATE: _____   S M T W T F S

MEMORIES MADE: _____
_____
_____
_____
_____
_____

TOUGH TIMES & LESSONS LEARNED: _____
_____
_____
_____
_____

What are you grateful for today?   Stressed Angry Tired Sad Happy Excited
_____

Did you know? The Ebbinghaus forgetting curve shows that students tend to forget a significant amount of learned information within days, emphasizing the importance of regular review.

DATE: _____ (S) (M) (T) (W) (T) (F) (S)

MONDAY MANNERS:

> Own up to your mistakes. In challenging situations, take responsibility without making excuses. Avoid blaming others—roommates, friends, professors, or parents. Acknowledge your role in the problem and focus on improving. Shifting blame is common but blaming is a completely useless activity. Instead of faulting a professor for a poor grade on a test or paper, search inward and notice where you could have improved. Recognize your power to make better choices, including a better investment of your time to learning and studying. If something seems unfair, seek solutions instead of just complaining about it.

MEMORIES MADE: _____
_____
_____
_____
_____

TOUGH TIMES & LESSONS LEARNED: _____
_____
_____
_____
_____

What are you grateful for today?   Stressed Angry Tired Sad Happy Excited
_____

REMEMBER! WAIT TO WRITE BELOW UNTIL THIS DAY NEXT YEAR!

DATE: _____ (S) (M) (T) (W) (T) (F) (S)

MEMORIES MADE: _____
_____
_____
_____
_____

TOUGH TIMES & LESSONS LEARNED: _____
_____
_____
_____
_____

What are you grateful for today?   Stressed Angry Tired Sad Happy Excited
_____

Did you know? Your eyes can adjust to light changes in as little as 0.1 seconds! Talk about superhero reflexes.

DATE: _____ (S) (M) (T) (W) (T) (F) (S)

TUESDAY TIPS:

> Build relationships with your professors; they're more than just lecturers. Whether in a large auditorium or a cozy seminar room, take a moment to introduce yourself and express gratitude after class. This small gesture can open doors to mentorship, advice, and opportunities. Engaging with your professors shows initiative and can greatly enrich your academic experience.

MEMORIES MADE: _____
_____
_____
_____
_____
_____

TOUGH TIMES & LESSONS LEARNED: _____
_____
_____
_____
_____

What are you grateful for today?
_____

Stressed Angry Tired Sad Happy Excited

REMEMBER! WAIT TO WRITE BELOW UNTIL THIS DAY NEXT YEAR!

DATE: _____ (S) (M) (T) (W) (T) (F) (S)

MEMORIES MADE: _____
_____
_____
_____
_____
_____

TOUGH TIMES & LESSONS LEARNED: _____
_____
_____
_____
_____

What are you grateful for today?
_____

Stressed Angry Tired Sad Happy Excited

Did you know? Cramming the night before is actually counterproductive? Spacing out your studying and getting enough sleep (7-8 hours!) enhances memory retention and cognitive performance. Think marathons, not sprints!

DATE: _____ (S) (M) (T) (W) (T) (F) (S)

WEDNESDAY (HUMP DAY!) HAPPY HACKS

> **Create an "awe album."** We covered "awe" earlier. So here's a happy hack wrinkle on "awe." Make some time to create an "awe album" or folder of pictures in your phone. Invest time scrolling through pictures and moving pictures that really inspire you into a folder with similar pictures. Purposefully add to it by capturing pictures of moments that inspire you. Take your time and move those truly awesome pictures into the folder. As you're doing this, don't rush through it. Pause and relive the moment of each picture. Soak it in a bit. Then don't forget to scroll through your "awe album" occasionally, especially when you're feeling down or stressed or even waiting in a long line. It can give you a boost and help you see the bigger awesome world out there.

MEMORIES MADE: _____
_____
_____
_____
_____

TOUGH TIMES & LESSONS LEARNED: _____
_____
_____
_____

What are you grateful for today?   Stressed Angry Tired Sad Happy Excited
_____

REMEMBER! WAIT TO WRITE BELOW UNTIL THIS DAY NEXT YEAR!

DATE: _____ (S) (M) (T) (W) (T) (F) (S)

MEMORIES MADE: _____
_____
_____
_____
_____

TOUGH TIMES & LESSONS LEARNED: _____
_____
_____
_____

What are you grateful for today?   Stressed Angry Tired Sad Happy Excited
_____

Did you know? Open communication is the golden key! Talk things out respectfully, actively listen, and be willing to compromise. Communication builds bridges, not walls.

DATE: _____ (S) (M) (T) (W) (T) (F) (S)

THURSDAY MYTHS:

> Myth: "I don't need to worry about my digital footprint."
>
> Reality: Your online presence can impact future job opportunities. Be mindful of what you post on social media. It's like leaving footprints in wet cement – they can set and be hard to change.

MEMORIES MADE: _____
_____
_____
_____
_____

TOUGH TIMES & LESSONS LEARNED: _____
_____
_____
_____
_____

What are you grateful for today?   Stressed Angry Tired Sad Happy Excited
_____

REMEMBER! WAIT TO WRITE BELOW UNTIL THIS DAY NEXT YEAR!

DATE: _____ (S) (M) (T) (W) (T) (F) (S)

MEMORIES MADE: _____
_____
_____
_____
_____

TOUGH TIMES & LESSONS LEARNED: _____
_____
_____
_____
_____

What are you grateful for today?   Stressed Angry Tired Sad Happy Excited
_____

Did you know? Your body is capable of producing aspirin; eating fruits and vegetables can trigger the production of salicylates, which are aspirin-like compounds.

DATE: _____ (S) (M) (T) (W) (T) (F) (S)

FRIDAY FILL IN THE BLANKS:

> "
> One lesson I learned outside of the classroom that has significantly impacted me is...
> _____
>
> and it changed my perspective by ...
> _____
> "

MEMORIES MADE: _____
_____
_____
_____
_____

TOUGH TIMES & LESSONS LEARNED: _____
_____
_____
_____

What are you grateful for today?   Stressed   Angry   Tired   Sad   Happy   Excited
_____

REMEMBER! WAIT TO WRITE BELOW UNTIL THIS DAY NEXT YEAR!

DATE: _____ (S) (M) (T) (W) (T) (F) (S)

MEMORIES MADE: _____
_____
_____
_____
_____

TOUGH TIMES & LESSONS LEARNED: _____
_____
_____
_____

What are you grateful for today?   Stressed   Angry   Tired   Sad   Happy   Excited
_____

Did you know? The average human produces 25,000 quarts of saliva in a lifetime, enough to fill two swimming pools. Now that's some serious spit!

DATE: _____ S M T W T F S

SATURDAY TED TALKS:

> If you find yourself stuck in a job you dread, this TED Talk "How to find work you love" by Scott Dinsmore offers hope! Forget climbing the wrong ladder. Find fulfillment through self-discovery and action. What truly matters to you? What energizes you? Explore different paths, talk to people in fields you admire, and don't be afraid to experiment. Remember, passionate work isn't just a dream, it's a choice. Take control, find your spark, and ignite a career you love!

MEMORIES MADE: _____
_____
_____
_____
_____
_____

TOUGH TIMES & LESSONS LEARNED: _____
_____
_____
_____
_____

What are you grateful for today?
_____

Stressed   Angry   Tired   Sad   Happy   Excited

REMEMBER! WAIT TO WRITE BELOW UNTIL THIS DAY NEXT YEAR!

DATE: _____ S M T W T F S

MEMORIES MADE: _____
_____
_____
_____
_____
_____

TOUGH TIMES & LESSONS LEARNED: _____
_____
_____
_____
_____

What are you grateful for today?
_____

Stressed   Angry   Tired   Sad   Happy   Excited

Did you know? The phrase "kick the bucket" is thought to have come from the method of hanging, where the person standing on a bucket would kick it away, leading to their death.

DATE: _____ (S) (M) (T) (W) (T) (F) (S)

SUNDAY STRESS BUSTERS:

> "Establishing a Consistent Routine. Developing a daily routine that includes dedicated time for studies, physical activity, relaxation, and adequate sleep can greatly assist in managing stress. A structured schedule helps in effectively managing your time and reduces the anxiety of unorganized tasks and responsibilities."

MEMORIES MADE: _____
_____
_____
_____
_____

TOUGH TIMES & LESSONS LEARNED:
_____
_____
_____
_____

What are you grateful for today?   Stressed Angry Tired Sad Happy Excited
_____

REMEMBER! WAIT TO WRITE BELOW UNTIL THIS DAY NEXT YEAR!

DATE: _____ (S) (M) (T) (W) (T) (F) (S)

MEMORIES MADE: _____
_____
_____
_____
_____

TOUGH TIMES & LESSONS LEARNED: _____
_____
_____
_____

What are you grateful for today?   Stressed Angry Tired Sad Happy Excited
_____

Did you know? You spend about 6 years of your life blinking!
Those eyelids work hard keeping your eyes fresh and protected.

DATE: _____ (S) (M) (T) (W) (T) (F) (S)

MONDAY MANNERS:

> Learn to genuinely apologize. A sincere apology doesn't include blame or excuses. For instance, with a humble heart you might say, "I'm truly sorry for what I did. I feel so bad. I hope for your forgiveness, understanding it may take time. How can I make it up to you?" Real apologies involve sincerity, a change of heart, and a genuine desire to restore what was damaged. A genuine apology, when done right, can restore relationships. Remember, people are more important than problems.

MEMORIES MADE: _____
_____
_____
_____
_____

TOUGH TIMES & LESSONS LEARNED: _____
_____
_____
_____

What are you grateful for today?
_____

Stressed Angry Tired Sad Happy Excited

REMEMBER! WAIT TO WRITE BELOW UNTIL THIS DAY NEXT YEAR!

DATE: _____ (S) (M) (T) (W) (T) (F) (S)

MEMORIES MADE: _____
_____
_____
_____
_____

TOUGH TIMES & LESSONS LEARNED: _____
_____
_____
_____

What are you grateful for today?
_____

Stressed Angry Tired Sad Happy Excited

Did you know? Limiting social media exposure before bed can improve sleep quality and reduce stress. Give your mind a digital detox at night for a calmer morning.

DATE: _____ S M T W T F S

TUESDAY TIPS:

> "Don't overcommit to extracurricular activities; find a balance. Okay, yes, get involved and do fun things, but don't let them consume you. Staying out super late or doing things that limit your study time can lead to more stress if your grades start to slip."

MEMORIES MADE: _____
_____
_____
_____
_____
_____

TOUGH TIMES & LESSONS LEARNED: _____
_____
_____
_____
_____

What are you grateful for today?
_____

Stressed Angry Tired Sad Happy Excited

REMEMBER! WAIT TO WRITE BELOW UNTIL THIS DAY NEXT YEAR!

DATE: _____ S M T W T F S

MEMORIES MADE: _____
_____
_____
_____
_____
_____

TOUGH TIMES & LESSONS LEARNED: _____
_____
_____
_____
_____

What are you grateful for today?
_____

Stressed Angry Tired Sad Happy Excited

Did you know? Learning basic financial skills like budgeting, investing, and debt management empowers you to take control of your finances and build a secure future. Educate yourself for financial stability!

DATE: _____ (S) (M) (T) (W) (T) (F) (S)

WEDNESDAY (HUMP DAY!) HAPPY HACKS:

> " When you are feeling frustrated, don't invalidate your emotional experience by thinking, "I shouldn't be feeling frustrated." This increases your brain's emotional reactivity, making the problem worse. Instead, remind yourself why it makes sense that you are feeling frustrated. For example, "I just bombed a test. It makes sense that I'm feeling frustrated." Validating your emotional experience helps reduce emotional reactivity so you can focus on what you want to get done instead of blaming yourself for feeling frustrated. "

MEMORIES MADE: _____
_____
_____
_____
_____

TOUGH TIMES & LESSONS LEARNED: _____
_____
_____
_____

What are you grateful for today?   Stressed Angry Tired Sad Happy Excited
_____

REMEMBER! WAIT TO WRITE BELOW UNTIL THIS DAY NEXT YEAR!

DATE: _____ (S) (M) (T) (W) (T) (F) (S)

MEMORIES MADE: _____
_____
_____
_____
_____

TOUGH TIMES & LESSONS LEARNED: _____
_____
_____
_____

What are you grateful for today?   Stressed Angry Tired Sad Happy Excited
_____

Did you know? Your brain uses 20% of your body's oxygen and blood supply – feed your head with healthy thoughts and delicious snacks!

DATE: _____ S M T W T F S

THURSDAY MYTHS:

> Myth: "College friendships are just temporary."
>
> Reality: Some of the friendships you form in college can last a lifetime. These relationships are forged through shared experiences and challenges, similar to how diamonds are formed under pressure. They may not all last, but some will shine for years.

MEMORIES MADE: _____
_____
_____
_____
_____
_____

TOUGH TIMES & LESSONS LEARNED: _____
_____
_____
_____
_____

What are you grateful for today?

Stressed Angry Tired Sad Happy Excited

_____

REMEMBER! WAIT TO WRITE BELOW UNTIL THIS DAY NEXT YEAR!

DATE: _____ S M T W T F S

MEMORIES MADE: _____
_____
_____
_____
_____
_____

TOUGH TIMES & LESSONS LEARNED: _____
_____
_____
_____
_____

What are you grateful for today?

Stressed Angry Tired Sad Happy Excited

_____

Did you know? Listening to music without lyrics, like classical or ambient music, can improve concentration and productivity while studying.

DATE: _____ (S) (M) (T) (W) (T) (F) (S)

FRIDAY FILL IN THE BLANKS:

> " The person I've met in college who has influenced me the most is...
> _____
>
> and the reason they have had such an impact is...
> _____ "

MEMORIES MADE: _____
_____
_____
_____
_____

TOUGH TIMES & LESSONS LEARNED: _____
_____
_____
_____
_____

What are you grateful for today?   Stressed Angry Tired Sad Happy Excited
_____

⬇ REMEMBER! WAIT TO WRITE BELOW UNTIL THIS DAY NEXT YEAR!

DATE: _____ (S) (M) (T) (W) (T) (F) (S)

MEMORIES MADE: _____
_____
_____
_____
_____

TOUGH TIMES & LESSONS LEARNED: _____
_____
_____
_____
_____

What are you grateful for today?   Stressed Angry Tired Sad Happy Excited
_____

Did you know? Celebrating small victories, like finishing a task or mastering a new skill, releases dopamine, the "reward" neurotransmitter, boosting motivation and promoting positive thinking. High five yourself!

DATE: _____ (S) (M) (T) (W) (T) (F) (S)

SATURDAY TED TALKS:

> Mel Robbins throws out the self-help fluff in her TED Talk, "How to stop screwing yourself over." Forget waiting for motivation! It's about taking action. When inspiration strikes, you have 5 seconds to act before your brain talks you out of it. Set your alarm earlier, say "I will" instead of "I want to," and break through self-doubt with action. This isn't magic, it's rewiring your brain for progress. So, start taking control, 5 seconds at a time!

MEMORIES MADE: _____
_____
_____
_____
_____
_____

TOUGH TIMES & LESSONS LEARNED: _____
_____
_____
_____
_____

What are you grateful for today?   Stressed Angry Tired Sad Happy Excited
_____

REMEMBER! WAIT TO WRITE BELOW UNTIL THIS DAY NEXT YEAR!

DATE: _____ (S) (M) (T) (W) (T) (F) (S)

MEMORIES MADE: _____
_____
_____
_____
_____
_____

TOUGH TIMES & LESSONS LEARNED: _____
_____
_____
_____
_____

What are you grateful for today?   Stressed Angry Tired Sad Happy Excited
_____

Did you know? Your body's ability to detect temperature is so precise that it can sense changes as small as 0.02 degrees Fahrenheit.

DATE: _____ S M T W T F S

SUNDAY STRESS BUSTERS:

> Maintaining Healthy Eating Habits: Eating a balanced and nutritious diet plays a crucial role in stress management. Avoid reliance on caffeine and sugar, which can lead to increased anxiety and energy crashes. Instead, focus on a diet rich in fruits, vegetables, lean proteins, and whole grains to fuel both your body and mind. Taking care of your body equates to less stress!

MEMORIES MADE: _____
_____
_____
_____
_____

TOUGH TIMES & LESSONS LEARNED: _____
_____
_____
_____
_____

What are you grateful for today?
_____

Stressed Angry Tired Sad Happy Excited

REMEMBER! WAIT TO WRITE BELOW UNTIL THIS DAY NEXT YEAR!

DATE: _____ S M T W T F S

MEMORIES MADE: _____
_____
_____
_____
_____

TOUGH TIMES & LESSONS LEARNED: _____
_____
_____
_____
_____

What are you grateful for today?
_____

Stressed Angry Tired Sad Happy Excited

Did you know? Listening to classical music before taking a test can calm your nerves and improve cognitive function. Mozart might be your secret weapon for exam success!

DATE: _____ (S) (M) (T) (W) (T) (F) (S)

MONDAY MANNERS:

> Respect other's apartments and living areas. As you get to know other students and make more friends, stay respectful of their places. Always knock. Don't assume you can help yourself to their snacks or food whenever you want. Respect their shoe policy and don't put your feet up on furniture. If you make a mess, clean it up. If you break something, replace it. When students get too comfortable, they tend to get too casual. Strive to be a guest that people look forward to having over—start with respect and asking about the living space rules.

MEMORIES MADE: _____

_____
_____
_____
_____
_____

TOUGH TIMES & LESSONS LEARNED: _____

_____
_____
_____
_____

What are you grateful for today?

_____ Stressed Angry Tired Sad Happy Excited

REMEMBER! WAIT TO WRITE BELOW UNTIL THIS DAY NEXT YEAR!

DATE: _____ (S) (M) (T) (W) (T) (F) (S)

MEMORIES MADE: _____

_____
_____
_____
_____
_____

TOUGH TIMES & LESSONS LEARNED: _____

_____
_____
_____
_____

What are you grateful for today?

_____ Stressed Angry Tired Sad Happy Excited

Did you know? The act of smiling, even if it's forced, can reduce stress and make you feel happier due to the release of endorphins.

DATE: _____ (S) (M) (T) (W) (T) (F) (S)

TUESDAY TIPS:

> Make it a habit to check your emails daily. Professors frequently use email to share crucial updates, academic opportunities, and important communications. Ignoring your inbox could lead to missing essential information, important deadlines, or valuable opportunities to participate and stand out. Staying on top of your emails ensures you're always in the loop and ready to make the most of your academic journey.

MEMORIES MADE: _____
_____
_____
_____
_____
_____

TOUGH TIMES & LESSONS LEARNED: _____
_____
_____
_____
_____

What are you grateful for today?

_____

Stressed Angry Tired Sad Happy Excited

REMEMBER! WAIT TO WRITE BELOW UNTIL THIS DAY NEXT YEAR!

DATE: _____ (S) (M) (T) (W) (T) (F) (S)

MEMORIES MADE: _____
_____
_____
_____
_____
_____

TOUGH TIMES & LESSONS LEARNED: _____
_____
_____
_____
_____

What are you grateful for today?

_____

Stressed Angry Tired Sad Happy Excited

Did you know? The phrase "rule of thumb" supposedly originates from an old English law that allowed men to beat their wives with sticks no thicker than their thumb, although there's considerable debate about the accuracy of this origin.

DATE: _____ (S) (M) (T) (W) (T) (F) (S)

WEDNESDAY (HUMP DAY!) HAPPY HACKS

> Eating a healthy diet can make you happier. Foods with good nutrients like omega-3s, vitamins, and antioxidants help keep your brain healthy and your mood stable. Eating less sugar helps avoid mood swings, and foods that are good for your gut can also improve your mood. Try some "happy foods" including dark chocolate, berries, bananas, nuts and seeds, leafy greens and yogurt! Everyone is different, and a good diet is just one part of being happy and healthy.

MEMORIES MADE: _____
_____
_____
_____
_____

TOUGH TIMES & LESSONS LEARNED: _____
_____
_____
_____
_____

What are you grateful for today?
_____

Stressed | Angry | Tired | Sad | Happy | Excited

REMEMBER! WAIT TO WRITE BELOW UNTIL THIS DAY NEXT YEAR!

DATE: _____ (S) (M) (T) (W) (T) (F) (S)

MEMORIES MADE: _____
_____
_____
_____
_____

TOUGH TIMES & LESSONS LEARNED: _____
_____
_____
_____
_____

What are you grateful for today?
_____

Stressed | Angry | Tired | Sad | Happy | Excited

Did you know? Taking intentional breaks, including short walks or relaxation techniques, can rejuvenate the mind and enhance overall happiness and productivity.

DATE: _____ (S) (M) (T) (W) (T) (F) (S)

THURSDAY MYTHS:

> Myth: "I can skip classes if I read the textbook."
>
> Reality: While textbooks are a valuable resource, they can't replace the nuances of a lecture. Professors often offer insights and explanations that aren't in the book. It's like choosing between reading a recipe and actually cooking the meal.

MEMORIES MADE: _____
_____
_____
_____
_____
_____

TOUGH TIMES & LESSONS LEARNED: _____
_____
_____
_____
_____

What are you grateful for today?   Stressed Angry Tired Sad Happy Excited
_____

> REMEMBER! WAIT TO WRITE BELOW UNTIL THIS DAY NEXT YEAR!

DATE: _____ (S) (M) (T) (W) (T) (F) (S)

MEMORIES MADE: _____
_____
_____
_____
_____
_____

TOUGH TIMES & LESSONS LEARNED: _____
_____
_____
_____
_____

What are you grateful for today?   Stressed Angry Tired Sad Happy Excited
_____

Did you know? Good posture prevents back pain and improves breathing, highlighting the importance of body alignment in overall health.

DATE: _____ S M T W T F S

FRIDAY FILL IN THE BLANKS:

" A subject or activity I never thought I would enjoy is ...
_____

and what it has taught me about myself is ...
_____ "

MEMORIES MADE: _____
_____
_____
_____
_____
_____

TOUGH TIMES & LESSONS LEARNED: _____
_____
_____
_____
_____

What are you grateful for today?
_____

Stressed Angry Tired Sad Happy Excited

REMEMBER! WAIT TO WRITE BELOW UNTIL THIS DAY NEXT YEAR!

DATE: _____ S M T W T F S

MEMORIES MADE: _____
_____
_____
_____
_____
_____

TOUGH TIMES & LESSONS LEARNED: _____
_____
_____
_____
_____

What are you grateful for today?
_____

Stressed Angry Tired Sad Happy Excited

Did you know? Packing your lunch most days can significantly save money on daily expenses and often lead to healthier eating choices. Brown bag it for budget and health!

DATE: _____ (S) (M) (T) (W) (T) (F) (S)

SATURDAY TED TALKS:

> Gaming to reduce stress!? In her TED talk "The Game That Can Give You 10 Extra Years of Life," Jane McGonigal discusses a game she designed to boost resilience and add years to your life. Called "SuperBetter," the game helps people tackle personal challenges, like health issues, by adopting a mindset similar to gaming. It involves setting goals, facing obstacles, seeking allies, and celebrating victories, just like in video games. By turning real-life struggles into a game, people can become more motivated and optimistic. McGonigal's research shows that this approach can reduce anxiety, depression, and increase mental resilience, potentially adding up to 10 extra years to your life.

MEMORIES MADE: _____
_____
_____
_____
_____
_____

TOUGH TIMES & LESSONS LEARNED: _____
_____
_____
_____
_____

What are you grateful for today?
_____

Stressed | Angry | Tired | Sad | Happy | Excited

REMEMBER! WAIT TO WRITE BELOW UNTIL THIS DAY NEXT YEAR!

DATE: _____ (S) (M) (T) (W) (T) (F) (S)

MEMORIES MADE: _____
_____
_____
_____
_____
_____

TOUGH TIMES & LESSONS LEARNED: _____
_____
_____
_____
_____

What are you grateful for today?
_____

Stressed | Angry | Tired | Sad | Happy | Excited

Did you know? The strongest muscle in your body is the gluteus maximus, aka your butt!
Thank it for all those uphill stair climbs and grocery hauls.

DATE: _____ (S) (M) (T) (W) (T) (F) (S)

SUNDAY STRESS BUSTERS:

> Practicing simple deep breathing exercises can offer a swift and potent remedy for stress relief. Begin by taking a deep breath in through your nose, allowing your lungs to fully expand. Pause briefly at the peak of your inhalation, then gently exhale through your mouth, releasing tension with the breath. This technique, easily done in any setting, is a powerful tool for soothing the mind and alleviating stress.

MEMORIES MADE: _____
_____
_____
_____
_____

TOUGH TIMES & LESSONS LEARNED:
_____
_____
_____
_____

What are you grateful for today?   Stressed Angry Tired Sad Happy Excited
_____

REMEMBER! WAIT TO WRITE BELOW UNTIL THIS DAY NEXT YEAR!

DATE: _____ (S) (M) (T) (W) (T) (F) (S)

MEMORIES MADE: _____
_____
_____
_____
_____

TOUGH TIMES & LESSONS LEARNED: _____
_____
_____
_____

What are you grateful for today?   Stressed Angry Tired Sad Happy Excited
_____

Did you know? Sound travels faster through water than air!
So, don't yell underwater if you want to stay discreet!

DATE: _____ (S) (M) (T) (W) (T) (F) (S)

MONDAY MANNERS:

> " Know how to talk about your interests. When you meet new people, one of the first questions asked is, "What do you like to do?" or "Tell me about yourself." While there isn't a "right" or "wrong" answer to this, please don't reply with "I don't know" or "Nothing, I'm pretty boring." You don't have to be a professional dancer to like swing dancing and you don't have to know everything about sports to enjoy games. If you're not sure what you like, try some new things. And you can change your interests as often as you like! Be ready to give a better answer! "

MEMORIES MADE: _____
_____
_____
_____
_____
_____

TOUGH TIMES & LESSONS LEARNED: _____
_____
_____
_____
_____

What are you grateful for today?   Stressed Angry Tired Sad Happy Excited
_____

REMEMBER! WAIT TO WRITE BELOW UNTIL THIS DAY NEXT YEAR!

DATE: _____ (S) (M) (T) (W) (T) (F) (S)

MEMORIES MADE: _____
_____
_____
_____
_____
_____

TOUGH TIMES & LESSONS LEARNED: _____
_____
_____
_____
_____

What are you grateful for today?   Stressed Angry Tired Sad Happy Excited
_____

Did you know? Your body has a unique type of hair, called vellus hair, which is fine and often invisible to the naked eye, covering most of your body.

DATE: _____ (S) (M) (T) (W) (T) (F) (S)

TUESDAY TIPS:

> **"** Communicate openly with roommates and establish ground rules. Whew···this one is HUGE! (if you have roommates :) Talk about things early and often. Don't let frustrations bottle up. Consider setting aside a regular time each week (Sunday nights?) to sit down and chat about how things are going, from dirty dishes to annoying habits. Happy roomies intentionally create organization, cleaning charts, and rules that everyone makes and lives by. Trust me, be open with each other and don't talk behind each other's backs! **"**

MEMORIES MADE: _____
_____
_____
_____
_____

TOUGH TIMES & LESSONS LEARNED: _____
_____
_____
_____
_____

What are you grateful for today?
_____

Stressed | Angry | Tired | Sad | Happy | Excited

REMEMBER! WAIT TO WRITE BELOW UNTIL THIS DAY NEXT YEAR!

DATE: _____ (S) (M) (T) (W) (T) (F) (S)

MEMORIES MADE: _____
_____
_____
_____
_____
_____

TOUGH TIMES & LESSONS LEARNED: _____
_____
_____
_____
_____

What are you grateful for today?
_____

Stressed | Angry | Tired | Sad | Happy | Excited

Did you know? The original purpose of summer vacation in the U.S. was not for leisure, but because it was too hot to study and because families needed help on the farm.

DATE: _____ Ⓢ Ⓜ Ⓣ Ⓦ Ⓣ Ⓕ Ⓢ

WEDNESDAY (HUMP DAY!) HAPPY HACKS:

> A happy "you" starts with resting right. It helps you think clearly, stay in a good mood, and handle emotions better. Not getting enough sleep can make you irritable and increase the risk of feeling sad or anxious. It's also related to weight gain, low energy and poor health. Restful sleep is essential for feeling happy and keeping your mind and body healthy. Yes, you're young and in college, but staying up crazy late and sleeping in just isn't great for your body and brain. Young adults between 18-25 need 7-9 hours of sleep per night. Want to be happier? Get your Zzz's!

MEMORIES MADE: _____
_____
_____
_____
_____

TOUGH TIMES & LESSONS LEARNED: _____
_____
_____
_____

What are you grateful for today?   Stressed Angry Tired Sad Happy Excited
_____

REMEMBER! WAIT TO WRITE BELOW UNTIL THIS DAY NEXT YEAR!

DATE: _____ Ⓢ Ⓜ Ⓣ Ⓦ Ⓣ Ⓕ Ⓢ

MEMORIES MADE: _____
_____
_____
_____
_____

TOUGH TIMES & LESSONS LEARNED: _____
_____
_____
_____

What are you grateful for today?   Stressed Angry Tired Sad Happy Excited
_____

Did you know? A full bladder is roughly the size of a soft ball, holding up to 500-800 ml of urine.
But it's not good for you to hold that much for too long!

DATE: _____ (S) (M) (T) (W) (T) (F) (S)

THURSDAY MYTHS:

> Myth: "I'll be able to maintain a long-distance relationship easily."
>
> Reality: Long-distance relationships are challenging, especially with the transitions college brings. It requires effort, trust, and communication. Think of it as maintaining a delicate plant – without the right care, it might not thrive.

MEMORIES MADE: _____
_____
_____
_____
_____
_____

TOUGH TIMES & LESSONS LEARNED: _____
_____
_____
_____
_____

What are you grateful for today?
_____   Stressed | Angry | Tired | Sad | Happy | Excited

REMEMBER! WAIT TO WRITE BELOW UNTIL THIS DAY NEXT YEAR!

DATE: _____ (S) (M) (T) (W) (T) (F) (S)

MEMORIES MADE: _____
_____
_____
_____
_____
_____

TOUGH TIMES & LESSONS LEARNED: _____
_____
_____
_____
_____

What are you grateful for today?
_____   Stressed | Angry | Tired | Sad | Happy | Excited

Did you know? Humans can make 10,000 different facial expressions to convey a wide range of emotions and communications. That's a ton of emojis!

DATE: _____   (S) (M) (T) (W) (T) (F) (S)

FRIDAY FILL IN THE BLANKS:

> " My favorite memory from this semester so far is... _____
>
> and it stands out to me because... _____ "

MEMORIES MADE: _____
_____
_____
_____
_____
_____

TOUGH TIMES & LESSONS LEARNED: _____
_____
_____
_____
_____

What are you grateful for today?   Stressed Angry Tired Sad Happy Excited
_____

⬇ REMEMBER! WAIT TO WRITE BELOW UNTIL THIS DAY NEXT YEAR!

DATE: _____   (S) (M) (T) (W) (T) (F) (S)

MEMORIES MADE: _____
_____
_____
_____
_____
_____

TOUGH TIMES & LESSONS LEARNED: _____
_____
_____
_____
_____

What are you grateful for today?   Stressed Angry Tired Sad Happy Excited
_____

Did you know? The term "sophomore" means "wise fool" in Greek, a nod to the learning process where students start to gain knowledge but may not have the full picture.

DATE: _____ (S) (M) (T) (W) (T) (F) (S)

SATURDAY TED TALKS:

> Neil Pasricha, in his TED Talk "The 3 A's of Awesome," reveals a simple recipe for a fulfilling life: Attitude, Awareness, and Authenticity. Cultivate a positive outlook, stay present and mindful of the good, and be true to yourself. These "A's" lead to meaningful connections, joyful moments, and a life you genuinely enjoy. Remember, awesome isn't about grand achievements, but about savoring the simple wonders and living authentically. So, embrace the 3 A's and watch your life flourish!

MEMORIES MADE: _____
_____
_____
_____
_____
_____

TOUGH TIMES & LESSONS LEARNED: _____
_____
_____
_____
_____

What are you grateful for today?
_____

Stressed Angry Tired Sad Happy Excited

REMEMBER! WAIT TO WRITE BELOW UNTIL THIS DAY NEXT YEAR!

DATE: _____ (S) (M) (T) (W) (T) (F) (S)

MEMORIES MADE: _____
_____
_____
_____
_____
_____

TOUGH TIMES & LESSONS LEARNED: _____
_____
_____
_____
_____

What are you grateful for today?
_____

Stressed Angry Tired Sad Happy Excited

Did you know? Your nose can detect over 1 trillion different scents!
No wonder some smells bring back vivid memories.

DATE: _____ (S) (M) (T) (W) (T) (F) (S)

SUNDAY STRESS BUSTERS:

> " Engaging in regular physical activity is an effective way to combat stress and elevate your mood. Options abound, from a brisk walk around campus to jogging or hitting the gym. Choose an exercise you genuinely enjoy and make it a staple in your weekly routine. This commitment to movement not only bolsters your physical well-being but also offers a valuable mental respite from the rigors of academic life, helping you to recharge and refocus. "

MEMORIES MADE: _____
_____
_____
_____
_____

TOUGH TIMES & LESSONS LEARNED: _____
_____
_____
_____

What are you grateful for today?   Stressed Angry Tired Sad Happy Excited
_____

REMEMBER! WAIT TO WRITE BELOW UNTIL THIS DAY NEXT YEAR!

DATE: _____ (S) (M) (T) (W) (T) (F) (S)

MEMORIES MADE: _____
_____
_____
_____
_____

TOUGH TIMES & LESSONS LEARNED: _____
_____
_____
_____

What are you grateful for today?   Stressed Angry Tired Sad Happy Excited
_____

Did you know? Acts of self-care, like a relaxing bath or reading a book, can greatly enhance mental well-being and positivity, crucial for managing the stresses of college life.

DATE: _____ (S) (M) (T) (W) (T) (F) (S)

MONDAY MANNERS:

> Cultivating friendships demands time and effort. One study from the University of Kansas suggests it takes approximately 40-60 hours for a casual friendship to develop, 80-100 hours to become "friends," and over 200 hours to become close friends. In a world of instant gratification, building strong bonds doesn't follow the same quick pace. To develop lasting connections, invest the necessary time and develop the patience as relationships grow. Start with a couple foundational elements—kindness and gratitude.

MEMORIES MADE: _____
_____
_____
_____
_____
_____

TOUGH TIMES & LESSONS LEARNED: _____
_____
_____
_____
_____

What are you grateful for today?   Stressed Angry Tired Sad Happy Excited
_____

REMEMBER! WAIT TO WRITE BELOW UNTIL THIS DAY NEXT YEAR!

DATE: _____ (S) (M) (T) (W) (T) (F) (S)

MEMORIES MADE: _____
_____
_____
_____
_____
_____

TOUGH TIMES & LESSONS LEARNED: _____
_____
_____
_____
_____

What are you grateful for today?   Stressed Angry Tired Sad Happy Excited
_____

Did you know? Opting for whole grains over refined grains provides sustained energy, fiber, and essential nutrients for optimal health. Choose brown over white!

DATE: _____ (S) (M) (T) (W) (T) (F) (S)

TUESDAY TIPS:

> Be open to making new friends and connections. You may have a friend or two that you love to do things with, and that's great! But consider your social life as the letter "U" that is open to people coming and going, instead of a closed-off letter "O." Make sense?

MEMORIES MADE: _____
_____
_____
_____
_____
_____

TOUGH TIMES & LESSONS LEARNED: _____
_____
_____
_____
_____

What are you grateful for today?
_____

Stressed Angry Tired Sad Happy Excited

REMEMBER! WAIT TO WRITE BELOW UNTIL THIS DAY NEXT YEAR!

DATE: _____ (S) (M) (T) (W) (T) (F) (S)

MEMORIES MADE: _____
_____
_____
_____
_____
_____

TOUGH TIMES & LESSONS LEARNED: _____
_____
_____
_____
_____

What are you grateful for today?
_____

Stressed Angry Tired Sad Happy Excited

Did you know? Your body produces enough heat in one day to boil a gallon of water!
You're like a walking human furnace.

DATE: _____ (S) (M) (T) (W) (T) (F) (S)

WEDNESDAY (HUMP DAY!) HAPPY HACKS

> Happy humble people silently go about doing good. True goodness doesn't need to draw attention to itself. Genuinely good people quietly lift others as they make their way through life—without need for recognition, fanfare or glory. Random acts of kindness and small and simple things are what make people great. Choose to be remembered for your kindness, not perceived greatness.

MEMORIES MADE: _____
_____
_____
_____
_____

TOUGH TIMES & LESSONS LEARNED: _____
_____
_____
_____
_____

What are you grateful for today?

Stressed | Angry | Tired | Sad | Happy | Excited

REMEMBER! WAIT TO WRITE BELOW UNTIL THIS DAY NEXT YEAR!

DATE: _____ (S) (M) (T) (W) (T) (F) (S)

MEMORIES MADE: _____
_____
_____
_____
_____

TOUGH TIMES & LESSONS LEARNED: _____
_____
_____
_____
_____

What are you grateful for today?

Stressed | Angry | Tired | Sad | Happy | Excited

Did you know? Regular participation in group activities, whether social, recreational, or support groups, can improve mental health by providing a sense of belonging and community.

DATE: _____ (S) (M) (T) (W) (T) (F) (S)

THURSDAY MYTHS:

> Myth: "I won't get stressed or overwhelmed."
>
> Reality: College can be stressful. It's normal to feel overwhelmed at times. The key is to develop coping strategies and seek support when needed. It's like carrying groceries – sometimes, you need to make multiple trips.

MEMORIES MADE: _____
_____
_____
_____
_____

TOUGH TIMES & LESSONS LEARNED: _____
_____
_____
_____
_____

What are you grateful for today?   Stressed Angry Tired Sad Happy Excited
_____

REMEMBER! WAIT TO WRITE BELOW UNTIL THIS DAY NEXT YEAR!

DATE: _____ (S) (M) (T) (W) (T) (F) (S)

MEMORIES MADE: _____
_____
_____
_____
_____

TOUGH TIMES & LESSONS LEARNED: _____
_____
_____
_____
_____

What are you grateful for today?   Stressed Angry Tired Sad Happy Excited
_____

Did you know? Your brain keeps developing until your late 40s, which means that college students' brains are still maturing and forming new connections.

DATE: _____ S M T W T F S

FRIDAY FILL IN THE BLANKS:

"The biggest change I've noticed in myself since starting college is...
_____

and it makes me feel...
_____"

MEMORIES MADE: _____
_____
_____
_____
_____

TOUGH TIMES & LESSONS LEARNED: _____
_____
_____
_____

What are you grateful for today?   Stressed Angry Tired Sad Happy Excited
_____

REMEMBER! WAIT TO WRITE BELOW UNTIL THIS DAY NEXT YEAR!

DATE: _____ S M T W T F S

MEMORIES MADE: _____
_____
_____
_____
_____

TOUGH TIMES & LESSONS LEARNED: _____
_____
_____
_____

What are you grateful for today?   Stressed Angry Tired Sad Happy Excited
_____

Did you know? The population of Earth is so large that if everyone stood shoulder-to-shoulder, we could make a line that would wrap around the equator 462 times! Imagine the world's longest conga line, with humans of all shapes and sizes.

DATE: _____ (S) (M) (T) (W) (T) (F) (S)

SATURDAY TED TALKS:

> In "Inside the Mind of a Master Procrastinator," Tim Urban humorously explains why people procrastinate. He describes a procrastinator's brain as having a Rational Decision-Maker and an Instant Gratification Monkey. The Monkey often takes control, leading to fun but unproductive activities. This lasts until the Panic Monster appears, usually when a deadline is close, scaring the Monkey away and forcing urgent work. Urban warns that for life goals with no deadlines, the Panic Monster never shows up, and things may never get done. He encourages tackling procrastination by being aware of it and considering the importance of time and life goals.

MEMORIES MADE: _____
_____
_____
_____
_____

TOUGH TIMES & LESSONS LEARNED: _____
_____
_____
_____
_____

What are you grateful for today?

Stressed | Angry | Tired | Sad | Happy | Excited

REMEMBER! WAIT TO WRITE BELOW UNTIL THIS DAY NEXT YEAR!

DATE: _____ (S) (M) (T) (W) (T) (F) (S)

MEMORIES MADE: _____
_____
_____
_____
_____

TOUGH TIMES & LESSONS LEARNED: _____
_____
_____
_____
_____

What are you grateful for today?

Stressed | Angry | Tired | Sad | Happy | Excited

Did you know? Humans and giraffes have the same number of neck vertebrae; despite their length difference, both have seven.

DATE: _____ (S) (M) (T) (W) (T) (F) (S)

SUNDAY STRESS BUSTERS:

> Set realistic and achievable goals for both your academic pursuits and personal growth. Aiming too high with unrealistic expectations can often lead to unnecessary stress and a sense of falling short. Concentrate on establishing smaller, manageable targets that you can confidently reach. This approach not only reduces stress but also fosters a sense of accomplishment and momentum, making larger goals seem more attainable over time.

MEMORIES MADE: _____
_____
_____
_____
_____

TOUGH TIMES & LESSONS LEARNED:
_____
_____
_____
_____

What are you grateful for today?
_____

Stressed | Angry | Tired | Sad | Happy | Excited

REMEMBER! WAIT TO WRITE BELOW UNTIL THIS DAY NEXT YEAR!

DATE: _____ (S) (M) (T) (W) (T) (F) (S)

MEMORIES MADE: _____
_____
_____
_____
_____

TOUGH TIMES & LESSONS LEARNED: _____
_____
_____
_____
_____

What are you grateful for today?
_____

Stressed | Angry | Tired | Sad | Happy | Excited

Did you know? Astronauts in space can grow up to two inches taller due to reduced gravity on their spines! Just don't pack your high heels for your space trip.

DATE: _____ (S) (M) (T) (W) (T) (F) (S)

MONDAY MANNERS:

> The law of attraction – you attract what you are. People tend to receive what they put out into the world. Want others to be more kind? Start with being more kind. Dislike drama? Refrain from being drawn into and contributing to it. Want more positivity? Be more positive and happier. Want better friends who are uplifting? Turn outward and start lifting others. Small changes can lead to significant improvements in yourself and your surroundings. Remember, the only person you can change is yourself. If you're not happy with your life, consider altering the energy you're putting into the world.

MEMORIES MADE: _____
_____
_____
_____
_____
_____

TOUGH TIMES & LESSONS LEARNED: _____
_____
_____
_____
_____

What are you grateful for today?   Stressed   Angry   Tired   Sad   Happy   Excited
_____

REMEMBER! WAIT TO WRITE BELOW UNTIL THIS DAY NEXT YEAR!

DATE: _____ (S) (M) (T) (W) (T) (F) (S)

MEMORIES MADE: _____
_____
_____
_____
_____
_____

TOUGH TIMES & LESSONS LEARNED: _____
_____
_____
_____
_____

What are you grateful for today?   Stressed   Angry   Tired   Sad   Happy   Excited
_____

Did you know? Your brain lights up like a disco ball when you anticipate what's coming next in a song! Music activates reward centers and prediction pathways, making it a delightful guessing game for your neurons.

DATE: _____ (S) (M) (T) (W) (T) (F) (S)

TUESDAY TIPS:

> "Budget your finances wisely; watch for unnecessary expenses. Whether you are working a bit on the side, you've saved a ton before college, or your parents are paying your way, be money smart! The money habits you create now could really pay off later. The key is tracking your money. Budgeting may not be "cool" but the wisest people on this planet create and stick to budgets!"

MEMORIES MADE: _____
_____
_____
_____
_____

TOUGH TIMES & LESSONS LEARNED: _____
_____
_____
_____
_____

What are you grateful for today?
_____

Stressed | Angry | Tired | Sad | Happy | Excited

REMEMBER! WAIT TO WRITE BELOW UNTIL THIS DAY NEXT YEAR!

DATE: _____ (S) (M) (T) (W) (T) (F) (S)

MEMORIES MADE: _____
_____
_____
_____
_____

TOUGH TIMES & LESSONS LEARNED: _____
_____
_____
_____
_____

What are you grateful for today?
_____

Stressed | Angry | Tired | Sad | Happy | Excited

Did you know? The phrase "sleep tight" might come from the days when mattresses were supported by ropes; sleeping tight meant the ropes were pulled tight, providing a well-sprung bed.

DATE: _____   S M T W T F S

WEDNESDAY (HUMP DAY!) HAPPY HACKS:

> Happy people prioritize what matters most. You will have all kinds of responsibilities in school and life. As you juggle multiples roles and tasks, remember that some of the balls you are trying to juggle and keep in the air are made of rubber and some are made of glass. Here's some wise counsel I once received: Decide which balls you are juggling are made of rubber and which ones are made of glass (the most important parts of your life). Never. Drop. The glass balls.

MEMORIES MADE: _____
_____
_____
_____
_____

TOUGH TIMES & LESSONS LEARNED: _____
_____
_____
_____

What are you grateful for today?   Stressed · Angry · Tired · Sad · Happy · Excited
_____

REMEMBER! WAIT TO WRITE BELOW UNTIL THIS DAY NEXT YEAR!

DATE: _____   S M T W T F S

MEMORIES MADE: _____
_____
_____
_____
_____

TOUGH TIMES & LESSONS LEARNED: _____
_____
_____
_____

What are you grateful for today?   Stressed · Angry · Tired · Sad · Happy · Excited
_____

Did you know? The human body's biochemical processes produce about half a liter of pure alcohol per day through fermentation processes. Think about that one for a minute...

DATE: _____ (S) (M) (T) (W) (T) (F) (S)

THURSDAY MYTHS:

> Myth: "I won't change my political or religious beliefs."
>
> Reality: College is a time of exploration and questioning. Your beliefs might evolve as you're exposed to new ideas and perspectives. It's like updating software; sometimes, your system needs new programming.

MEMORIES MADE: _____
_____
_____
_____
_____

TOUGH TIMES & LESSONS LEARNED: _____
_____
_____
_____
_____

What are you grateful for today?   Stressed Angry Tired Sad Happy Excited
_____

⬇ REMEMBER! WAIT TO WRITE BELOW UNTIL THIS DAY NEXT YEAR!

DATE: _____ (S) (M) (T) (W) (T) (F) (S)

MEMORIES MADE: _____
_____
_____
_____
_____

TOUGH TIMES & LESSONS LEARNED: _____
_____
_____
_____
_____

What are you grateful for today?   Stressed Angry Tired Sad Happy Excited
_____

Did you know? Malala Yousafzai, a young Pakistani activist shot for advocating for girls' education, survived and became the youngest Nobel Prize laureate. Her unwavering commitment to her cause shows the power of courage and determination in the face of adversity.

DATE: _____ (S) (M) (T) (W) (T) (F) (S)

FRIDAY FILL IN THE BLANKS:

> "
> The most interesting person I've met in college is...
> _____
>
> and what makes them interesting is...
> _____
> "

MEMORIES MADE: _____
_____
_____
_____
_____

TOUGH TIMES & LESSONS LEARNED: _____
_____
_____
_____
_____

What are you grateful for today?   Stressed Angry Tired Sad Happy Excited
_____

↳ REMEMBER! WAIT TO WRITE BELOW UNTIL THIS DAY NEXT YEAR!

DATE: _____ (S) (M) (T) (W) (T) (F) (S)

MEMORIES MADE: _____
_____
_____
_____
_____
_____

TOUGH TIMES & LESSONS LEARNED: _____
_____
_____
_____
_____

What are you grateful for today?   Stressed Angry Tired Sad Happy Excited
_____

Did you know? Music and language share processing power in the brain! This cross-wiring helps with speech development, memory, and even reading skills. So, sing along and boost your brainpower!

DATE: _____ S M T W T F S

SATURDAY TED TALKS:

> Forget just listing past jobs! Jason Shen, in his TED Talk, urges job seekers to focus on "ability," not experience. He argues our potential often outgrows our resumes. Highlight skills, problem-solving, eagerness to learn, and a growth mindset. Showcase your adaptability and passion, proving you can thrive in new situations. Remember, companies need talent, not just experience. So, focus on what you can do, not where you've been, and open doors to exciting new possibilities!

MEMORIES MADE: _____
_____
_____
_____
_____

TOUGH TIMES & LESSONS LEARNED: _____
_____
_____
_____
_____

What are you grateful for today?
_____

Stressed | Angry | Tired | Sad | Happy | Excited

REMEMBER! WAIT TO WRITE BELOW UNTIL THIS DAY NEXT YEAR!

DATE: _____ S M T W T F S

MEMORIES MADE: _____
_____
_____
_____
_____

TOUGH TIMES & LESSONS LEARNED: _____
_____
_____
_____
_____

What are you grateful for today?
_____

Stressed | Angry | Tired | Sad | Happy | Excited

Did you know? Outdoor exercises like hiking or cycling provide not only physical benefits but also vitamin D from sunlight, offering a dual advantage for health.

DATE: _____ (S) (M) (T) (W) (T) (F) (S)

SUNDAY STRESS BUSTERS:

> **"** Learning to focus on what really matters in life AND what you can control will help you think about stress differently. On the <u>next page</u> you'll see two circles that overlap. One circle represents all the things in your life that REALLY matter. The other circle represents what you can control. Go ahead and make a list of those things in your life that REALLY matter and another list of things you can control. Then where those two things overlap is the place where you should try to focus in life - things that BOTH really matter and that you can control. Remind yourself of those things you worry about that you have little or no control over. **"**

MEMORIES MADE: _____
_____
_____
_____
_____

TOUGH TIMES & LESSONS LEARNED: _____
_____
_____
_____
_____

What are you grateful for today?   Stressed Angry Tired Sad Happy Excited
_____

REMEMBER! WAIT TO WRITE BELOW UNTIL THIS DAY NEXT YEAR!

DATE: _____ (S) (M) (T) (W) (T) (F) (S)

MEMORIES MADE: _____
_____
_____
_____
_____
_____

TOUGH TIMES & LESSONS LEARNED: _____
_____
_____
_____
_____

What are you grateful for today?   Stressed Angry Tired Sad Happy Excited
_____

Did you know? Spending time with animals, like petting a dog or watching birds, can lower cortisol levels and increase feelings of calmness and well-being.

LIST OF THINGS THAT REALLY MATTER IN YOUR LIFE:

LIST OF THINGS THAT YOU CAN CONTROL IN YOUR LIFE:

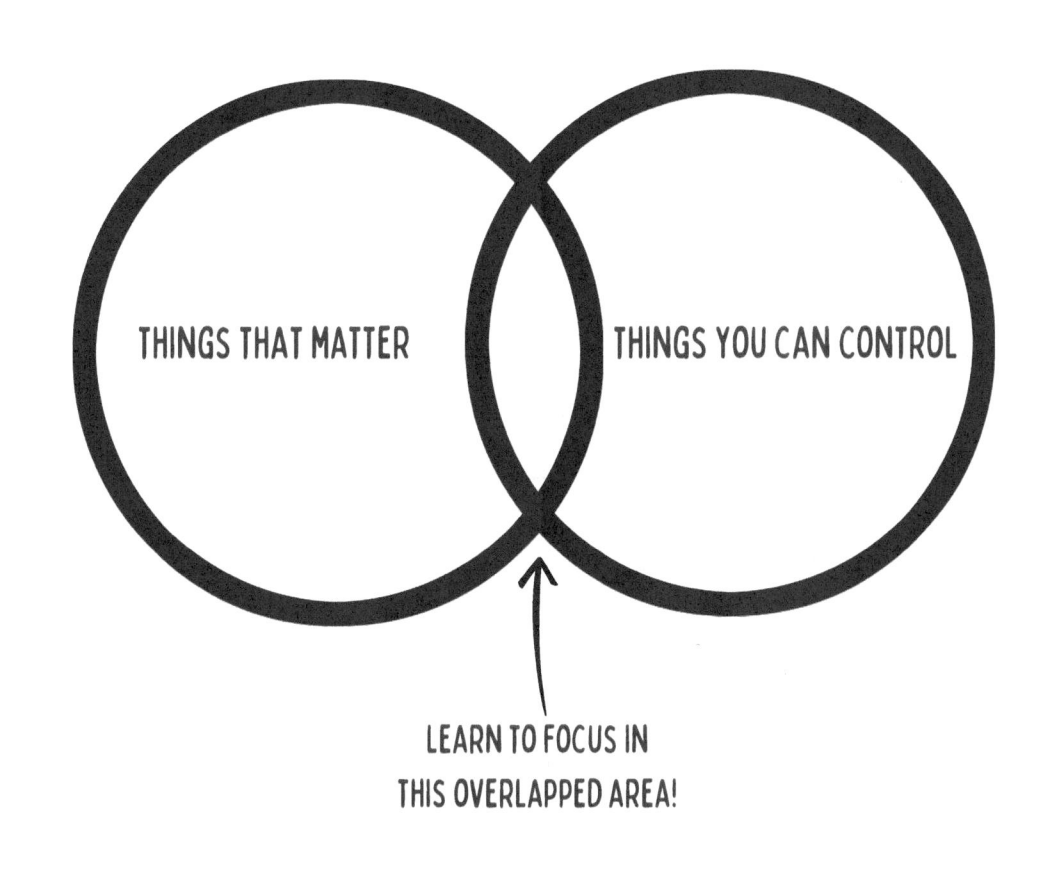

THINGS THAT MATTER — **THINGS YOU CAN CONTROL**

LEARN TO FOCUS IN THIS OVERLAPPED AREA!

DATE: _____   (S) (M) (T) (W) (T) (F) (S)

MONDAY MANNERS:

> Prioritize presence over phone distractions. DON'T IGNORE THIS ONE! When you're with others, give them your all-in attention! Quit scrolling and snapping. Enjoy who you are with and what you are doing rather than wondering what other friends might be doing elsewhere. Try putting your phone on silent or disable notifications. Being fully present with others will deepen connections and strengthen relationships. If you are expecting an important text or call, give others a heads up. Embrace the habit of being fully present for a more fulfilling life and meaningful connections.

MEMORIES MADE: _____
_____
_____
_____
_____
_____

TOUGH TIMES & LESSONS LEARNED: _____
_____
_____
_____
_____

What are you grateful for today?   Stressed Angry Tired Sad Happy Excited
_____

REMEMBER! WAIT TO WRITE BELOW UNTIL THIS DAY NEXT YEAR!

DATE: _____   (S) (M) (T) (W) (T) (F) (S)

MEMORIES MADE: _____
_____
_____
_____
_____
_____

TOUGH TIMES & LESSONS LEARNED: _____
_____
_____
_____
_____

What are you grateful for today?   Stressed Angry Tired Sad Happy Excited
_____

Did you know? The human body has more than 650 muscles, which work together to move, support the skeleton, and maintain posture. Pump em' up!

DATE: _____ (S) (M) (T) (W) (T) (F) (S)

TUESDAY TIPS:

> "Avoid the path of least resistance. Courses are not just about doing well and getting good grades or finishing with a high GPA. It's not something you just get through, hoping to magically change by graduation. College is an awesome time for personal growth and development. Just doing the minimum is like having a fancy car without an engine; it might look good, but it's missing what really matters inside. Learn to love learning."

MEMORIES MADE: _____
_____
_____
_____
_____

TOUGH TIMES & LESSONS LEARNED: _____
_____
_____
_____

What are you grateful for today?
_____

Stressed Angry Tired Sad Happy Excited

↙ REMEMBER! WAIT TO WRITE BELOW UNTIL THIS DAY NEXT YEAR!

DATE: _____ (S) (M) (T) (W) (T) (F) (S)

MEMORIES MADE: _____
_____
_____
_____
_____

TOUGH TIMES & LESSONS LEARNED: _____
_____
_____
_____

What are you grateful for today?
_____

Stressed Angry Tired Sad Happy Excited

Did you know? Expressing emotions, whether through writing (different than whining), art, or conversation, can lead to increased happiness and emotional well-being in college students.

DATE: _____ (S) (M) (T) (W) (T) (F) (S)

WEDNESDAY (HUMP DAY!) HAPPY HACKS:

> "Explore internships and part-time jobs for practical experience. Heck, even volunteer to work with professors in their labs if you can. You've heard it before, "it's not what you know but who you know." Okay, both are super important, but you will need experience in your area! Plus, again, if you're even remotely considering grad school, most want to know what experience you have."

MEMORIES MADE: _____
_____
_____
_____
_____

TOUGH TIMES & LESSONS LEARNED: _____
_____
_____
_____
_____

What are you grateful for today?   Stressed Angry Tired Sad Happy Excited
_____

> REMEMBER! WAIT TO WRITE BELOW UNTIL THIS DAY NEXT YEAR!

DATE: _____ (S) (M) (T) (W) (T) (F) (S)

MEMORIES MADE: _____
_____
_____
_____
_____

TOUGH TIMES & LESSONS LEARNED: _____
_____
_____
_____
_____

What are you grateful for today?   Stressed Angry Tired Sad Happy Excited
_____

Did you know? You sneeze at an average speed of 100 miles per hour!
Watch out, world! Ka-chow!

DATE: _____ (S) (M) (T) (W) (T) (F) (S)

THURSDAY MYTHS:

> Myth: "I have to go abroad to have a complete college experience."
>
> Reality: While studying abroad can be enriching, it's not the only path to a fulfilling college experience. Engaging in campus life, internships, and local community projects can also be incredibly rewarding. It's like choosing between different travel destinations – each offers its own unique experiences.

MEMORIES MADE: _____
_____
_____
_____
_____
_____

TOUGH TIMES & LESSONS LEARNED: _____
_____
_____
_____
_____

What are you grateful for today?   Stressed · Angry · Tired · Sad · Happy · Excited
_____

REMEMBER! WAIT TO WRITE BELOW UNTIL THIS DAY NEXT YEAR!

DATE: _____ (S) (M) (T) (W) (T) (F) (S)

MEMORIES MADE: _____
_____
_____
_____
_____
_____

TOUGH TIMES & LESSONS LEARNED: _____
_____
_____
_____
_____

What are you grateful for today?   Stressed · Angry · Tired · Sad · Happy · Excited
_____

Did you know? You are more bacteria than human cells! Embrace the good bacteria that keep you healthy. But wash those hands often!

DATE: _____ (S) (M) (T) (W) (T) (F) (S)

FRIDAY FILL IN THE BLANKS:

> My favorite brand(s) of clothing is...
> _____
>
> and my favorite item(s) is...
> _____

MEMORIES MADE: _____
_____
_____
_____
_____

TOUGH TIMES & LESSONS LEARNED: _____
_____
_____
_____
_____

What are you grateful for today?
_____

Stressed Angry Tired Sad Happy Excited

↙ REMEMBER! WAIT TO WRITE BELOW UNTIL THIS DAY NEXT YEAR!

DATE: _____ (S) (M) (T) (W) (T) (F) (S)

MEMORIES MADE: _____
_____
_____
_____
_____

TOUGH TIMES & LESSONS LEARNED: _____
_____
_____
_____
_____

What are you grateful for today?
_____

Stressed Angry Tired Sad Happy Excited

Did you know? The tradition of throwing graduation caps in the air originated at the United States Naval Academy in 1912 when graduates were first given caps to toss.

DATE: _____ (S) (M) (T) (W) (T) (F) (S)

SATURDAY TED TALKS:

> Matt Walker, in his TED Talk "Sleep is Your Superpower," argues that sleep isn't a luxury, but a biological necessity. He exposes the dangers of sleep deprivation, highlighting its impact on learning, memory, immunity, and even our genes. He debunks myths about "catching up" on sleep and emphasizes the importance of consistent, quality sleep (7-8 hours) for optimal brain and body function. He calls for a cultural shift in valuing sleep, urging us to prioritize it for personal and societal well-being. Remember, "Sleep is your superpower," and neglecting it weakens your mind and body's potential.

MEMORIES MADE: _____
_____
_____
_____
_____

TOUGH TIMES & LESSONS LEARNED: _____
_____
_____
_____

What are you grateful for today?

Stressed | Angry | Tired | Sad | Happy | Excited

REMEMBER! WAIT TO WRITE BELOW UNTIL THIS DAY NEXT YEAR!

DATE: _____ (S) (M) (T) (W) (T) (F) (S)

MEMORIES MADE: _____
_____
_____
_____
_____

TOUGH TIMES & LESSONS LEARNED: _____
_____
_____
_____

What are you grateful for today?

Stressed | Angry | Tired | Sad | Happy | Excited

Did you know? Practicing forgiveness, including self-forgiveness, can lead to lower levels of anxiety, depression, and major psychiatric disorders, promoting emotional healing.

DATE: _____ (S) (M) (T) (W) (T) (F) (S)

SUNDAY STRESS BUSTERS:

> "Paying close attention to how and what you eat can really affect how stressed you feel. Try to notice what's on your plate, enjoy every mouthful, and don't eat just because you're stressed. Eating this way helps your body digest food better and can make you feel better about your meals. When you eat slowly and without distractions, you're more likely to eat the right amount and enjoy your food more. This can lead to feeling better both physically and mentally."

MEMORIES MADE: _____
_____
_____
_____
_____

TOUGH TIMES & LESSONS LEARNED: _____
_____
_____
_____

What are you grateful for today?   Stressed Angry Tired Sad Happy Excited
_____

REMEMBER! WAIT TO WRITE BELOW UNTIL THIS DAY NEXT YEAR!

DATE: _____ (S) (M) (T) (W) (T) (F) (S)

MEMORIES MADE: _____
_____
_____
_____
_____

TOUGH TIMES & LESSONS LEARNED: _____
_____
_____
_____

What are you grateful for today?   Stressed Angry Tired Sad Happy Excited
_____

Did you know? Dancing can improve mental health by combining physical exercise, creative expression, and social interaction, enhancing mood and reducing stress. So go ahead and get your groove on!

DATE: _____ (S) (M) (T) (W) (T) (F) (S)

MONDAY MANNERS:

> Answer the door with a smile. Greet the visitor with a warm "hello." If it's someone there to see your roommate, invite them in while you go find them. Talk with the person while you are waiting for the roommate to arrive. If it's family members of your roommate, be especially positive and kind! Being kind and respectful in the doorway is a manner to learn and take with you for your entire life. First impressions are especially important. A warm welcome starts with a smile, eye contact, and a greeting.

MEMORIES MADE: _____
_____
_____
_____
_____
_____

TOUGH TIMES & LESSONS LEARNED: _____
_____
_____
_____
_____

What are you grateful for today?   Stressed Angry Tired Sad Happy Excited
_____

REMEMBER! WAIT TO WRITE BELOW UNTIL THIS DAY NEXT YEAR!

DATE: _____ (S) (M) (T) (W) (T) (F) (S)

MEMORIES MADE: _____
_____
_____
_____
_____
_____

TOUGH TIMES & LESSONS LEARNED: _____
_____
_____
_____
_____

What are you grateful for today?   Stressed Angry Tired Sad Happy Excited
_____

Did you know? Your eyes are always the same size from birth, but your nose and ears never stop growing.

DATE: _____ (S) (M) (T) (W) (T) (F) (S)

TUESDAY TIPS:

> Use office hours to clarify doubts and build rapport with professors. If you're thinking about going to grad school, this is super important. You are going to need letters of recommendation, so getting to know professors and getting help are both important! And go in early in the semester, not toward the end when you're stressed and desperate. Professors don't like that. Just sayin...

MEMORIES MADE: _____
_____
_____
_____
_____
_____

TOUGH TIMES & LESSONS LEARNED: _____
_____
_____
_____
_____

What are you grateful for today?   Stressed Angry Tired Sad Happy Excited
_____

REMEMBER! WAIT TO WRITE BELOW UNTIL THIS DAY NEXT YEAR!

DATE: _____ (S) (M) (T) (W) (T) (F) (S)

MEMORIES MADE: _____
_____
_____
_____
_____
_____

TOUGH TIMES & LESSONS LEARNED: _____
_____
_____
_____
_____

What are you grateful for today?   Stressed Angry Tired Sad Happy Excited
_____

Did you know? Laughter can serve as a mini workout; it engages the abdominal muscles and even burns calories, combining health benefits with joy. Go bust a gut! :)

DATE: _____ (S) (M) (T) (W) (T) (F) (S)

WEDNESDAY (HUMP DAY!) HAPPY HACKS

> You only control your troubles. When you experience struggles in life, most fall into one of three categories: trials, troubles, and afflictions. There are subtle differences. Trials are struggles that happen because we live in a wild unpredictable world—cancer, earthquakes and diseases are common examples. They aren't necessarily anyone's "fault," Troubles come as a result of decisions WE make. Afflictions arise because of the choices of others. We only have control over one of these. Choose to focus on those things in your life that YOU have control over.

MEMORIES MADE: _____
_____
_____
_____
_____

TOUGH TIMES & LESSONS LEARNED: _____
_____
_____
_____

What are you grateful for today?   Stressed Angry Tired Sad Happy Excited
_____

REMEMBER! WAIT TO WRITE BELOW UNTIL THIS DAY NEXT YEAR!

DATE: _____ (S) (M) (T) (W) (T) (F) (S)

MEMORIES MADE: _____
_____
_____
_____
_____

TOUGH TIMES & LESSONS LEARNED: _____
_____
_____
_____

What are you grateful for today?   Stressed Angry Tired Sad Happy Excited
_____

Did you know? The world's largest pizza ever made measured 132 feet in diameter and contained over 130,000 slices! Imagine the pizza parties you could throw with that! That's some serious dough!

DATE: _____   S M T W T F S

THURSDAY MYTHS:

> Myth: "I can handle everything by myself."
>
> Reality: It's okay to ask for help. Whether it's academic support, mental health resources, or just leaning on friends, seeking assistance is a sign of strength, not weakness. It's like trying to move a couch by yourself – sometimes, you need an extra set of hands.

MEMORIES MADE: _____
_____
_____
_____
_____
_____

TOUGH TIMES & LESSONS LEARNED: _____
_____
_____
_____
_____

What are you grateful for today?   Stressed Angry Tired Sad Happy Excited
_____

REMEMBER! WAIT TO WRITE BELOW UNTIL THIS DAY NEXT YEAR!

DATE: _____   S M T W T F S

MEMORIES MADE: _____
_____
_____
_____
_____
_____

TOUGH TIMES & LESSONS LEARNED: _____
_____
_____
_____
_____

What are you grateful for today?   Stressed Angry Tired Sad Happy Excited
_____

Did you know? The phrase "steal someone's thunder" originated from the playwright John Dennis, who invented a new method for simulating the sound of thunder for his plays. When his method was copied, it was said that others had "stolen his thunder."

DATE: _____ (S) (M) (T) (W) (T) (F) (S)

FRIDAY FILL IN THE BLANKS:

> "
> My favorite way to relax is...
> _____
>
> especially when...
> _____
> "

MEMORIES MADE: _____
_____
_____
_____
_____

TOUGH TIMES & LESSONS LEARNED: _____
_____
_____
_____

What are you grateful for today?
_____

Stressed | Angry | Tired | Sad | Happy | Excited

REMEMBER! WAIT TO WRITE BELOW UNTIL THIS DAY NEXT YEAR!

DATE: _____ (S) (M) (T) (W) (T) (F) (S)

MEMORIES MADE: _____
_____
_____
_____
_____

TOUGH TIMES & LESSONS LEARNED: _____
_____
_____
_____

What are you grateful for today?
_____

Stressed | Angry | Tired | Sad | Happy | Excited

Did you know? The phrase "under the weather" comes from sailors who, feeling seasick due to the weather, would go below deck to feel better, thus being "under the weather."

DATE: _____   (S) (M) (T) (W) (T) (F) (S)

SATURDAY TED TALKS:

> In his TED talk "Why We All Need to Practice Emotional First Aid," Guy Winch argues that we should treat our emotional pain as we do physical pain. He explains that we often neglect psychological injuries like rejection or failure, which can impact our mental health and life satisfaction. Winch stresses the importance of being mindful of emotional pain and taking immediate steps to heal psychological wounds through practices like reframing our thinking, affirming our self-worth, and combating rumination. Practicing emotional first aid helps us recover faster and fosters better long-term mental health.

MEMORIES MADE: _____
_____
_____
_____
_____
_____

TOUGH TIMES & LESSONS LEARNED: _____
_____
_____
_____
_____

What are you grateful for today?   Stressed Angry Tired Sad Happy Excited
_____

REMEMBER! WAIT TO WRITE BELOW UNTIL THIS DAY NEXT YEAR!

DATE: _____   (S) (M) (T) (W) (T) (F) (S)

MEMORIES MADE: _____
_____
_____
_____
_____
_____

TOUGH TIMES & LESSONS LEARNED: _____
_____
_____
_____
_____

What are you grateful for today?   Stressed Angry Tired Sad Happy Excited
_____

Did you know? Maintaining strong social connections and nurturing meaningful relationships promotes happiness, reduces stress, and strengthens the immune system. Connect for greater well-being!

DATE: _____ (S) (M) (T) (W) (T) (F) (S)

SUNDAY STRESS BUSTERS:

> "Try different ways to relax like tightening and then loosening your muscles, imagining peaceful places, or listening to calm music. These activities can lower your stress and make you feel more at peace. Adding these simple practices to your daily life can really help keep stress under control and make you feel more relaxed. It's good to experiment and find out which one works best for you, so you can use it whenever you need to calm down and feel better."

MEMORIES MADE: _____
_____
_____
_____
_____

TOUGH TIMES & LESSONS LEARNED:
_____
_____
_____
_____

What are you grateful for today?

Stressed | Angry | Tired | Sad | Happy | Excited

REMEMBER! WAIT TO WRITE BELOW UNTIL THIS DAY NEXT YEAR!

DATE: _____ (S) (M) (T) (W) (T) (F) (S)

MEMORIES MADE: _____
_____
_____
_____
_____
_____

TOUGH TIMES & LESSONS LEARNED: _____
_____
_____
_____
_____

What are you grateful for today?

Stressed | Angry | Tired | Sad | Happy | Excited

Did you know? The concept of 'office hours' in academia originated from the idea of professors being available in their offices for a set time each week to meet with students.

DATE: _____ (S) (M) (T) (W) (T) (F) (S)

MONDAY MANNERS:

> Make appreciation a habit. Express gratitude regularly, especially to professors, parents, roommates, friends, servers and anyone else that does something nice — whether it's part of their job or not. Make thanking others a habit, acknowledging the numerous people who go out of their way to help you. Regular expressions of gratitude foster appreciation and increase others' willingness to assist you in the future. The happiest people in this world are those who take time to notice and thank others for the small and simple things they say and do. Be grateful and express it regularly!

MEMORIES MADE: _____
_____
_____
_____
_____
_____

TOUGH TIMES & LESSONS LEARNED: _____
_____
_____
_____
_____

What are you grateful for today? Stressed | Angry | Tired | Sad | Happy | Excited
_____

REMEMBER! WAIT TO WRITE BELOW UNTIL THIS DAY NEXT YEAR!

DATE: _____ (S) (M) (T) (W) (T) (F) (S)

MEMORIES MADE: _____
_____
_____
_____
_____
_____

TOUGH TIMES & LESSONS LEARNED: _____
_____
_____
_____
_____

What are you grateful for today? Stressed | Angry | Tired | Sad | Happy | Excited
_____

Did you know? Humans are bioluminescent and glow in the dark, but the light that we emit is 1,000 times weaker than our human eyes are able to pick up.

DATE: _____ (S) (M) (T) (W) (T) (F) (S)

TUESDAY TIPS:

> " Be proactive in seeking out career advice and counseling. Counselors are just plain cool. Go visit a career counselor and you'll be grateful (they LOVE when you visit!). And then go chat with people who are in your profession. Talk to them about what it's like – what they love and don't like about their job. You really need to love what you do. The best way to know is get some experience doing it and talking to others who have done it. Start with a counselor! "

MEMORIES MADE: _____
_____
_____
_____
_____

TOUGH TIMES & LESSONS LEARNED: _____
_____
_____
_____

What are you grateful for today?
_____

Stressed | Angry | Tired | Sad | Happy | Excited

REMEMBER! WAIT TO WRITE BELOW UNTIL THIS DAY NEXT YEAR!

DATE: _____ (S) (M) (T) (W) (T) (F) (S)

MEMORIES MADE: _____
_____
_____
_____
_____

TOUGH TIMES & LESSONS LEARNED: _____
_____
_____
_____

What are you grateful for today?
_____

Stressed | Angry | Tired | Sad | Happy | Excited

Did you know? Digital eye strain, or "computer vision syndrome," affects about 50% of computer users, causing symptoms like dry eyes, headache, blurred vision, and neck pain.

DATE: _____ (S) (M) (T) (W) (T) (F) (S)

WEDNESDAY (HUMP DAY!) HAPPY HACKS:

> Want to know the secret to getting happy fast? Turn outward and serve someone else! Helping others makes us happy because it creates a feel-good sensation called the "helper's high." When we do good things for others, our brains release endorphins, making us feel happier. Also, helping people connects us with them, gives us a sense of purpose, and helps us see life from a different perspective. This focus on others instead of ourselves can make us feel more grateful and understanding. In simple terms, if you're feeling down, ask yourself what you can do to improve the lives of those around you. Then notice the nudge and follow the feeling!

MEMORIES MADE: _____
_____
_____
_____
_____
_____

TOUGH TIMES & LESSONS LEARNED: _____
_____
_____
_____
_____

What are you grateful for today?
_____

Stressed | Angry | Tired | Sad | Happy | Excited

REMEMBER! WAIT TO WRITE BELOW UNTIL THIS DAY NEXT YEAR!

DATE: _____ (S) (M) (T) (W) (T) (F) (S)

MEMORIES MADE: _____
_____
_____
_____
_____
_____

TOUGH TIMES & LESSONS LEARNED: _____
_____
_____
_____
_____

What are you grateful for today?
_____

Stressed | Angry | Tired | Sad | Happy | Excited

Did you know? Social media platforms use algorithms designed to keep users engaged for as long as possible, sometimes leading to addictive behaviors and overuse.

DATE: _____ (S) (M) (T) (W) (T) (F) (S)

THURSDAY MYTHS:

> Myth: "I can party hard and still excel academically."
>
> Reality: Balance is key. Excessive partying can take a toll on your academic performance and health. It's important to have fun, but also to prioritize your responsibilities. It's like a seesaw — too much weight on one side and everything tips over.

MEMORIES MADE: _____
_____
_____
_____
_____
_____

TOUGH TIMES & LESSONS LEARNED: _____
_____
_____
_____
_____
_____

What are you grateful for today?   Stressed Angry Tired Sad Happy Excited
_____

REMEMBER! WAIT TO WRITE BELOW UNTIL THIS DAY NEXT YEAR!

DATE: _____ (S) (M) (T) (W) (T) (F) (S)

MEMORIES MADE: _____
_____
_____
_____
_____
_____

TOUGH TIMES & LESSONS LEARNED: _____
_____
_____
_____
_____
_____

What are you grateful for today?   Stressed Angry Tired Sad Happy Excited
_____

Did you know? Strong relationships with family and friends are crucial for happiness in college, providing support and a sense of belonging. Stay connected with your peeps!

DATE: _____ Ⓢ Ⓜ Ⓣ Ⓦ Ⓣ Ⓕ Ⓢ

FRIDAY FILL IN THE BLANKS:

" The most inspiring person in my life is...
_____

because...
_____ "

MEMORIES MADE: _____
_____
_____
_____
_____
_____

TOUGH TIMES & LESSONS LEARNED: _____
_____
_____
_____
_____

What are you grateful for today?   Stressed Angry Tired Sad Happy Excited
_____

> REMEMBER! WAIT TO WRITE BELOW UNTIL THIS DAY NEXT YEAR!

DATE: _____ Ⓢ Ⓜ Ⓣ Ⓦ Ⓣ Ⓕ Ⓢ

MEMORIES MADE: _____
_____
_____
_____
_____
_____

TOUGH TIMES & LESSONS LEARNED: _____
_____
_____
_____
_____

What are you grateful for today?   Stressed Angry Tired Sad Happy Excited
_____

Did you know? Collaborating with classmates on projects not only strengthens understanding but also hones communication and teamwork skills, valuable assets for any career path.

DATE: _____ (S) (M) (T) (W) (T) (F) (S)

SATURDAY TED TALKS:

> In Malcolm Gladwell's TED Talk, "Choice, Happiness, and Spaghetti Sauce," he uses the story of Howard Moskowitz, a marketing researcher, to challenge the idea of a "one-size-fits-all" approach to consumer preferences. Moskowitz studied spaghetti sauce and discovered diverse taste preferences, rejecting the pursuit of a perfect sauce. This leads to Gladwell's central message: embracing human variability is key to understanding happiness and success. He applies this to areas like business, education, and personal choices, highlighting that catering to individual needs, rather than seeking universal solutions, leads to better outcomes and greater satisfaction. In sum, Gladwell's message is: celebrate your unique sauce recipe, and don't underestimate the power of variety!

MEMORIES MADE: _____
_____
_____
_____
_____
_____

TOUGH TIMES & LESSONS LEARNED: _____
_____
_____
_____
_____

What are you grateful for today?
_____

Stressed Angry Tired Sad Happy Excited

↩ REMEMBER! WAIT TO WRITE BELOW UNTIL THIS DAY NEXT YEAR!

DATE: _____ (S) (M) (T) (W) (T) (F) (S)

MEMORIES MADE: _____
_____
_____
_____
_____
_____

TOUGH TIMES & LESSONS LEARNED: _____
_____
_____
_____
_____

What are you grateful for today?
_____

Stressed Angry Tired Sad Happy Excited

Did you know? Sharing the load means lighter shoulders! Rotate chores fairly, contribute to cleaning common areas, and be mindful of messes you create.
Teamwork makes the living space dream work.

DATE: _____ (S) (M) (T) (W) (T) (F) (S)

SUNDAY STRESS BUSTERS:

> Laughing and enjoying yourself is an excellent way to reduce stress. You can watch funny movies or shows, tell jokes with your friends, or do anything else that makes you giggle. Laughing helps to make you feel lighter and less burdened by the stresses of school. It's like laughter gives your mind a break from worrying and helps you feel happier. So, finding time to laugh and have fun isn't just enjoyable; it's also really good for your well-being.

MEMORIES MADE: _____
_____
_____
_____
_____

TOUGH TIMES & LESSONS LEARNED: _____
_____
_____
_____

What are you grateful for today?
_____

Stressed Angry Tired Sad Happy Excited

REMEMBER! WAIT TO WRITE BELOW UNTIL THIS DAY NEXT YEAR!

DATE: _____ (S) (M) (T) (W) (T) (F) (S)

MEMORIES MADE: _____
_____
_____
_____
_____

TOUGH TIMES & LESSONS LEARNED: _____
_____
_____
_____

What are you grateful for today?
_____

Stressed Angry Tired Sad Happy Excited

Did you know? Engaging in hobbies you enjoy, like painting, writing, or playing music, can be a powerful tool for stress relief and creative expression. Here's another picture to color! :)

DRAWING AND DOODLING WHILE TAKING SOME DEEP BREATHS CAN HELP YOU RELAX AND FEEL LESS STRESSED!

DATE: _____ (S) (M) (T) (W) (T) (F) (S)

MONDAY MANNERS:

> Get the door for others. Whether it is your roommate with their arms full or someone pushing a stroller at a store, observe what's going on and jump at the chance to help someone with the door. Keep your eyes up and attuned to the needs of others. See a person in a wheelchair or and elderly person getting ready to enter a restaurant? Hop up and hold the door open. Notice when there is someone coming in behind you and open the door for them. These small acts of service contribute to creating a better, kinder world. First observe, then serve!

MEMORIES MADE: _____
_____
_____
_____
_____
_____

TOUGH TIMES & LESSONS LEARNED: _____
_____
_____
_____
_____

What are you grateful for today?
_____

Stressed   Angry   Tired   Sad   Happy   Excited

REMEMBER! WAIT TO WRITE BELOW UNTIL THIS DAY NEXT YEAR!

DATE: _____ (S) (M) (T) (W) (T) (F) (S)

MEMORIES MADE: _____
_____
_____
_____
_____
_____

TOUGH TIMES & LESSONS LEARNED: _____
_____
_____
_____
_____

What are you grateful for today?
_____

Stressed   Angry   Tired   Sad   Happy   Excited

Did you know? Studying for 1 hour before going to bed can help you remember facts better the next morning. Just try to go to bed before midnight for best retention!

DATE: _____ (S) (M) (T) (W) (T) (F) (S)

TUESDAY TIPS:

> Take breaks and engage in stress-relief activities. This is another mental health checkup. Don't use breaks to procrastinate, but plan breaks and reward yourself when you have put in the time. Plus, breaks give your brain a chance to soak it all in. Physical activities are especially helpful for your brain AND your body. The key is to be "all-in" with whatever you are doing, whether it's studying or taking a break. And shut off your phone when you are engaged in an activity that takes concentration! The notifications will trigger your brain to check things and distract you!

MEMORIES MADE: _____
_____
_____
_____
_____

TOUGH TIMES & LESSONS LEARNED: _____
_____
_____
_____
_____

What are you grateful for today?   Stressed Angry Tired Sad Happy Excited
_____

REMEMBER! WAIT TO WRITE BELOW UNTIL THIS DAY NEXT YEAR!

DATE: _____ (S) (M) (T) (W) (T) (F) (S)

MEMORIES MADE: _____
_____
_____
_____
_____

TOUGH TIMES & LESSONS LEARNED: _____
_____
_____
_____

What are you grateful for today?   Stressed Angry Tired Sad Happy Excited
_____

Did you know? Laughing for 10-15 minutes per day can help reduce stress hormones. Find the lighter side of life and make some great memories with others by laughing!

DATE: _____ (S) (M) (T) (W) (T) (F) (S)

WEDNESDAY (HUMP DAY!) HAPPY HACKS:

> "Learn to label your thinking. When you catch yourself thinking something negative, like "I'm a failure," try saying, "I'm having the thought that I'm a failure" instead. This little change helps you see these thoughts as just things your mind is saying, not facts. It's like stepping back and realizing these are just words in your head, not truths about you. This helps make the bad feelings less intense, because you're not taking those thoughts so seriously anymore. Remember, thoughts are just thoughts and they don't control you or your behavior."

MEMORIES MADE: _____
_____
_____
_____
_____
_____

TOUGH TIMES & LESSONS LEARNED: _____
_____
_____
_____
_____

What are you grateful for today?

Stressed | Angry | Tired | Sad | Happy | Excited
_____

REMEMBER! WAIT TO WRITE BELOW UNTIL THIS DAY NEXT YEAR!

DATE: _____ (S) (M) (T) (W) (T) (F) (S)

MEMORIES MADE: _____
_____
_____
_____
_____
_____

TOUGH TIMES & LESSONS LEARNED: _____
_____
_____
_____
_____

What are you grateful for today?

Stressed | Angry | Tired | Sad | Happy | Excited
_____

Did you know? A study in the "Journal of Social and Clinical Psychology" found that limiting social media use to 30 minutes a day resulted in significant reductions in levels of anxiety, depression, and loneliness.

DATE: _____ Ⓢ Ⓜ Ⓣ Ⓦ Ⓣ Ⓕ Ⓢ

THURSDAY MYTHS:

> Myth: "I don't need to think about my career until my senior year."
>
> Reality: Starting to plan your career early can give you an edge. Internships, networking, and exploring career options should begin sooner rather than later. It's like planting a garden – the sooner you start, the better the harvest.

MEMORIES MADE: _____
_____
_____
_____
_____
_____

TOUGH TIMES & LESSONS LEARNED: _____
_____
_____
_____
_____

What are you grateful for today?
_____

Stressed | Angry | Tired | Sad | Happy | Excited

REMEMBER! WAIT TO WRITE BELOW UNTIL THIS DAY NEXT YEAR!

DATE: _____ Ⓢ Ⓜ Ⓣ Ⓦ Ⓣ Ⓕ Ⓢ

MEMORIES MADE: _____
_____
_____
_____
_____
_____

TOUGH TIMES & LESSONS LEARNED: _____
_____
_____
_____
_____

What are you grateful for today?
_____

Stressed | Angry | Tired | Sad | Happy | Excited

Did you know? The average human walks around 110,000 miles in a lifetime.
Try to get your 10,000 steps in for better physical and mental health!

DATE: _____ (S) (M) (T) (W) (T) (F) (S)

FRIDAY FILL IN THE BLANKS:

" The best gift I ever received was...
_____

and it meant a lot because...
_____ "

MEMORIES MADE: _____
_____
_____
_____
_____

TOUGH TIMES & LESSONS LEARNED: _____
_____
_____
_____
_____

What are you grateful for today?
_____

Stressed Angry Tired Sad Happy Excited

REMEMBER! WAIT TO WRITE BELOW UNTIL THIS DAY NEXT YEAR!

DATE: _____ (S) (M) (T) (W) (T) (F) (S)

MEMORIES MADE: _____
_____
_____
_____
_____

TOUGH TIMES & LESSONS LEARNED: _____
_____
_____
_____
_____

What are you grateful for today?
_____

Stressed Angry Tired Sad Happy Excited

Did you know? Saving 10% of your income can help you become financially secure over time.
If you get into the habit while you're young, it will really PAY off when you're older!

DATE: _____ (S) (M) (T) (W) (T) (F) (S)

SATURDAY TED TALKS:

> In his TED talk, "The art and science of happiness," Professor Arthur Brooks flips the script on traditional happiness pursuits like "bucket lists," arguing true joy lies in deep connections and meaningful goals. He debunks the myth of money leading to happiness and instead emphasizes the power of strong social bonds, volunteering, and personal growth. He challenges the "comparison trap" and advocates for gratitude practices. His message boils down to this: find purpose, build relationships, savor small joys, and happiness will follow.

MEMORIES MADE: _____
_____
_____
_____
_____

TOUGH TIMES & LESSONS LEARNED: _____
_____
_____
_____
_____

What are you grateful for today?
_____

Stressed | Angry | Tired | Sad | Happy | Excited

REMEMBER! WAIT TO WRITE BELOW UNTIL THIS DAY NEXT YEAR!

DATE: _____ (S) (M) (T) (W) (T) (F) (S)

MEMORIES MADE: _____
_____
_____
_____
_____

TOUGH TIMES & LESSONS LEARNED: _____
_____
_____
_____
_____

What are you grateful for today?
_____

Stressed | Angry | Tired | Sad | Happy | Excited

Did you know? The phrase "wear your heart on your sleeve" comes from the Middle Ages, when knights might wear the colors of the lady they represented in jousts, literally or symbolically wearing their affections for all to see.

DATE: _____ (S) (M) (T) (W) (T) (F) (S)

SUNDAY STRESS BUSTERS:

> "More water = less stress? Drinking enough water is super important for keeping your energy up and staying in a good mood. Not having enough water can make it harder to think clearly and can make you feel more stressed out. Make sure you're drinking plenty of water all day long. It helps your brain work better and keeps you feeling good. So, carrying a water bottle with you and sipping from it throughout the day can really help you stay hydrated and feel better overall."

MEMORIES MADE: _____
_____
_____
_____
_____

TOUGH TIMES & LESSONS LEARNED: _____
_____
_____
_____

What are you grateful for today?
_____

Stressed | Angry | Tired | Sad | Happy | Excited

REMEMBER! WAIT TO WRITE BELOW UNTIL THIS DAY NEXT YEAR!

DATE: _____ (S) (M) (T) (W) (T) (F) (S)

MEMORIES MADE: _____
_____
_____
_____
_____

TOUGH TIMES & LESSONS LEARNED: _____
_____
_____
_____

What are you grateful for today?
_____

Stressed | Angry | Tired | Sad | Happy | Excited

Did you know? Taking regular study breaks helps boost retention and understanding of study material. Try 20 or 25 minutes of studying (with no phone interruptions) then get up and take a break!

DATE: _____ S M T W T F S

MONDAY MANNERS:

> Avoid whispering in front of others as it creates discomfort, changes group dynamics, and may hurt feelings. Whispering in a movie may be appropriate, but when you're with others in a group setting, choose a better time for private conversations. Whispering can make people feel self-conscious and left out. When others are whispering, we often think they are talking about us. Consider how you'd feel in such situations and strive to create a more inclusive and comfortable environment. If a conversation isn't meant for a group, wait for a more appropriate time to discuss it privately.

MEMORIES MADE: _____
_____
_____
_____
_____
_____

TOUGH TIMES & LESSONS LEARNED: _____
_____
_____
_____
_____

What are you grateful for today?   Stressed Angry Tired Sad Happy Excited
_____

REMEMBER! WAIT TO WRITE BELOW UNTIL THIS DAY NEXT YEAR!

DATE: _____ S M T W T F S

MEMORIES MADE: _____
_____
_____
_____
_____
_____

TOUGH TIMES & LESSONS LEARNED: _____
_____
_____
_____
_____

What are you grateful for today?   Stressed Angry Tired Sad Happy Excited
_____

Did you know? Stress levels go down after spending just 20 minutes outside in nature. Even going for a quick walk outside to get some fresh air can work wonders! Deep breaths and soak in the sights!

DATE: _____ (S) (M) (T) (W) (T) (F) (S)

TUESDAY TIPS:

> Be open to diverse perspectives and cultures. Remind yourself that everyone you ever meet can teach you something. This is especially true for those who are different than you. Even when you disagree with others who are different than you, learn to disagree with respect and civility. There is so much to learn in life. Be humble and open – slow to judge and quick to listen and love.

MEMORIES MADE: _____
_____
_____
_____
_____
_____

TOUGH TIMES & LESSONS LEARNED: _____
_____
_____
_____
_____

What are you grateful for today?
_____

Stressed | Angry | Tired | Sad | Happy | Excited

REMEMBER! WAIT TO WRITE BELOW UNTIL THIS DAY NEXT YEAR!

DATE: _____ (S) (M) (T) (W) (T) (F) (S)

MEMORIES MADE: _____
_____
_____
_____
_____
_____

TOUGH TIMES & LESSONS LEARNED: _____
_____
_____
_____
_____

What are you grateful for today?
_____

Stressed | Angry | Tired | Sad | Happy | Excited

Did you know? Forgiving others has been shown to reduce anxiety, depression and stress levels.
Remember, people are more important than problems and projects.

DATE: _____ S M T W T F S

WEDNESDAY (HUMP DAY!) HAPPY HACKS

> Anger can wreck your happiness. Anger is poisonous. It alters our perspective and we view others as obstacles in our way. It changes our vision, we don't see things as they are. We see things as we are. We don't see the whole picture. We see what we want to see, what we're staring at. Anger turns us inward. We can't see others' perspective when we're stuck focusing on ourselves. When we are upset about something, we treat others in a harsher way. In this way, when we get angry, we lose positive energy. And we lose the ability to see with compassion and empathy. If life is about connection, then anger is primarily about disconnection and destruction.

MEMORIES MADE: _____
_____
_____
_____
_____

TOUGH TIMES & LESSONS LEARNED: _____
_____
_____
_____
_____

What are you grateful for today?   Stressed   Angry   Tired   Sad   Happy   Excited
_____

REMEMBER! WAIT TO WRITE BELOW UNTIL THIS DAY NEXT YEAR!

DATE: _____ S M T W T F S

MEMORIES MADE: _____
_____
_____
_____
_____

TOUGH TIMES & LESSONS LEARNED: _____
_____
_____
_____
_____

What are you grateful for today?   Stressed   Angry   Tired   Sad   Happy   Excited
_____

Did you know? Researchers believe yawning helps cool the brain and improves focus/alertness. Just be sure to turn away or close your mouth a bit. Nobody wants to see your tonsils!

DATE: _____ (S) (M) (T) (W) (T) (F) (S)

THURSDAY MYTHS:

> Myth: "My major determines my career path."
>
> Reality: Your major doesn't lock you into a specific career. Many people find jobs in fields unrelated to their major. Think of your major as a starting point, not a final destination. Between 30-50% of students will change their major before graduation!

MEMORIES MADE: _____
_____
_____
_____
_____
_____

TOUGH TIMES & LESSONS LEARNED: _____
_____
_____
_____
_____
_____

What are you grateful for today?   Stressed Angry Tired Sad Happy Excited
_____

> REMEMBER! WAIT TO WRITE BELOW UNTIL THIS DAY NEXT YEAR!

DATE: _____ (S) (M) (T) (W) (T) (F) (S)

MEMORIES MADE: _____
_____
_____
_____
_____
_____

TOUGH TIMES & LESSONS LEARNED: _____
_____
_____
_____
_____

What are you grateful for today?   Stressed Angry Tired Sad Happy Excited
_____

Did you know? Endorphins released when falling in love are chemically similar to pain relievers. Don't fall too fast! You might be feeling a "high" and not be thinking straight! Take it slow yo!

DATE: _____ (S) (M) (T) (W) (T) (F) (S)

FRIDAY FILL IN THE BLANKS:

> "
> My favorite type of weather is...
> _____
>
> and I love it because...
> _____
> "

MEMORIES MADE: _____
_____
_____
_____
_____

TOUGH TIMES & LESSONS LEARNED: _____
_____
_____
_____
_____

What are you grateful for today?
_____

Stressed | Angry | Tired | Sad | Happy | Excited

REMEMBER! WAIT TO WRITE BELOW UNTIL THIS DAY NEXT YEAR!

DATE: _____ (S) (M) (T) (W) (T) (F) (S)

MEMORIES MADE: _____
_____
_____
_____
_____

TOUGH TIMES & LESSONS LEARNED: _____
_____
_____
_____
_____

What are you grateful for today?
_____

Stressed | Angry | Tired | Sad | Happy | Excited

Did you know? The average person has between 1,000 to 2,000 dreams a year.
(Hmm...I wonder how many of those we actually remember).

DATE: _____ (S) (M) (T) (W) (T) (F) (S)

SATURDAY TED TALKS:

> In his insightful TED Talk titled "The habits of happiness," Matthieu Ricard, a Buddhist monk, challenges the common belief that happiness is a matter of chance. He argues that happiness is, in fact, a skill that can be developed and nurtured through practice. By consciously choosing positivity over negativity, anchoring ourselves in the present moment, and embracing meditation, we can journey towards true joy. Ricard emphasizes that cultivating gratitude and kindness can create a resilient inner sanctuary of happiness, one that doesn't waver with life's ups and downs. He encourages us to actively train our minds, to seek joy from within, and to allow our inner happiness to flourish and thrive, regardless of external circumstances.

MEMORIES MADE: _____
_____
_____
_____
_____

TOUGH TIMES & LESSONS LEARNED: _____
_____
_____
_____
_____

What are you grateful for today?   Stressed Angry Tired Sad Happy Excited
_____

REMEMBER! WAIT TO WRITE BELOW UNTIL THIS DAY NEXT YEAR!

DATE: _____ (S) (M) (T) (W) (T) (F) (S)

MEMORIES MADE: _____
_____
_____
_____
_____

TOUGH TIMES & LESSONS LEARNED: _____
_____
_____
_____
_____

What are you grateful for today?   Stressed Angry Tired Sad Happy Excited
_____

Did you know? Learning a new skill improves memory by signaling the brain to "blossom". Just think, you could learn the harmonica and drive your roommates nuts! At least you'll have a better memory! :)

DATE: _____ (S) (M) (T) (W) (T) (F) (S)

SUNDAY STRESS BUSTERS:

> Cutting down on caffeine helps keep stress in check and makes sleep better. Too much caffeine from drinks like coffee, tea, and energy drinks can make you feel more anxious and mess up your sleep. Try to drink less of these, especially later in the day and at night, so they don't keep you awake or make you feel jittery. Lowering your caffeine can help you feel calmer and get better rest, which is good for lowering stress.

MEMORIES MADE: _____
_____
_____
_____
_____
_____

TOUGH TIMES & LESSONS LEARNED: _____
_____
_____
_____
_____

What are you grateful for today?
_____

Stressed | Angry | Tired | Sad | Happy | Excited

REMEMBER! WAIT TO WRITE BELOW UNTIL THIS DAY NEXT YEAR!

DATE: _____ (S) (M) (T) (W) (T) (F) (S)

MEMORIES MADE: _____
_____
_____
_____
_____
_____

TOUGH TIMES & LESSONS LEARNED: _____
_____
_____
_____
_____

What are you grateful for today?
_____

Stressed | Angry | Tired | Sad | Happy | Excited

Did you know? Exercising 3 hours after studying has been found to boost long-term memory.
Just don't start exercising at 3am or it will keep you up all night!

DATE: _____ (S) (M) (T) (W) (T) (F) (S)

MONDAY MANNERS:

> Create a safety code word. It's wise to come up with a safety code word with your roommates, friends, parents, siblings, or others you trust for those moments you feel unsafe or want to leave. Agree on a word or phrase to discreetly communicate discomfort, such as "fish" or "snowman." :) Plan a response for when this code is used in a text or call. In situations that don't feel right, caring friends and parents want to prioritize your safety. This code serves as a signal that you need help or need an excuse to get out of challenging situations.

MEMORIES MADE: _____
_____
_____
_____
_____

TOUGH TIMES & LESSONS LEARNED: _____
_____
_____
_____
_____

What are you grateful for today?   Stressed Angry Tired Sad Happy Excited
_____

➤ REMEMBER! WAIT TO WRITE BELOW UNTIL THIS DAY NEXT YEAR!

DATE: _____ (S) (M) (T) (W) (T) (F) (S)

MEMORIES MADE: _____
_____
_____
_____
_____

TOUGH TIMES & LESSONS LEARNED: _____
_____
_____
_____
_____

What are you grateful for today?   Stressed Angry Tired Sad Happy Excited
_____

Did you know? Setting a timer can help minimize distractions and improve productivity. So break out your phone or even a good ol' kitchen timer and study away til she rings!

DATE: _____ (S) (M) (T) (W) (T) (F) (S)

TUESDAY TIPS:

> Join study groups for collaborative learning. We get it. Study groups aren't for everybody. But chances are you will have some group work in classes and you're likely to work in teams and groups in your career. Learn to work well in groups. Pull your weight. Be on time. Contribute in meaningful ways. Listen to others. Don't procrastinate. Be reliable, dependable and coachable. Nobody likes to work in groups with a slacker. Don't be the slacker. Just sayin.

MEMORIES MADE: _____
_____
_____
_____
_____

TOUGH TIMES & LESSONS LEARNED: _____
_____
_____
_____
_____

What are you grateful for today?   Stressed Angry Tired Sad Happy Excited
_____

REMEMBER! WAIT TO WRITE BELOW UNTIL THIS DAY NEXT YEAR!

DATE: _____ (S) (M) (T) (W) (T) (F) (S)

MEMORIES MADE: _____
_____
_____
_____
_____

TOUGH TIMES & LESSONS LEARNED: _____
_____
_____
_____
_____

What are you grateful for today?   Stressed Angry Tired Sad Happy Excited
_____

Did you know that the adult human skeleton is quite dynamic? It's not just a static structure; it actually renews itself approximately every 10 years through a natural process called bone remodeling. Who knew!?

DATE: _____   (S) (M) (T) (W) (T) (F) (S)

WEDNESDAY (HUMP DAY!) HAPPY HACKS:

> Another gratitude happy hack! You now have a list of people in your life you're so grateful for right? Take a look at your list and write a letter to one of the people. A handwritten letter is best (typed letter can work too). Open up in your letter and express your appreciation. Be specific. Several ways you can share this, starting with the most powerful: 1. The next time you are with this person, read it to him/her out loud. Grab a tissue—just sayin. Or, 2. Call the person/FaceTime and read it to him/her. Or 3. Email or mail the letter to the person. This gratitude hack can be a gamechanger!

MEMORIES MADE: _____
_____
_____
_____
_____

TOUGH TIMES & LESSONS LEARNED: _____
_____
_____
_____

What are you grateful for today?   Stressed Angry Tired Sad Happy Excited

REMEMBER! WAIT TO WRITE BELOW UNTIL THIS DAY NEXT YEAR!

DATE: _____   (S) (M) (T) (W) (T) (F) (S)

MEMORIES MADE: _____
_____
_____
_____
_____

TOUGH TIMES & LESSONS LEARNED: _____
_____
_____
_____

What are you grateful for today?   Stressed Angry Tired Sad Happy Excited

Did you know? People who donate time or money tend to be happier and have better health.
Start now by just donating even a little to a cause you care about.

DATE: _____ (S) (M) (T) (W) (T) (F) (S)

THURSDAY MYTHS:

> "
> Myth: "I can only study in the library."
>
> Reality: Find a study spot that works for you, whether it's a coffee shop, your dorm room, or a park. Different environments suit different people. It's like finding the perfect spot to relax – everyone has their preference.
> "

MEMORIES MADE: _____
_____
_____
_____
_____
_____

TOUGH TIMES & LESSONS LEARNED: _____
_____
_____
_____
_____

What are you grateful for today?   Stressed Angry Tired Sad Happy Excited
_____

REMEMBER! WAIT TO WRITE BELOW UNTIL THIS DAY NEXT YEAR!

DATE: _____ (S) (M) (T) (W) (T) (F) (S)

MEMORIES MADE: _____
_____
_____
_____
_____
_____

TOUGH TIMES & LESSONS LEARNED: _____
_____
_____
_____
_____

What are you grateful for today?   Stressed Angry Tired Sad Happy Excited
_____

Did you know? Our brains are more active in the morning than evening, peaking around noon. Take advantage of these power hours and do things that require focus and concentration.

DATE: _____ (S) (M) (T) (W) (T) (F) (S)

FRIDAY FILL IN THE BLANKS:

> Life check! Your future self (and your kids!) may be interested in what the price of different things are right now. Fill in the blank for the average price of the following:
>
> Oil change: _____ Loaf of bread: _____
>
> Large pizza from a chain: _____ Monthly cell phone plan: _____
>
> Last pair of your shoes (brand too!): _____ Pack of gum: _____

MEMORIES MADE: _____
_____
_____
_____
_____
_____

TOUGH TIMES & LESSONS LEARNED: _____
_____
_____
_____
_____

What are you grateful for today?
_____

Stressed | Angry | Tired | Sad | Happy | Excited

REMEMBER! WAIT TO WRITE BELOW UNTIL THIS DAY NEXT YEAR!

DATE: _____ (S) (M) (T) (W) (T) (F) (S)

MEMORIES MADE: _____
_____
_____
_____
_____
_____

TOUGH TIMES & LESSONS LEARNED: _____
_____
_____
_____
_____

What are you grateful for today?
_____

Stressed | Angry | Tired | Sad | Happy | Excited

Did you know? Using mnemonic devices helps boost memory and recall of learned information. Acronyms, visual imagery, rhymes, and chunking are all mnemonic strategies that can make remembering facts, numbers, and details much easier.

DATE: _____ (S) (M) (T) (W) (T) (F) (S)

SATURDAY TED TALKS:

> In his TED Talk, "The happy secret to better work," Shawn Achor flips the script. He argues that happiness doesn't lead to success, but rather, success often arises from being happy. By focusing on positive thinking, practicing gratitude, and savoring small wins, you can boost optimism, creativity, and productivity. Think "happy brain, happy results!" This positive outlook fuels resilience, making you better equipped to handle challenges. Ditch the stress, cultivate optimism, and watch your work (and life) flourish!

MEMORIES MADE: _____
_____
_____
_____
_____

TOUGH TIMES & LESSONS LEARNED: _____
_____
_____
_____

What are you grateful for today?   Stressed Angry Tired Sad Happy Excited
_____

REMEMBER! WAIT TO WRITE BELOW UNTIL THIS DAY NEXT YEAR!

DATE: _____ (S) (M) (T) (W) (T) (F) (S)

MEMORIES MADE: _____
_____
_____
_____
_____

TOUGH TIMES & LESSONS LEARNED: _____
_____
_____
_____

What are you grateful for today?   Stressed Angry Tired Sad Happy Excited
_____

Did you know? When feeling stressed, splash your face with cold water to trigger the mammalian diving reflex. Seriously, give this one a try!

DATE: _____ (S) (M) (T) (W) (T) (F) (S)

SUNDAY STRESS BUSTERS:

> Make sure to pencil in time for fun stuff, like watching movies, walking in nature, or going to events at school. Taking breaks for fun helps balance out work or study time and keeps stress down. It's just as important as all the serious stuff because it gives your brain a rest and can make you feel happier and more relaxed. So, remember to plan some chill time and enjoy the things you love to do!

MEMORIES MADE: _____
_____
_____
_____
_____

TOUGH TIMES & LESSONS LEARNED: _____
_____
_____
_____

What are you grateful for today?
_____

Stressed | Angry | Tired | Sad | Happy | Excited

REMEMBER! WAIT TO WRITE BELOW UNTIL THIS DAY NEXT YEAR!

DATE: _____ (S) (M) (T) (W) (T) (F) (S)

MEMORIES MADE: _____
_____
_____
_____
_____

TOUGH TIMES & LESSONS LEARNED: _____
_____
_____
_____

What are you grateful for today?
_____

Stressed | Angry | Tired | Sad | Happy | Excited

Did you know? Talking to yourself out loud can improve focus for problem solving and decision making. Just don't do it in an elevator with others or while standing in a line ;)

DATE: _____ (S) (M) (T) (W) (T) (F) (S)

MONDAY MANNERS:

> Don't play the "ratings" game. Reject the practice of rating people's looks or bodies, as it's always hurtful and inappropriate. Refrain from asking others to rate you; your worth is much more than a subjective number. Rating games and apps may seem harmless but have serious consequences, such as damaged feelings, self-esteem, and even suicidal thoughts. Instead, view others as people who have thoughts, feelings, fears, and goals. Refusing to engage in these games is a positive initial step, and actively discouraging them is even better for promoting a healthier perspective on others.

MEMORIES MADE: _____
_____
_____
_____
_____
_____

TOUGH TIMES & LESSONS LEARNED: _____
_____
_____
_____
_____

What are you grateful for today?   Stressed Angry Tired Sad Happy Excited
_____

REMEMBER! WAIT TO WRITE BELOW UNTIL THIS DAY NEXT YEAR!

DATE: _____ (S) (M) (T) (W) (T) (F) (S)

MEMORIES MADE: _____
_____
_____
_____
_____
_____

TOUGH TIMES & LESSONS LEARNED: _____
_____
_____
_____
_____

What are you grateful for today?   Stressed Angry Tired Sad Happy Excited
_____

Did you know? Getting sunlight exposure in the morning, versus midday, produces more vitamin D. And probably reduces the chance of a sunburn!

DATE: _____   S M T W T F S

TUESDAY TIPS:

> Learn how to manage finances and build credit responsibly. You can (and should) start building credit early. Like right now. A good credit score is key when you apply for a car loan, mortgage and credit cards. You can start by having a parent or guardian add you as an authorized user on their credit card and/or opening a student credit card (specialized for students). But be wise and talk to others about smart ways to build credit.

MEMORIES MADE: _____
_____
_____
_____
_____
_____

TOUGH TIMES & LESSONS LEARNED: _____
_____
_____
_____
_____

What are you grateful for today?
_____

Stressed Angry Tired Sad Happy Excited

REMEMBER! WAIT TO WRITE BELOW UNTIL THIS DAY NEXT YEAR!

DATE: _____   S M T W T F S

MEMORIES MADE: _____
_____
_____
_____
_____
_____

TOUGH TIMES & LESSONS LEARNED: _____
_____
_____
_____
_____

What are you grateful for today?
_____

Stressed Angry Tired Sad Happy Excited

Did you know? Memories trigger similar brain activity as the event originally perceived. This means when you remember something, your brain lights up in much the same way as when you first experienced it, making memories feel vivid and sometimes as real as the moment they happened.

DATE: _____ S M T W T F S

WEDNESDAY (HUMP DAY!) HAPPY HACKS

> "Find happiness in your own family history! Diving into your family history and genealogy can boost happiness and meaning. It creates a sense of identity and belonging by connecting you to your ancestors. It also strengthens family bonds, as shared stories and histories create deeper connections among living relatives. Additionally, learning about ancestors' challenges and achievements can be inspiring and offer a perspective on one's own life. You could start by calling a grandparent and asking them about their life, stories, trials, and triumphs! You can also visit free websites such as familysearch.org. Give it a try!"

MEMORIES MADE: _____
_____
_____
_____
_____
_____

TOUGH TIMES & LESSONS LEARNED: _____
_____
_____
_____
_____

What are you grateful for today?   Stressed   Angry   Tired   Sad   Happy   Excited
_____

REMEMBER! WAIT TO WRITE BELOW UNTIL THIS DAY NEXT YEAR!

DATE: _____ S M T W T F S

MEMORIES MADE: _____
_____
_____
_____
_____
_____

TOUGH TIMES & LESSONS LEARNED: _____
_____
_____
_____
_____

What are you grateful for today?   Stressed   Angry   Tired   Sad   Happy   Excited
_____

Did you know? Plants like snake plant and aloe vera improve air quality and mental health.
Plus, aloe plant is great for treating burns! Come on! Buy a plant! Even a cute little succulent.

DATE: _____ (S) (M) (T) (W) (T) (F) (S)

THURSDAY MYTHS:

> Myth: "College professors are just there to lecture."
>
> Reality: Professors can be mentors, advisors, and valuable connections for your career. Building relationships with them can open doors to opportunities beyond the classroom. Trust me, we went into this because we like working with students!

MEMORIES MADE: _____
_____
_____
_____
_____

TOUGH TIMES & LESSONS LEARNED: _____
_____
_____
_____
_____

What are you grateful for today?
_____

Stressed | Angry | Tired | Sad | Happy | Excited

REMEMBER! WAIT TO WRITE BELOW UNTIL THIS DAY NEXT YEAR!

DATE: _____ (S) (M) (T) (W) (T) (F) (S)

MEMORIES MADE: _____
_____
_____
_____
_____

TOUGH TIMES & LESSONS LEARNED: _____
_____
_____
_____

What are you grateful for today?
_____

Stressed | Angry | Tired | Sad | Happy | Excited

Did you know? Using visual imagery techniques before exams improves information recall. By creating mental pictures of what you're studying, you can better remember the material during the test, almost like having a mental cheat sheet!

DATE: _____ S M T W T F S

FRIDAY FILL IN THE BLANKS:

> " The most enjoyable part of my daily routine is...
> _____
>
> and I love it because...
> _____ "

MEMORIES MADE: _____
_____
_____
_____
_____

TOUGH TIMES & LESSONS LEARNED: _____
_____
_____
_____
_____

What are you grateful for today?   Stressed Angry Tired Sad Happy Excited
_____

⬇ REMEMBER! WAIT TO WRITE BELOW UNTIL THIS DAY NEXT YEAR!

DATE: _____ S M T W T F S

MEMORIES MADE: _____
_____
_____
_____
_____

TOUGH TIMES & LESSONS LEARNED: _____
_____
_____
_____
_____

What are you grateful for today?   Stressed Angry Tired Sad Happy Excited
_____

Did you know? Meeting a best friend triggers the same neurological reactions as receiving a reward. So, make time to meet up with your besties, back home and your new buddies.

DATE: _____ S M T W T F S

SATURDAY TED TALKS:

> Katie Hood, in her TED Talk unveils the difference between healthy and unhealthy love. Forget drama and chaos. Healthy love respects your boundaries, fosters trust, and encourages growth. Unhealthy love, however, is controlling, manipulative, and isolates you from others. Remember, true love empowers you, not diminishes you. Choose relationships that build you up, not tear you down. Find love that celebrates your individuality and supports your journey!

MEMORIES MADE: _____
_____
_____
_____
_____
_____

TOUGH TIMES & LESSONS LEARNED: _____
_____
_____
_____
_____
_____

What are you grateful for today?   Stressed Angry Tired Sad Happy Excited
_____

> REMEMBER! WAIT TO WRITE BELOW UNTIL THIS DAY NEXT YEAR!

DATE: _____ S M T W T F S

MEMORIES MADE: _____
_____
_____
_____
_____
_____

TOUGH TIMES & LESSONS LEARNED: _____
_____
_____
_____
_____
_____

What are you grateful for today?   Stressed Angry Tired Sad Happy Excited
_____

Did you know? Smiling even when unhappy can lift your mood due to smile feedback mechanisms.
So if you're happy (or even unhappy) and you know it, smile and show it (or fake it)!

DATE: _____ (S) (M) (T) (W) (T) (F) (S)

SUNDAY STRESS BUSTERS:

> "Turning on some music is a great way to chill out and cut down on stress. You can jam to your favorite songs, find cool new music, or just play some gentle instrumental tunes to calm your thoughts. Music has a way of making you feel more relaxed and can even make your day better. So when you're feeling wound up or just need a break, let music be your go-to helper for a quick and easy way to relax and feel good."

MEMORIES MADE: _____
_____
_____
_____
_____

TOUGH TIMES & LESSONS LEARNED: _____
_____
_____
_____

What are you grateful for today? Stressed Angry Tired Sad Happy Excited
_____

REMEMBER! WAIT TO WRITE BELOW UNTIL THIS DAY NEXT YEAR!

DATE: _____ (S) (M) (T) (W) (T) (F) (S)

MEMORIES MADE: _____
_____
_____
_____
_____

TOUGH TIMES & LESSONS LEARNED: _____
_____
_____
_____

What are you grateful for today? Stressed Angry Tired Sad Happy Excited
_____

Did you know? Your sense of smell is the strongest of all senses and is closely linked to memory, more so than any other sense. This is why a certain scent can instantly take you back to a moment in your past, evoking emotions and memories as if you were there again.

DATE: _____ (S) (M) (T) (W) (T) (F) (S)

MONDAY MANNERS:

> Earn others' trust. Whether it's a roommate, friend, or parent who shares something in confidence, be respectful and keep it 100% confidential. Keep secrets and what others say confidential unless there is a serious safety risk. Trust not only forms the foundation of friendships but the foundation of romantic and all other relationships. Trust is slowly earned and easily burned. Breaking trust strains relationships—especially those you are living with. Strive to embody the loyalty and trustworthiness you seek in a friend.

MEMORIES MADE: _____
_____
_____
_____
_____

TOUGH TIMES & LESSONS LEARNED: _____
_____
_____
_____

What are you grateful for today?   Stressed Angry Tired Sad Happy Excited
_____

REMEMBER! WAIT TO WRITE BELOW UNTIL THIS DAY NEXT YEAR!

DATE: _____ (S) (M) (T) (W) (T) (F) (S)

MEMORIES MADE: _____
_____
_____
_____
_____

TOUGH TIMES & LESSONS LEARNED: _____
_____
_____
_____

What are you grateful for today?   Stressed Angry Tired Sad Happy Excited
_____

Did you know the average newborn urinates about 20 times per day?
Kidneys process fluid waste as muscles and organs develop after birth.

DATE: _____ (S) (M) (T) (W) (T) (F) (S)

TUESDAY TIPS:

> In his book, The Power of Habit, Charles Duhigg refers to a "keystone habit" as a fundamental habit that, once established, can trigger the development of multiple positive behaviors and create widespread changes in a person's life. Keystone habits have a ripple effect, leading to the formation of additional good habits and positive changes that extend beyond the initial habit itself. For example, regular exercise is often cited as a keystone habit because it can lead to better eating habits, improved discipline in other areas, increased energy levels, and overall better mental health. What is your "keystone habit?"

MEMORIES MADE: _____
_____
_____
_____
_____

TOUGH TIMES & LESSONS LEARNED: _____
_____
_____
_____
_____

What are you grateful for today?   Stressed Angry Tired Sad Happy Excited
_____

REMEMBER! WAIT TO WRITE BELOW UNTIL THIS DAY NEXT YEAR!

DATE: _____ (S) (M) (T) (W) (T) (F) (S)

MEMORIES MADE: _____
_____
_____
_____
_____

TOUGH TIMES & LESSONS LEARNED: _____
_____
_____
_____
_____

What are you grateful for today?   Stressed Angry Tired Sad Happy Excited
_____

Did you know your body needs 13 vitamins and 16 minerals for good health?
These essential micronutrients enable metabolic, neural, and musculoskeletal function.

DATE: _____ (S) (M) (T) (W) (T) (F) (S)

WEDNESDAY (HUMP DAY!) HAPPY HACKS:

> "Mom! My journal says you should pay for me to get a massage!" See how that one goes over! Haha! But seriously, massage can boost happiness by helping you relax and feel less pain. A massage causes your body to release endorphins, which are chemicals that make you feel good. This can also lower stress hormones like cortisol, making you feel more peaceful and happy. Regular massages can also help you sleep better, and good sleep is important for staying in a good mood and doing your best in college! The touch you get during a massage can also make you feel emotionally comforted and cared for. So, massages are a great way to feel more comfortable physically, less stressed, and generally happier and more relaxed. Uh···Mom??

MEMORIES MADE: _____
_____
_____
_____
_____

TOUGH TIMES & LESSONS LEARNED: _____
_____
_____
_____

What are you grateful for today?   Stressed Angry Tired Sad Happy Excited
_____

REMEMBER! WAIT TO WRITE BELOW UNTIL THIS DAY NEXT YEAR!

DATE: _____ (S) (M) (T) (W) (T) (F) (S)

MEMORIES MADE: _____
_____
_____
_____
_____

TOUGH TIMES & LESSONS LEARNED: _____
_____
_____
_____

What are you grateful for today?   Stressed Angry Tired Sad Happy Excited
_____

Did you know? About one-third of adults smile more than 20 times per day. Sadly, 14% smile less than 5 times per day. Children smile up to 400 times per day. Get your smile on!

DATE: _____ (S) (M) (T) (W) (T) (F) (S)

THURSDAY MYTHS:

> "Myth: College is only about getting a degree."
>
> Reality: College is also about personal growth, exploring interests, and building life skills. The experiences and relationships you develop are just as valuable as your degree. Think of it as a journey, not just a destination.

MEMORIES MADE: _____
_____
_____
_____
_____
_____

TOUGH TIMES & LESSONS LEARNED: _____
_____
_____
_____
_____

What are you grateful for today? Stressed Angry Tired Sad Happy Excited
_____

REMEMBER! WAIT TO WRITE BELOW UNTIL THIS DAY NEXT YEAR!

DATE: _____ (S) (M) (T) (W) (T) (F) (S)

MEMORIES MADE: _____
_____
_____
_____
_____
_____

TOUGH TIMES & LESSONS LEARNED: _____
_____
_____
_____
_____

What are you grateful for today? Stressed Angry Tired Sad Happy Excited
_____

Did you know? We speak an average of 16,000 words per day? That doesn't include all the unspoken words we think about! Be kind with how you speak to yourself!

DATE: _____ (S) (M) (T) (W) (T) (F) (S)

FRIDAY FILL IN THE BLANKS:

> "
> The person I've met in college who has influenced me the most is...
> _____
>
> and the reason they have had such an impact is...
> _____
> "

MEMORIES MADE: _____
_____
_____
_____

TOUGH TIMES & LESSONS LEARNED: _____
_____
_____
_____

What are you grateful for today?
_____

Stressed Angry Tired Sad Happy Excited

⮕ REMEMBER! WAIT TO WRITE BELOW UNTIL THIS DAY NEXT YEAR!

DATE: _____ (S) (M) (T) (W) (T) (F) (S)

MEMORIES MADE: _____
_____
_____
_____

TOUGH TIMES & LESSONS LEARNED: _____
_____
_____
_____

What are you grateful for today?
_____

Stressed Angry Tired Sad Happy Excited

Did you know? There are countless things trying to get your attention. The greatest gift you can give someone else is not your time, it's your undivided attention. A remarkable and wonderful gift indeed!

DATE: _____ (S) (M) (T) (W) (T) (F) (S)

SATURDAY TED TALKS:

> In her TED Talk "Why we laugh," laughter expert Sophie Scott dives into the science of our giggles. Forget forced chuckles, true laughter thrives on connection and surprise. Studies show we're 30 times more likely to laugh with others, bonding over unexpected humor. She breaks down the biology, revealing laughter's stress-busting powers and its unique sound resonating with others. From tickles to stand-up, Scott explores the diverse triggers and emphasizes laughter's role as a social glue. So, embrace genuine connection, seek out the surprising, and let that joyful noise ring out!

MEMORIES MADE: _____
_____
_____
_____
_____
_____

TOUGH TIMES & LESSONS LEARNED: _____
_____
_____
_____
_____
_____

What are you grateful for today?
_____

Stressed   Angry   Tired   Sad   Happy   Excited

REMEMBER! WAIT TO WRITE BELOW UNTIL THIS DAY NEXT YEAR!

DATE: _____ (S) (M) (T) (W) (T) (F) (S)

MEMORIES MADE: _____
_____
_____
_____
_____
_____

TOUGH TIMES & LESSONS LEARNED: _____
_____
_____
_____
_____
_____

What are you grateful for today?
_____

Stressed   Angry   Tired   Sad   Happy   Excited

Did you know? Lasting happiness is not about getting what you want.
It's striving toward what is meaningful.

DATE: _____ (S) (M) (T) (W) (T) (F) (S)

SUNDAY STRESS BUSTERS:

> "Resilience is our ability to recover from difficulties, strengthened by proactive habits such as regular exercise, practicing mindfulness, maintaining a healthy diet, and ensuring adequate sleep. These positive routines boost our overall wellbeing, making us better equipped to handle life's stresses and challenges. Additionally, reactive strategies, such as deep breathing during stressful moments, or changing your posture, which will change how you feel, helps manage negative emotions on the spot. Together, these practices fortify our mental and emotional resilience, enabling us to navigate adversity more effectively."

MEMORIES MADE: _____
_____
_____
_____
_____
_____

TOUGH TIMES & LESSONS LEARNED: _____
_____
_____
_____
_____

What are you grateful for today?   Stressed Angry Tired Sad Happy Excited
_____

REMEMBER! WAIT TO WRITE BELOW UNTIL THIS DAY NEXT YEAR!

DATE: _____ (S) (M) (T) (W) (T) (F) (S)

MEMORIES MADE: _____
_____
_____
_____
_____
_____

TOUGH TIMES & LESSONS LEARNED: _____
_____
_____
_____
_____

What are you grateful for today?   Stressed Angry Tired Sad Happy Excited
_____

Did you know? You are always broadcasting a message to the world, starting with your facial expressions and posture and attitude. Pay attention to your countenance!

DATE: _____ (S) (M) (T) (W) (T) (F) (S)

MONDAY MANNERS:

> Master the art of active listening by fully engaging with the speaker. Face them, put your phone down, maintain eye contact, and nod with occasional "uh huh." Refrain from interrupting, judging, or planning your response prematurely. Stay focused, ask questions, and paraphrase to ensure understanding. In a world lacking good listeners, this skill sets you apart. Effective listeners excel as students, friends, and employees, fostering a sense of value and understanding. Though challenging, practicing genuine listening proves worthwhile in enhancing connections and communication.

MEMORIES MADE: _____
_____
_____
_____
_____
_____

TOUGH TIMES & LESSONS LEARNED: _____
_____
_____
_____
_____

What are you grateful for today?
_____

Stressed | Angry | Tired | Sad | Happy | Excited

REMEMBER! WAIT TO WRITE BELOW UNTIL THIS DAY NEXT YEAR!

DATE: _____ (S) (M) (T) (W) (T) (F) (S)

MEMORIES MADE: _____
_____
_____
_____
_____
_____

TOUGH TIMES & LESSONS LEARNED: _____
_____
_____
_____
_____

What are you grateful for today?
_____

Stressed | Angry | Tired | Sad | Happy | Excited

Did you know? The micro moments in life can lead to macro changes and improvements in health, happiness, and positive well-being? Send a text of kindness and see what happens.

DATE: _____ S M T W T F S

TUESDAY TIPS:

> You can read all the anxiety advice in the world, but none of it matters unless YOU. TAKE. ACTION. To feel better you have to ruthlessly focus your efforts on those things that reduce your anxiety, and increase positive emotions, and stop doing the things that keep you down, tense, and awake at night. One of the absolute best ways to start feeling better is exercise. And sleep. And eating right. Get those puppies in order and it will create an upward spiral. But if you want to feel better, you've got to change up some habits and take action my friend.

MEMORIES MADE: _____
_____
_____
_____
_____
_____

TOUGH TIMES & LESSONS LEARNED: _____
_____
_____
_____
_____

What are you grateful for today?   Stressed Angry Tired Sad Happy Excited
_____

REMEMBER! WAIT TO WRITE BELOW UNTIL THIS DAY NEXT YEAR!

DATE: _____ S M T W T F S

MEMORIES MADE: _____
_____
_____
_____
_____
_____

TOUGH TIMES & LESSONS LEARNED: _____
_____
_____
_____
_____

What are you grateful for today?   Stressed Angry Tired Sad Happy Excited
_____

Did you know? The happiest people on this planet are those who focus less on looking good and more on being good and doing good for others.

DATE: _____ (S) (M) (T) (W) (T) (F) (S)

WEDNESDAY (HUMP DAY!) HAPPY HACKS

> Soak in some sunshine! Yep, sunshine helps make people happy. When you're in the sun, your body creates vitamin D, which is good for your mood. The sun also helps keep your body clock in check, leading to better sleep and more alertness. Plus, sunlight increases serotonin, a brain chemical that makes you feel happy. Being in the sun usually means you're outside doing fun activities, which can also make you feel good. Sunny days tend to make people feel more cheerful and positive. It's important, though, to balance getting enough sun with protecting your skin—don't get a painful sunburn! In short, being in the sun in moderation can really help improve your mood and make you feel happier (and the fresh air is good for you too)!

MEMORIES MADE: _____
_____
_____
_____
_____

TOUGH TIMES & LESSONS LEARNED: _____
_____
_____
_____
_____

What are you grateful for today?   Stressed Angry Tired Sad Happy Excited
_____

REMEMBER! WAIT TO WRITE BELOW UNTIL THIS DAY NEXT YEAR!

DATE: _____ (S) (M) (T) (W) (T) (F) (S)

MEMORIES MADE: _____
_____
_____
_____
_____

TOUGH TIMES & LESSONS LEARNED: _____
_____
_____
_____

What are you grateful for today?   Stressed Angry Tired Sad Happy Excited
_____

Did you know? Fear kills more dreams than failure ever will!
Enjoy today and face the future with faith!

DATE: _____ S M T W T F S

THURSDAY MYTHS:

> Myth: "I'll be living in luxury in my dorm room."
>
> Reality: Dorm rooms are typically basic and require sharing space with others. It's a lesson in minimalism and creativity in utilizing small spaces. Think of it as a crash course in 'Tiny House Living' - college edition.

MEMORIES MADE: _____
_____
_____
_____
_____
_____

TOUGH TIMES & LESSONS LEARNED: _____
_____
_____
_____
_____

What are you grateful for today?
_____

Stressed Angry Tired Sad Happy Excited

REMEMBER! WAIT TO WRITE BELOW UNTIL THIS DAY NEXT YEAR!

DATE: _____ S M T W T F S

MEMORIES MADE: _____
_____
_____
_____
_____
_____

TOUGH TIMES & LESSONS LEARNED: _____
_____
_____
_____
_____

What are you grateful for today?
_____

Stressed Angry Tired Sad Happy Excited

Did you know? If you live in violation of your virtues and values,
it is difficult to be truly happy and have peace. Live true to the real you.

DATE: _____ (S) (M) (T) (W) (T) (F) (S)

FRIDAY FILL IN THE BLANKS:

> "I feel happiest in college when ...
> _____
>
> because...
> _____"

MEMORIES MADE: _____
_____
_____
_____
_____

TOUGH TIMES & LESSONS LEARNED: _____
_____
_____
_____

What are you grateful for today?   Stressed Angry Tired Sad Happy Excited
_____

REMEMBER! WAIT TO WRITE BELOW UNTIL THIS DAY NEXT YEAR!

DATE: _____ (S) (M) (T) (W) (T) (F) (S)

MEMORIES MADE: _____
_____
_____
_____
_____

TOUGH TIMES & LESSONS LEARNED: _____
_____
_____
_____

What are you grateful for today?   Stressed Angry Tired Sad Happy Excited
_____

Did you know chemical signals in the brain cause roughly 20% of college students to feel depressed? Counseling, self-care, and JOURNALING can help manage mood.

DATE: _____ (S) (M) (T) (W) (T) (F) (S)

SATURDAY TED TALKS:

> Sleep isn't a luxury, says scientist Russell Foster! In his TED Talk "Why do we sleep." he debunks popular theories like sleep for restoration or energy conservation. Instead, he focuses on sleep as brain processing and memory consolidation. Studies show sleep deprivation cripples learning and creativity. So, ditch the all-nighters and prioritize consistent, quality sleep (7-8 hours). Foster even hints at using sleep patterns to predict mental health. Remember, sleep isn't just rest, it's your brain's power nap for peak performance.

MEMORIES MADE: _____
_____
_____
_____
_____

TOUGH TIMES & LESSONS LEARNED: _____
_____
_____
_____
_____

What are you grateful for today?   Stressed Angry Tired Sad Happy Excited
_____

> REMEMBER! WAIT TO WRITE BELOW UNTIL THIS DAY NEXT YEAR!

DATE: _____ (S) (M) (T) (W) (T) (F) (S)

MEMORIES MADE: _____
_____
_____
_____
_____

TOUGH TIMES & LESSONS LEARNED: _____
_____
_____
_____
_____

What are you grateful for today?   Stressed Angry Tired Sad Happy Excited
_____

Did you know 58% of college graduates move back home after getting their degree?
It can provide a stable transition to full independence (just talk to your parents first!).

DATE: _____ (S) (M) (T) (W) (T) (F) (S)

SUNDAY STRESS BUSTERS:

> Less stress? Learn the ABCs. Sue Johnson's ABCDE model involves five steps: Adversity, Beliefs, Consequences, Disputation, and Energization. It starts with identifying a challenging event (Adversity), examining the beliefs that arise from it (Beliefs), understanding the emotional and behavioral Consequences of those beliefs, actively challenging and Disputing irrational or unhelpful beliefs, and finally, feeling Energized or transformed by adopting more rational, supportive beliefs, leading to healthier emotional outcomes and behaviors. Search it up to learn more!

MEMORIES MADE: _____
_____
_____
_____
_____

TOUGH TIMES & LESSONS LEARNED: _____
_____
_____
_____
_____

What are you grateful for today?   Stressed Angry Tired Sad Happy Excited
_____

REMEMBER! WAIT TO WRITE BELOW UNTIL THIS DAY NEXT YEAR!

DATE: _____ (S) (M) (T) (W) (T) (F) (S)

MEMORIES MADE: _____
_____
_____
_____
_____

TOUGH TIMES & LESSONS LEARNED: _____
_____
_____
_____
_____

What are you grateful for today?   Stressed Angry Tired Sad Happy Excited
_____

Did you know the first year of college is linked to the greatest intellectual growth over one's lifetime? New social and academic exposure promotes development.

DATE: _____ (S) (M) (T) (W) (T) (F) (S)

MONDAY MANNERS:

> Contribute your share in group projects. We get it, not everyone is thrilled with group projects, but they are much worse when one person doesn't do their part. Don't procrastinate, especially on group projects. Dive in and do your part. A collective effort lightens the load for everyone. Your work ethic swiftly shapes your reputation, with a positive one opening doors to various opportunities. At the very least, fulfill your responsibilities on time, and whenever possible, go the extra mile. Being a reliable person garners rewards as others come to count on you.

MEMORIES MADE: _____
_____
_____
_____
_____
_____

TOUGH TIMES & LESSONS LEARNED: _____
_____
_____
_____
_____

What are you grateful for today?   Stressed Angry Tired Sad Happy Excited
_____

REMEMBER! WAIT TO WRITE BELOW UNTIL THIS DAY NEXT YEAR!

DATE: _____ (S) (M) (T) (W) (T) (F) (S)

MEMORIES MADE: _____
_____
_____
_____
_____
_____

TOUGH TIMES & LESSONS LEARNED: _____
_____
_____
_____
_____

What are you grateful for today?   Stressed Angry Tired Sad Happy Excited
_____

Did you know highlighted textbook passages are 15% less memorable than hand-written notes? Writing engages more neural connections.

DATE: _____ S M T W T F S

TUESDAY TIPS:

> Be aware of the "law of little things" and the "law of least effort." The law of little things simply reminds us that most of what is good in life, from physical and mental health to love and relationships, is strengthened from many "little" things. Small acts of kindness, consistent exercise and eating well, etc. Similarly, the "law of least effort" means it tends to be easier in life to give the least effort possible. It's easier to sleep in than wake up early. It's easier to watch TV or scroll social media than study or read. It's easier to stay home than go out with friends. Intentional effort with consistent "little things" will lead to a happier, more fulfilling life.

MEMORIES MADE: _____
_____
_____
_____
_____

TOUGH TIMES & LESSONS LEARNED: _____
_____
_____
_____
_____

What are you grateful for today?   Stressed Angry Tired Sad Happy Excited
_____

REMEMBER! WAIT TO WRITE BELOW UNTIL THIS DAY NEXT YEAR!

DATE: _____ S M T W T F S

MEMORIES MADE: _____
_____
_____
_____
_____

TOUGH TIMES & LESSONS LEARNED: _____
_____
_____
_____
_____

What are you grateful for today?   Stressed Angry Tired Sad Happy Excited
_____

Did you know 50% of college students feel overwhelmed by academic expectations?
Utilize resources like tutoring, counseling, and time management skills.

DATE: _____   (S) (M) (T) (W) (T) (F) (S)

WEDNESDAY (HUMP DAY!) HAPPY HACKS:

> Happiness depends on how you interpret your world and everything that happens to you. We are interpreting machines, interpreting every moment of every day. Success in life and relationship quality depends on how we interpret small and large interactions and experiences. Mihaly Csikszentmihalyi once said, "Happiness, in fact, is a condition that must be prepared for, cultivated, and defended privately by each person. People who learn to control inner experience will be able to determine the quality of their lives, which is as close as any of us can come to being happy." Pay close attention to how you interpret and control inner experiences, especially stressful ones.

MEMORIES MADE: _____
_____
_____
_____
_____
_____

TOUGH TIMES & LESSONS LEARNED: _____
_____
_____
_____
_____

What are you grateful for today?   Stressed Angry Tired Sad Happy Excited
_____

REMEMBER! WAIT TO WRITE BELOW UNTIL THIS DAY NEXT YEAR!

DATE: _____   (S) (M) (T) (W) (T) (F) (S)

MEMORIES MADE: _____
_____
_____
_____
_____
_____

TOUGH TIMES & LESSONS LEARNED: _____
_____
_____
_____
_____

What are you grateful for today?   Stressed Angry Tired Sad Happy Excited
_____

Did you know participating in extracurricular activities makes you 24% more likely to get hired after college? Leadership and teamwork skills appeal to employers.

DATE: _____ S M T W T F S

THURSDAY MYTHS:

> Myth: "I can easily maintain a long-distance friendship with my high school friends."
> Reality: Keeping up long-distance friendships takes effort. You'll both be busy with new experiences, but with effort, communication, and occasional visits, these friendships can endure and evolve. It's like tending a garden – regular care keeps it flourishing.

MEMORIES MADE: _____
_____
_____
_____
_____

TOUGH TIMES & LESSONS LEARNED: _____
_____
_____
_____
_____

What are you grateful for today?   Stressed Angry Tired Sad Happy Excited
_____

REMEMBER! WAIT TO WRITE BELOW UNTIL THIS DAY NEXT YEAR!

DATE: _____ S M T W T F S

MEMORIES MADE: _____
_____
_____
_____
_____
_____

TOUGH TIMES & LESSONS LEARNED: _____
_____
_____
_____
_____

What are you grateful for today?   Stressed Angry Tired Sad Happy Excited
_____

Did you know eight out of ten millionaires hold a bachelor's degree?
College provides tools for building wealth long-term. Stay in school!

DATE: _____   S M T W T F S

FRIDAY FILL IN THE BLANKS:

> "A surprising lesson college has taught me about life is ...
> _____
>
> and it's impactful because...
> _____"

MEMORIES MADE: _____
_____
_____
_____
_____

TOUGH TIMES & LESSONS LEARNED: _____
_____
_____
_____
_____

What are you grateful for today?   Stressed Angry Tired Sad Happy Excited
_____

⬅ REMEMBER! WAIT TO WRITE BELOW UNTIL THIS DAY NEXT YEAR!

DATE: _____   S M T W T F S

MEMORIES MADE: _____
_____
_____
_____
_____

TOUGH TIMES & LESSONS LEARNED: _____
_____
_____
_____
_____

What are you grateful for today?   Stressed Angry Tired Sad Happy Excited
_____

Did you know a kitchen sink holds roughly 200,000 different bacterial cells per square inch? Microbes thrive on moist surfaces like sink drains. Don't play the 5-second rule with the sink!

DATE: _____ (S) (M) (T) (W) (T) (F) (S)

SATURDAY TED TALKS:

> In her TED Talk, Celeste Headlee shares ten powerful rules for having better conversations. She emphasizes the importance of truly listening, being present, and keeping an open mind. Headlee argues that genuine engagement, rather than just exchanging information, is key to meaningful communication. Her insightful tips, including using open-ended questions and avoiding pontificating, offer practical guidance for improving dialogue in both personal and professional interactions, leading to more productive and enriching conversations.

MEMORIES MADE: _____
_____
_____
_____
_____

TOUGH TIMES & LESSONS LEARNED: _____
_____
_____
_____

What are you grateful for today?   Stressed Angry Tired Sad Happy Excited
_____

REMEMBER! WAIT TO WRITE BELOW UNTIL THIS DAY NEXT YEAR!

DATE: _____ (S) (M) (T) (W) (T) (F) (S)

MEMORIES MADE: _____
_____
_____
_____
_____

TOUGH TIMES & LESSONS LEARNED: _____
_____
_____
_____

What are you grateful for today?   Stressed Angry Tired Sad Happy Excited
_____

Did you know students who use dating apps average a GPA .18 lower than non-users'?
Focus supports success.

DATE: _____ (S) (M) (T) (W) (T) (F) (S)

SUNDAY STRESS BUSTERS:

> Understanding that stress is shaped by our perception, not just the events themselves, offers a powerful strategy for stress reduction. When confronted with potential stressors, reframe them as opportunities for growth or learning rather than insurmountable obstacles. By adopting a more positive and resilient outlook, you can significantly lessen the impact of stress on your well-being, transforming challenges into valuable experiences that contribute to personal development and strength. Remember: stress is NOT what happens, it's a matter of how you are viewing what happens.

MEMORIES MADE: _____
_____
_____
_____
_____
_____

TOUGH TIMES & LESSONS LEARNED: _____
_____
_____
_____
_____

What are you grateful for today?
_____

Stressed Angry Tired Sad Happy Excited

REMEMBER! WAIT TO WRITE BELOW UNTIL THIS DAY NEXT YEAR!

DATE: _____ (S) (M) (T) (W) (T) (F) (S)

MEMORIES MADE: _____
_____
_____
_____
_____
_____

TOUGH TIMES & LESSONS LEARNED: _____
_____
_____
_____
_____

What are you grateful for today?
_____

Stressed Angry Tired Sad Happy Excited

Did you know undergraduates who studied 3 or more hours per day were most satisfied looking back? Hard work brings achievement.

DATE: _____ (S) (M) (T) (W) (T) (F) (S)

MONDAY MANNERS:

> "Don't ghost people who text you. When your parents or other adults message you, they usually have info to share, not just to chat. A simple thumbs up or reply works wonders. If they ask something or need a response, don't leave them hanging—give it pronto. It's way easier and more respectful than waiting for a reminder. Quick replies show you're on top of it! If you're unsure, say you'll get back to them. This works with friends and roommates too—it stinks to be ignored!"

MEMORIES MADE: _____
_____
_____
_____
_____
_____

TOUGH TIMES & LESSONS LEARNED: _____
_____
_____
_____
_____
_____

What are you grateful for today?
_____

Stressed | Angry | Tired | Sad | Happy | Excited

REMEMBER! WAIT TO WRITE BELOW UNTIL THIS DAY NEXT YEAR!

DATE: _____ (S) (M) (T) (W) (T) (F) (S)

MEMORIES MADE: _____
_____
_____
_____
_____
_____

TOUGH TIMES & LESSONS LEARNED: _____
_____
_____
_____
_____
_____

What are you grateful for today?
_____

Stressed | Angry | Tired | Sad | Happy | Excited

Did you know by junior year over 80% of students express certainty about their career path?
Discovering your interests takes time and effort. Be patient my friends!

DATE: _____ S M T W T F S

TUESDAY TIPS:

> Confronting and overcoming our greatest fears—fear of failure, fear for our personal safety, and fear of being rejected—is a pivotal journey towards personal growth. Facing the fear of failure empowers us to take risks and learn from setbacks. Addressing fears for our safety helps us build resilience and confidence in navigating life's uncertainties. Overcoming the fear of rejection teaches us the value of authenticity and the strength found in vulnerability. Together, these triumphs forge a path to a more courageous and fulfilled life.

MEMORIES MADE: _____
_____
_____
_____
_____
_____

TOUGH TIMES & LESSONS LEARNED: _____
_____
_____
_____
_____

What are you grateful for today?   Stressed Angry Tired Sad Happy Excited
_____

REMEMBER! WAIT TO WRITE BELOW UNTIL THIS DAY NEXT YEAR!

DATE: _____ S M T W T F S

MEMORIES MADE: _____
_____
_____
_____
_____
_____

TOUGH TIMES & LESSONS LEARNED: _____
_____
_____
_____
_____

What are you grateful for today?   Stressed Angry Tired Sad Happy Excited
_____

Did you know college students are twice as likely to have their identity or property stolen than other adults? Protect sensitive information. Don't dish out your life story online!

DATE: _____ S M T W T F S

WEDNESDAY (HUMP DAY!) HAPPY HACKS

> "Practice mental subtraction. This happy hack is simple but powerful. Go back to your gratitude list of people, places, experiences, and things. Then mentally subtract one of those from your life. Ask yourself, "What would my life be like without⋯" then fill in the blank with something from your list. Hopefully you feel more gratitude and appreciation for that person or part of your life. When you're walking across campus, waiting in line somewhere, or just brushing your teeth at night, pause and think about how much you seriously have and enjoy in life. Then mentally subtract it. What would your life be like without hot running water, for example? Yep, it's good to be grateful."

MEMORIES MADE: _____
_____
_____
_____
_____

TOUGH TIMES & LESSONS LEARNED: _____
_____
_____
_____

What are you grateful for today? Stressed Angry Tired Sad Happy Excited
_____

REMEMBER! WAIT TO WRITE BELOW UNTIL THIS DAY NEXT YEAR!

DATE: _____ S M T W T F S

MEMORIES MADE: _____
_____
_____
_____
_____

TOUGH TIMES & LESSONS LEARNED: _____
_____
_____
_____

What are you grateful for today? Stressed Angry Tired Sad Happy Excited
_____

Did you know undergraduates who take a course requiring 20 pages of writing are more likely to graduate? Extensive writing promotes analytical skills. Embrace those papers!

DATE: _____   S M T W T F S

THURSDAY MYTHS:

> Myth: "I'll never feel like I belong."
>
> Reality: Adjusting to college life takes time. It's common to feel out of place initially, but as you engage with the campus community, you'll find your niche. It's like being a new character in a TV show – it takes a few episodes to develop your storyline.

MEMORIES MADE: _____
_____
_____
_____
_____
_____

TOUGH TIMES & LESSONS LEARNED: _____
_____
_____
_____
_____

What are you grateful for today?   Stressed   Angry   Tired   Sad   Happy   Excited
_____

REMEMBER! WAIT TO WRITE BELOW UNTIL THIS DAY NEXT YEAR!

DATE: _____   S M T W T F S

MEMORIES MADE: _____
_____
_____
_____
_____
_____

TOUGH TIMES & LESSONS LEARNED: _____
_____
_____
_____
_____

What are you grateful for today?   Stressed   Angry   Tired   Sad   Happy   Excited
_____

Did you know students with origami experience show heightened spatial reasoning and memory skills? Creative hobbies build helpful brain networks. Go crazy and learn how to fold paper!

DATE: _____ (S) (M) (T) (W) (T) (F) (S)

FRIDAY FILL IN THE BLANKS:

> "A subject that has become unexpectedly meaningful to me is...
> _____
>
> and it resonates with me because...
> _____"

MEMORIES MADE: _____
_____
_____
_____
_____
_____

TOUGH TIMES & LESSONS LEARNED: _____
_____
_____
_____
_____

What are you grateful for today?   Stressed Angry Tired Sad Happy Excited
_____

REMEMBER! WAIT TO WRITE BELOW UNTIL THIS DAY NEXT YEAR!

DATE: _____ (S) (M) (T) (W) (T) (F) (S)

MEMORIES MADE: _____
_____
_____
_____
_____
_____

TOUGH TIMES & LESSONS LEARNED: _____
_____
_____
_____
_____

What are you grateful for today?   Stressed Angry Tired Sad Happy Excited
_____

Did you know 20% of students report memory gaps after drinking that qualify as blackouts?
Even occasional heavy drinking has consequences. Make good choices.

DATE: _____   S M T W T F S

SATURDAY TED TALKS:

> In her TED Talk, Julia Dhar proposes that productive disagreement can lead to innovation and progress. She emphasizes the importance of seeing disagreement as an opportunity rather than a threat, and suggests engaging with opposing views respectfully and with an open mind. By focusing on shared goals and values, Dhar believes we can find common ground and transform debates into collaborative problem-solving sessions, enriching our collective understanding and solutions.

MEMORIES MADE: _____
_____
_____
_____
_____

TOUGH TIMES & LESSONS LEARNED: _____
_____
_____
_____

What are you grateful for today?   Stressed Angry Tired Sad Happy Excited
_____

REMEMBER! WAIT TO WRITE BELOW UNTIL THIS DAY NEXT YEAR!

DATE: _____   S M T W T F S

MEMORIES MADE: _____
_____
_____
_____
_____

TOUGH TIMES & LESSONS LEARNED: _____
_____
_____
_____

What are you grateful for today?   Stressed Angry Tired Sad Happy Excited
_____

Did you know 65% of college grads have regrets about their major, school, or academic choices?
No path is perfect - focus on growth. But don't be afraid to change majors along the way.

DATE: _____ (S) (M) (T) (W) (T) (F) (S)

SUNDAY STRESS BUSTERS:

> "What lights are blinking in your life? Your emotions act as a dashboard in your car, each one signaling something important about your internal state, much like how various indicators in a car alert you to different conditions. Stress, worry, sadness, disgust, and fear are not just feelings; they are crucial signals that tell you when something needs your attention, just as a fuel gauge or engine light does. By paying attention to these emotional signals, you can better understand your needs and navigate your life more effectively. When stressed, pause and ask yourself what these signals are telling you."

MEMORIES MADE: _____
_____
_____
_____
_____

TOUGH TIMES & LESSONS LEARNED:
_____
_____
_____
_____

What are you grateful for today?   Stressed Angry Tired Sad Happy Excited
_____

REMEMBER! WAIT TO WRITE BELOW UNTIL THIS DAY NEXT YEAR!

DATE: _____ (S) (M) (T) (W) (T) (F) (S)

MEMORIES MADE: _____
_____
_____
_____
_____

TOUGH TIMES & LESSONS LEARNED: _____
_____
_____
_____

What are you grateful for today?   Stressed Angry Tired Sad Happy Excited
_____

Did you know students rank relationship drama, sleep issues, and depression as bigger impediments to academic success than partying? Take care of your mental health.

DATE: _____ S M T W T F S

MONDAY MANNERS:

> Discuss money with sensitivity. Avoid asking roommates or friends how much their parents make, how big their house is, or what kind of cars they drive. Don't pry into others' financial details or brag about what you own or received for your birthday or graduation. Talking about money is okay, but digging for specific information about others isn't. If you have serious money-related inquiries, consult your parents or Google average salaries for different careers. Feel free to share good deals with friends but do so tactfully. Remember a person's worth has nothing to do with money.

MEMORIES MADE: _____
_____
_____
_____
_____

TOUGH TIMES & LESSONS LEARNED: _____
_____
_____
_____

What are you grateful for today?   Stressed Angry Tired Sad Happy Excited
_____

REMEMBER! WAIT TO WRITE BELOW UNTIL THIS DAY NEXT YEAR!

DATE: _____ S M T W T F S

MEMORIES MADE: _____
_____
_____
_____
_____

TOUGH TIMES & LESSONS LEARNED: _____
_____
_____
_____

What are you grateful for today?   Stressed Angry Tired Sad Happy Excited
_____

Did you know 60% of undergraduate students report feeling lonely on campus?
Making friends takes effort but builds essential social connections.

DATE: _____ (S) (M) (T) (W) (T) (F) (S)

TUESDAY TIPS:

> " The ripple effects of enhanced physical activity extend far beyond just fitness improvements. Research indicates that engaging in regular exercise can lead to a cascade of positive lifestyle changes, including healthier eating habits, increased productivity at work, a reduction in cigarette smoking, heightened patience, diminished stress levels, and even improved financial management. These interconnected benefits underscore the profound impact that physical well-being can have on various aspects of our lives, promoting a holistic approach to health and personal development. "

MEMORIES MADE: _____
_____
_____
_____
_____

TOUGH TIMES & LESSONS LEARNED: _____
_____
_____
_____

What are you grateful for today?   Stressed Angry Tired Sad Happy Excited
_____

REMEMBER! WAIT TO WRITE BELOW UNTIL THIS DAY NEXT YEAR!

DATE: _____ (S) (M) (T) (W) (T) (F) (S)

MEMORIES MADE: _____
_____
_____
_____
_____

TOUGH TIMES & LESSONS LEARNED: _____
_____
_____
_____

What are you grateful for today?   Stressed Angry Tired Sad Happy Excited
_____

Did you know students who live on campus have GPAs .44 points higher on average than commuters? Immersive college living promotes success.

DATE: _____   (S) (M) (T) (W) (T) (F) (S)

WEDNESDAY (HUMP DAY!) HAPPY HACKS:

> " Start your day in a positive way. Findings from research suggest that how you start your day in the morning can have a profound effect on your mood for the rest of the day. Rather than waking up and scrolling through your phone or hitting snooze a few times, try changing it up. Here's a few ideas. Start with drinking a full glass of water. Try exercising, yoga, even stretching to get your body going, which kickstarts your brain. Some people benefit from meditation or prayer. Others read something positive and uplifting, watch an uplifting video on YouTube, or send a positive text to someone. Try changing up your morning routine to change how the rest of your day goes! "

MEMORIES MADE: _____
_____
_____
_____
_____

TOUGH TIMES & LESSONS LEARNED: _____
_____
_____
_____

What are you grateful for today?   Stressed Angry Tired Sad Happy Excited
_____

> REMEMBER! WAIT TO WRITE BELOW UNTIL THIS DAY NEXT YEAR!

DATE: _____   (S) (M) (T) (W) (T) (F) (S)

MEMORIES MADE: _____
_____
_____
_____
_____

TOUGH TIMES & LESSONS LEARNED: _____
_____
_____
_____

What are you grateful for today?   Stressed Angry Tired Sad Happy Excited
_____

Did you know eight hours before an exam, studying hard facts boosts retention more than trying to grasp conceptual relationships? Understand key principles well in advance.

DATE: _____ (S) (M) (T) (W) (T) (F) (S)

THURSDAY MYTHS:

> Myth: "I can't change my roommate if we don't get along."
>
> Reality: Most colleges have a process for addressing roommate conflicts. Communication is key, but if things don't work out, there are options to switch. It's not a life sentence – you have choices.

MEMORIES MADE: _____
_____
_____
_____
_____
_____

TOUGH TIMES & LESSONS LEARNED: _____
_____
_____
_____
_____

What are you grateful for today?

Stressed | Angry | Tired | Sad | Happy | Excited
_____

REMEMBER! WAIT TO WRITE BELOW UNTIL THIS DAY NEXT YEAR!

DATE: _____ (S) (M) (T) (W) (T) (F) (S)

MEMORIES MADE: _____
_____
_____
_____
_____
_____

TOUGH TIMES & LESSONS LEARNED: _____
_____
_____
_____
_____

What are you grateful for today?

Stressed | Angry | Tired | Sad | Happy | Excited
_____

Did you know college graduates are more likely to receive employer-sponsored health insurance? Higher degrees provide long-term lifestyle benefits.

DATE: _____   S M T W T F S

FRIDAY FILL IN THE BLANKS:

> "A lifestyle change I've made since starting college is ...
> _____
>
> and it resonates with me because...
> _____"

MEMORIES MADE: _____
_____
_____
_____
_____
_____

TOUGH TIMES & LESSONS LEARNED: _____
_____
_____
_____
_____

What are you grateful for today?   Stressed Angry Tired Sad Happy Excited
_____

REMEMBER! WAIT TO WRITE BELOW UNTIL THIS DAY NEXT YEAR!

DATE: _____   S M T W T F S

MEMORIES MADE: _____
_____
_____
_____
_____
_____

TOUGH TIMES & LESSONS LEARNED: _____
_____
_____
_____
_____

What are you grateful for today?   Stressed Angry Tired Sad Happy Excited
_____

Did you know the more devices students use for academic reading, the worse they comprehend concepts? Minimize digital distraction when studying complex material.

DATE: _____ (S) (M) (T) (W) (T) (F) (S)

SATURDAY TED TALKS:

> In her TED Talk, "Why some people find exercise harder than others," Emily Balcetis explains that it's not just willpower, but perception plays a key role. Her research shows people with a wider field of vision see exercise as physically demanding, leading to less motivation. The solution? Smaller screens, narrower visual focus, and focusing on progress, not distance. By altering their perception, even those who find exercise difficult can find joy and success in movement. So, ditch the wide-screen gym TVs, focus on your personal progress, and unlock your inner exercise enthusiast!

MEMORIES MADE: _____
_____
_____
_____
_____
_____

TOUGH TIMES & LESSONS LEARNED: _____
_____
_____
_____
_____

What are you grateful for today?   Stressed Angry Tired Sad Happy Excited
_____

REMEMBER! WAIT TO WRITE BELOW UNTIL THIS DAY NEXT YEAR!

DATE: _____ (S) (M) (T) (W) (T) (F) (S)

MEMORIES MADE: _____
_____
_____
_____
_____
_____

TOUGH TIMES & LESSONS LEARNED: _____
_____
_____
_____
_____

What are you grateful for today?   Stressed Angry Tired Sad Happy Excited
_____

Did you know joining one student organization makes you 19% more likely to graduate college?
Building community and support systems helps persistence. Go get involved!

DATE: _____ (S) (M) (T) (W) (T) (F) (S)

SUNDAY STRESS BUSTERS:

> Want to stress less? Prioritize your sleep! Research indicates that missing out on just 90 minutes of sleep can reduce your alertness by 33%. Interestingly, high achievers are often those who prioritize their sleep, averaging 8 hours and 36 minutes each night. This contrasts with the average American, who gets only about 6 hours and 51 minutes of sleep during the week. Adequate sleep is essential for peak performance and reaching your full potential, so it's important not to dismiss it as mere laziness but as a critical component of success.

MEMORIES MADE: _____
_____
_____
_____
_____
_____

TOUGH TIMES & LESSONS LEARNED: _____
_____
_____
_____
_____

What are you grateful for today?
_____

Stressed Angry Tired Sad Happy Excited

REMEMBER! WAIT TO WRITE BELOW UNTIL THIS DAY NEXT YEAR!

DATE: _____ (S) (M) (T) (W) (T) (F) (S)

MEMORIES MADE: _____
_____
_____
_____
_____
_____

TOUGH TIMES & LESSONS LEARNED: _____
_____
_____
_____
_____

What are you grateful for today?
_____

Stressed Angry Tired Sad Happy Excited

Did you know the average student takes 5.2 years to finish a 4-year bachelor's degree?
Changing majors or taking fewer classes at times is common.

DATE: _____ (S) (M) (T) (W) (T) (F) (S)

MONDAY MANNERS:

> Happy people learn to focus their time and attention on what is really important and what they can control. While there will be many times you wish you could control your roommates, friends, romantic partners or parents, you will be happier when you focus on what you can control. And there are very few things in life that are really super duper important. Stay calm and keep the big picture in mind. What is important? What can you control? Shift from worrying about little things and trying to control people to focusing your energy on shaping the life you desire.

MEMORIES MADE: _____

_____
_____
_____
_____
_____

TOUGH TIMES & LESSONS LEARNED: _____

_____
_____
_____
_____

What are you grateful for today?   Stressed Angry Tired Sad Happy Excited
_____

REMEMBER! WAIT TO WRITE BELOW UNTIL THIS DAY NEXT YEAR!

DATE: _____ (S) (M) (T) (W) (T) (F) (S)

MEMORIES MADE: _____

_____
_____
_____
_____
_____

TOUGH TIMES & LESSONS LEARNED: _____

_____
_____
_____
_____

What are you grateful for today?   Stressed Angry Tired Sad Happy Excited
_____

Did you know eight out of ten students feel anxious about their financial circumstances?
Seeking aid and budgeting helps ease money concerns that can impact studies.

DATE: _____ (S) (M) (T) (W) (T) (F) (S)

TUESDAY TIPS:

> Jeff Olson, the creator of Live Happy, points out that it's the little adjustments made consistently over time that lead to real change. Just as a single greasy meal won't ruin your health, one healthy smoothie won't make you fit overnight. Similarly, a single workout session won't build your muscles instantly, nor will one good moment instantly strengthen a relationship or boost long-term happiness. True progress in overall well-being rarely happens in an instant; it requires steady and persistent effort. We created the acronym S.C.A.R.E.D. Small Changes Are Really Effective…Dude.

MEMORIES MADE: _____
_____
_____
_____
_____
_____

TOUGH TIMES & LESSONS LEARNED: _____
_____
_____
_____
_____

What are you grateful for today?   Stressed Angry Tired Sad Happy Excited
_____

REMEMBER! WAIT TO WRITE BELOW UNTIL THIS DAY NEXT YEAR!

DATE: _____ (S) (M) (T) (W) (T) (F) (S)

MEMORIES MADE: _____
_____
_____
_____
_____
_____

TOUGH TIMES & LESSONS LEARNED: _____
_____
_____
_____
_____

What are you grateful for today?   Stressed Angry Tired Sad Happy Excited
_____

Did you know skipping breakfast hinders memory, attention, and problem-solving in students? Proper nutrition aids cognition. Your mom was right - it's the most important meal of the day!

DATE: _____ S M T W T F S

WEDNESDAY (HUMP DAY!) HAPPY HACKS

> Is there someone you feel you need to thank for something that happened months or years ago? It's never too late to thank. In fact, research suggests there is power in expressing gratitude long after the experience has happened. In some cases, even more powerful than expressing gratitude in the moment because gratitude expressed after time shows that a person is still thinking about it. Think of something specific someone has done for you in the past and reach out with genuine thanks and let them know how much it still means to you.

MEMORIES MADE: _____
_____
_____
_____
_____

TOUGH TIMES & LESSONS LEARNED: _____
_____
_____
_____
_____

What are you grateful for today?   Stressed Angry Tired Sad Happy Excited
_____

REMEMBER! WAIT TO WRITE BELOW UNTIL THIS DAY NEXT YEAR!

DATE: _____ S M T W T F S

MEMORIES MADE: _____
_____
_____
_____
_____

TOUGH TIMES & LESSONS LEARNED: _____
_____
_____
_____
_____

What are you grateful for today?   Stressed Angry Tired Sad Happy Excited
_____

Did you know? The human body can survive without the stomach, 75% of the liver, one kidney, one lung, and virtually every organ from the pelvic and groin area.

DATE: _____ (S) (M) (T) (W) (T) (F) (S)

THURSDAY MYTHS:

> Myth: "I need to be extroverted to enjoy college."
>
> Reality: College offers diverse experiences suitable for all personalities. Introverts can find enjoyment in smaller group settings or individual activities. It's not a one-size-fits-all; there's something for everyone.

MEMORIES MADE: _____
_____
_____
_____
_____

TOUGH TIMES & LESSONS LEARNED: _____
_____
_____
_____

What are you grateful for today?
_____

Stressed | Angry | Tired | Sad | Happy | Excited

REMEMBER! WAIT TO WRITE BELOW UNTIL THIS DAY NEXT YEAR!

DATE: _____ (S) (M) (T) (W) (T) (F) (S)

MEMORIES MADE: _____
_____
_____
_____
_____

TOUGH TIMES & LESSONS LEARNED: _____
_____
_____
_____

What are you grateful for today?
_____

Stressed | Angry | Tired | Sad | Happy | Excited

Did you know? Setting realistic goals and celebrating small wins keeps you motivated and builds confidence. Remember, progress over perfection!

DATE: _____ (S) (M) (T) (W) (T) (F) (S)

FRIDAY FILL IN THE BLANKS:

> Life check! Your future self (and your kids!) may be interested in what the price of different things are right now. Fill in the blank for the average price of the following:
>
> Ream of paper: A pack of double AA batteries:
>
> A standard LED light bulb: Monthly gym pass:
>
> A smart phone case: A bottled water:

MEMORIES MADE: _____
_____
_____
_____
_____
_____

TOUGH TIMES & LESSONS LEARNED: _____
_____
_____
_____
_____

What are you grateful for today?

Stressed | Angry | Tired | Sad | Happy | Excited

REMEMBER! WAIT TO WRITE BELOW UNTIL THIS DAY NEXT YEAR!

DATE: _____ (S) (M) (T) (W) (T) (F) (S)

MEMORIES MADE: _____
_____
_____
_____
_____
_____

TOUGH TIMES & LESSONS LEARNED: _____
_____
_____
_____
_____

What are you grateful for today?

Stressed | Angry | Tired | Sad | Happy | Excited

Did you know? Color-coding study materials can improve organization and memory recall, making it a useful tactic for visual learners.

DATE: _____ S M T W T F S

SATURDAY TED TALKS:

> In Sandra Aamodt's TED Talk, "Why dieting doesn't usually work," she argues that dieting sets us up for failure. Our brains are hardwired to resist deprivation, triggering cravings and making weight loss unsustainable. She exposes the limitations of willpower and the dangers of yo-yo dieting on metabolism and self-esteem. Instead, she proposes a flexible, intuitive approach based on mindfulness and healthy habits. Listen to your body, prioritize nutrient-rich food, and ditch the restriction mindset. Remember, a healthy relationship with food, not dieting, is the key to lasting wellness.

MEMORIES MADE: _____
_____
_____
_____
_____

TOUGH TIMES & LESSONS LEARNED: _____
_____
_____
_____

What are you grateful for today?
_____

Stressed | Angry | Tired | Sad | Happy | Excited

> REMEMBER! WAIT TO WRITE BELOW UNTIL THIS DAY NEXT YEAR!

DATE: _____ S M T W T F S

MEMORIES MADE: _____
_____
_____
_____
_____

TOUGH TIMES & LESSONS LEARNED: _____
_____
_____
_____

What are you grateful for today?
_____

Stressed | Angry | Tired | Sad | Happy | Excited

Did you know? In a study of over 10,000 participants across 37 nations, kindness was rated as the most important quality women and men seek in romantic partners.

DATE: _____ (S) (M) (T) (W) (T) (F) (S)

SUNDAY STRESS BUSTERS:

> Attending skill-building workshops offered by many colleges is a proactive way to address college-related stress. These workshops, often focusing on stress management, time management, and effective study techniques, provide students with practical skills and strategies. Learning these skills can significantly help in navigating the pressures and challenges of college life, leading to a more manageable and successful academic journey.

MEMORIES MADE: _____
_____
_____
_____
_____

TOUGH TIMES & LESSONS LEARNED:
_____
_____
_____
_____

What are you grateful for today?
_____

Stressed | Angry | Tired | Sad | Happy | Excited

REMEMBER! WAIT TO WRITE BELOW UNTIL THIS DAY NEXT YEAR!

DATE: _____ (S) (M) (T) (W) (T) (F) (S)

MEMORIES MADE: _____
_____
_____
_____
_____

TOUGH TIMES & LESSONS LEARNED: _____
_____
_____
_____
_____

What are you grateful for today?
_____

Stressed | Angry | Tired | Sad | Happy | Excited

Did you know? The average smartphone user touches their phone 2,617 times a day, according to research by Dscout, highlighting the extensive interaction people have with their devices.

DATE: _____ (S) (M) (T) (W) (T) (F) (S)

MONDAY MANNERS:

> Be mindful of your nonverbal cues—voice tone, facial expressions, and body language—as they greatly impact how others perceive you. Be aware of your tone, as it may come across as harsh or snarky. Seek input from those who care about you and be open to improvement. There's nothing wrong with being yourself; the key is ensuring your external presentation aligns with your true self. If people often misunderstand you, it could be due to your tone or body language. Embracing feedback helps make small adjustments, fostering better relationships, increased confidence, and comfort in being authentic.

MEMORIES MADE: _____
_____
_____
_____
_____
_____

TOUGH TIMES & LESSONS LEARNED: _____
_____
_____
_____
_____

What are you grateful for today?
_____

Stressed | Angry | Tired | Sad | Happy | Excited

REMEMBER! WAIT TO WRITE BELOW UNTIL THIS DAY NEXT YEAR!

DATE: _____ (S) (M) (T) (W) (T) (F) (S)

MEMORIES MADE: _____
_____
_____
_____
_____
_____

TOUGH TIMES & LESSONS LEARNED: _____
_____
_____
_____
_____

What are you grateful for today?
_____

Stressed | Angry | Tired | Sad | Happy | Excited

Did you know? Your body's cells are constantly dying and being replaced, with nearly 98% of the atoms in your body replaced yearly.

DATE: _____ (S) (M) (T) (W) (T) (F) (S)

TUESDAY TIPS:

> Attend career fairs and workshops to explore future opportunities. These can actually be pretty eye-opening and important. Speak up when you're there. Talk with as many people as you can. They can give you free insights into different careers and opportunities. Again, it may just be building a relationship with those you speak with at the career fair. And they might know somebody who knows somebody who can help you now or in the future. Seriously, grow your social network as much as you can in your young years.

MEMORIES MADE: _____
_____
_____
_____
_____

TOUGH TIMES & LESSONS LEARNED: _____
_____
_____
_____
_____

What are you grateful for today?

Stressed   Angry   Tired   Sad   Happy   Excited

REMEMBER! WAIT TO WRITE BELOW UNTIL THIS DAY NEXT YEAR!

DATE: _____ (S) (M) (T) (W) (T) (F) (S)

MEMORIES MADE: _____
_____
_____
_____
_____

TOUGH TIMES & LESSONS LEARNED: _____
_____
_____
_____
_____

What are you grateful for today?

Stressed   Angry   Tired   Sad   Happy   Excited

Did you know? Taking the stairs instead of the elevator burns extra calories, strengthens leg muscles, and improves cardiovascular health. Climb your way to fitness!

DATE: _____ (S) (M) (T) (W) (T) (F) (S)

WEDNESDAY (HUMP DAY!) HAPPY HACKS:

> For a bit more happiness in your life, try an "awe walk." An "awe walk" is where you notice and focus on the amazing things around you while walking, and research says it can make you happier. Taking a walk where you intentionally slow down can help you pay attention to the moment and help you feel more connected to the world. Seeing beautiful or impressive things can reduce stress and make you feel thankful. Walking in nature, often part of awe walks, also lifts your mood and calms you down. Doing awe walks regularly can help you feel more relaxed and satisfied with life, leading to more happiness. So, get out there and notice all the cool things around you on your next "awe walk!"

MEMORIES MADE: _____
_____
_____
_____
_____
_____

TOUGH TIMES & LESSONS LEARNED: _____
_____
_____
_____
_____

What are you grateful for today?

Stressed Angry Tired Sad Happy Excited

REMEMBER! WAIT TO WRITE BELOW UNTIL THIS DAY NEXT YEAR!

DATE: _____ (S) (M) (T) (W) (T) (F) (S)

MEMORIES MADE: _____
_____
_____
_____
_____
_____

TOUGH TIMES & LESSONS LEARNED: _____
_____
_____
_____
_____

What are you grateful for today?

Stressed Angry Tired Sad Happy Excited

Did you know? Cultivating an attitude of forgiveness, including self-forgiveness, can lead to increased happiness and reduced stress, especially important in the dynamic college environment.

DATE: _____ (S) (M) (T) (W) (T) (F) (S)

THURSDAY MYTHS:

> Myth: "I must study something practical to be successful."
>
> Reality: Studying what you love can lead to a fulfilling career. Success isn't just measured in income but in satisfaction and happiness in your work. It's like choosing a favorite ice cream flavor — pick what you genuinely enjoy.

MEMORIES MADE: _____
_____
_____
_____
_____

TOUGH TIMES & LESSONS LEARNED: _____
_____
_____
_____
_____

What are you grateful for today?   Stressed Angry Tired Sad Happy Excited
_____

REMEMBER! WAIT TO WRITE BELOW UNTIL THIS DAY NEXT YEAR!

DATE: _____ (S) (M) (T) (W) (T) (F) (S)

MEMORIES MADE: _____
_____
_____
_____
_____

TOUGH TIMES & LESSONS LEARNED: _____
_____
_____
_____
_____

What are you grateful for today?   Stressed Angry Tired Sad Happy Excited
_____

Did you know? Choosing whole grains over refined grains provides fiber, essential vitamins, and minerals, promoting digestive health and lowering the risk of chronic diseases.
Go for the whole grains!

DATE: _____ (S) (M) (T) (W) (T) (F) (S)

FRIDAY FILL IN THE BLANKS:

> "What are the pros and cons of AI and why?
> _____
> _____
> _____
> _____"

MEMORIES MADE: _____
_____
_____
_____
_____

TOUGH TIMES & LESSONS LEARNED: _____
_____
_____
_____
_____

What are you grateful for today?   Stressed Angry Tired Sad Happy Excited
_____

⬅ REMEMBER! WAIT TO WRITE BELOW UNTIL THIS DAY NEXT YEAR!

DATE: _____ (S) (M) (T) (W) (T) (F) (S)

MEMORIES MADE: _____
_____
_____
_____
_____

TOUGH TIMES & LESSONS LEARNED: _____
_____
_____
_____
_____

What are you grateful for today?   Stressed Angry Tired Sad Happy Excited
_____

Did you know? The world's quietest room is located at Microsoft's headquarters in Washington, where the sound level is measured in decibels below the threshold of human hearing. Imagine stepping into a room so quiet you could hear the beating of your own heart!

DATE: _____ (S) (M) (T) (W) (T) (F) (S)

SATURDAY TED TALKS:

> In his TED Talk, "One more reason to get a good night's sleep." neuroscientist Jeff Iliff unveils a surprising reason to prioritize sleep: brain cleansing! During slumber, a glymphatic system flushes out harmful toxins like beta-amyloid, linked to Alzheimer's. Skipping sleep lets these toxins build up, harming brain health. Iliff emphasizes quality sleep (7-8 hours) as essential for this nightly brainwash. So, hit the hay early, let your brain detox, and wake up sharper, healthier, and with a cleaner mind!

MEMORIES MADE: _____
_____
_____
_____
_____
_____

TOUGH TIMES & LESSONS LEARNED: _____
_____
_____
_____
_____

What are you grateful for today?
_____

Stressed | Angry | Tired | Sad | Happy | Excited

REMEMBER! WAIT TO WRITE BELOW UNTIL THIS DAY NEXT YEAR!

DATE: _____ (S) (M) (T) (W) (T) (F) (S)

MEMORIES MADE: _____
_____
_____
_____
_____
_____

TOUGH TIMES & LESSONS LEARNED: _____
_____
_____
_____
_____

What are you grateful for today?
_____

Stressed | Angry | Tired | Sad | Happy | Excited

Did you know? Incorporating balance and coordination exercises into your routine can reduce the risk of falls, especially important as we age.

DATE: _____   (S) (M) (T) (W) (T) (F) (S)

SUNDAY STRESS BUSTERS:

> " Breathing fresh air by spending time outdoors, particularly in green spaces, is a natural and effective way to uplift your mood and alleviate stress. The serenity and beauty of nature can have a calming effect, helping to clear your mind and rejuvenate your spirit. Regularly schedule time to step outside, be it for a leisurely walk around campus or a more adventurous visit to a nearby park, to harness these benefits and enhance your overall well-being. "

MEMORIES MADE: _____
_____
_____
_____
_____

TOUGH TIMES & LESSONS LEARNED: _____
_____
_____
_____

What are you grateful for today?   Stressed   Angry   Tired   Sad   Happy   Excited
_____

👉 REMEMBER! WAIT TO WRITE BELOW UNTIL THIS DAY NEXT YEAR!

DATE: _____   (S) (M) (T) (W) (T) (F) (S)

MEMORIES MADE: _____
_____
_____
_____
_____

TOUGH TIMES & LESSONS LEARNED: _____
_____
_____
_____

What are you grateful for today?   Stressed   Angry   Tired   Sad   Happy   Excited
_____

Did you know? Kissing transfers less germs than a handshake! While a handshake can swap millions of bacteria, a passionate kiss might only transfer around 1,000 microbes.

WORD PUZZLE TIME - COLLEGE EDITION!

Finals
Syllabus
Tutor
Assignment
Mascot
Essay

Dorms
ACT
College
University
Professor
Sports

READY FOR A BIGGER CHALLENGE? TRY MAGIC SQUARE PUZZLES!

Magic Squares are square grids with a special arrangement of numbers in such a way that every row, column and diagonal adds up to the same numbers. This sum is called the "magic sum."

Magic Sum = 33

8	15	
		9
	7	

Magic Sum = 36

11		15
		8
9	14	

Magic Sum = 45

	13	
11		
	17	12

DATE: _____ S M T W T F S

MONDAY MANNERS:

> Embrace boredom and downtime as a skill. Many of us automatically reach for our phones when we become bored, whether we are with others or alone. Instead of reaching for your phone when you're bored, try catching yourself and just be still for a few minutes. Take a few deep breaths and spend a few minutes with uninterrupted thinking. Some research even suggests free-time and boredom aids brain function, sparking solutions, boosting mental health, unveiling new hobbies, clarifying thoughts, and promoting mindfulness. A few minutes of downtime daily yields numerous positive benefits. Try breathing before scrolling.

MEMORIES MADE: _____
_____
_____
_____
_____
_____

TOUGH TIMES & LESSONS LEARNED: _____
_____
_____
_____
_____

What are you grateful for today?   Stressed Angry Tired Sad Happy Excited
_____

REMEMBER! WAIT TO WRITE BELOW UNTIL THIS DAY NEXT YEAR!

DATE: _____ S M T W T F S

MEMORIES MADE: _____
_____
_____
_____
_____
_____

TOUGH TIMES & LESSONS LEARNED: _____
_____
_____
_____
_____

What are you grateful for today?   Stressed Angry Tired Sad Happy Excited
_____

Did you know? Your stomach growls because your muscles churn, not hunger. Even when your stomach's empty, muscles contract to move food residue around, causing those familiar growling noises.

DATE: _____ (S) (M) (T) (W) (T) (F) (S)

TUESDAY TIPS:

> " Keep an eye on scholarship and financial aid opportunities. Every year there are tons of scholarships and all kinds of financial aid that goes unused because students don't apply for it. Talk to the kind folks at the financial aid office. They are driven to help you find ways to save you money and can show you plenty of financial aid opportunities! "

MEMORIES MADE: _____
_____
_____
_____
_____

TOUGH TIMES & LESSONS LEARNED: _____
_____
_____
_____
_____

What are you grateful for today?
_____

Stressed | Angry | Tired | Sad | Happy | Excited

REMEMBER! WAIT TO WRITE BELOW UNTIL THIS DAY NEXT YEAR!

DATE: _____ (S) (M) (T) (W) (T) (F) (S)

MEMORIES MADE: _____
_____
_____
_____
_____

TOUGH TIMES & LESSONS LEARNED: _____
_____
_____
_____
_____

What are you grateful for today?
_____

Stressed | Angry | Tired | Sad | Happy | Excited

Did you know? We dream every night, even if we don't remember them. The brain cycles through REM sleep stages every night, which is when dreaming occurs. However, if you wake up during non-REM sleep, you're less likely to recall the dream.

DATE: _____ (S) (M) (T) (W) (T) (F) (S)

WEDNESDAY (HUMP DAY!) HAPPY HACKS:

> Find and soak in the good stuff. We're all born with a negativity bias—we notice imperfections in others, things that bug us, and threats to our well-being. And negativity is powerful. We're drawn to negative stuff! Positivity takes intentionality. The principle? You will always find what you're looking for. If you look for the good in a person or a situation, you will eventually find it. Complainers will always find things to complain about. People who are intentionally grateful will always find things to be grateful for. It's good to get good at finding the good. And there is good all around you.

MEMORIES MADE: _____
_____
_____
_____
_____
_____

TOUGH TIMES & LESSONS LEARNED: _____
_____
_____
_____
_____

What are you grateful for today?
_____

Stressed | Angry | Tired | Sad | Happy | Excited

REMEMBER! WAIT TO WRITE BELOW UNTIL THIS DAY NEXT YEAR!

DATE: _____ (S) (M) (T) (W) (T) (F) (S)

MEMORIES MADE: _____
_____
_____
_____
_____
_____

TOUGH TIMES & LESSONS LEARNED: _____
_____
_____
_____
_____

What are you grateful for today?
_____

Stressed | Angry | Tired | Sad | Happy | Excited

Did you know? The term "cold feet" stems originally from a military term, soldiers who had "cold feet" were those who were too scared to move. It now refers to a loss of courage or confidence in any situation.

DATE: _____ (S) (M) (T) (W) (T) (F) (S)

THURSDAY MYTHS:

> "
> Myth: "I'll be able to easily balance work, study, and social life."
>
> Reality: Finding the perfect balance is challenging and often requires adjustments. Prioritize tasks and manage your time wisely. It's like being a DJ, mixing tracks – sometimes you need to adjust the levels to get the sound just right.
> "

MEMORIES MADE: _____
_____
_____
_____
_____
_____

TOUGH TIMES & LESSONS LEARNED: _____
_____
_____
_____
_____

What are you grateful for today?
_____

Stressed | Angry | Tired | Sad | Happy | Excited

⬅ REMEMBER! WAIT TO WRITE BELOW UNTIL THIS DAY NEXT YEAR!

DATE: _____ (S) (M) (T) (W) (T) (F) (S)

MEMORIES MADE: _____
_____
_____
_____
_____
_____

TOUGH TIMES & LESSONS LEARNED: _____
_____
_____
_____
_____

What are you grateful for today?
_____

Stressed | Angry | Tired | Sad | Happy | Excited

Did you know? Lightning strikes the Earth about 44 times every second. That's over 3 million strikes a day! Lightning is a powerful force, and each strike can heat the air around it to over 50,000 degrees Fahrenheit!

DATE: _____   S M T W T F S

FRIDAY FILL IN THE BLANKS:

> An aspect of college life I'm grateful for is...
> _____
>
> because it has...
> _____

MEMORIES MADE: _____
_____
_____
_____
_____

TOUGH TIMES & LESSONS LEARNED: _____
_____
_____
_____
_____

What are you grateful for today?

Stressed   Angry   Tired   Sad   Happy   Excited

REMEMBER! WAIT TO WRITE BELOW UNTIL THIS DAY NEXT YEAR!

DATE: _____   S M T W T F S

MEMORIES MADE: _____
_____
_____
_____
_____

TOUGH TIMES & LESSONS LEARNED: _____
_____
_____
_____
_____

What are you grateful for today?

Stressed   Angry   Tired   Sad   Happy   Excited

Did you know? It takes 20 milliseconds longer to react to something sad than happy. Scientists believe this may be because negative emotions require more complex processing in the brain.

DATE: _____ (S) (M) (T) (W) (T) (F) (S)

SATURDAY TED TALKS:

> In Guy Winch's TED Talk, "How to fix a broken heart," he dives into the science of heartbreak. Forget quick fixes, healing takes time. First, acknowledge your pain, don't idealize the past. Understand that heartbreak is like a physical wound, it needs gentle care. Focus on self-compassion and resilience. Connect with friends, engage in activities you enjoy, nurture yourself. Avoid rebound relationships, they often complicate healing. Remember, heartbreak hurts, but it doesn't have to break you. With time and compassion, you'll heal, grow stronger, and find love again.

MEMORIES MADE: _____
_____
_____
_____
_____

TOUGH TIMES & LESSONS LEARNED: _____
_____
_____
_____

What are you grateful for today?
_____

Stressed | Angry | Tired | Sad | Happy | Excited

REMEMBER! WAIT TO WRITE BELOW UNTIL THIS DAY NEXT YEAR!

DATE: _____ (S) (M) (T) (W) (T) (F) (S)

MEMORIES MADE: _____
_____
_____
_____
_____

TOUGH TIMES & LESSONS LEARNED: _____
_____
_____
_____

What are you grateful for today?
_____

Stressed | Angry | Tired | Sad | Happy | Excited

Did you know? We use all of our brains, not just 10%! While some areas are more active for specific tasks, different parts of the brain work together to create our thoughts, feelings, and actions.

DATE: _____ (S) (M) (T) (W) (T) (F) (S)

SUNDAY STRESS BUSTERS:

> "Using visualization techniques involves creating a mental image of a positive outcome or a serene environment, which can serve as a powerful tool in managing stress. By vividly imagining a tranquil scene or envisioning yourself succeeding in a stressful scenario, you can significantly lower anxiety levels, elevate your mood, and better equip yourself to face challenging situations with confidence and calmness. Incorporating this practice into your daily routine can lead to improved mental resilience and well-being."

MEMORIES MADE: _____
_____
_____
_____
_____

TOUGH TIMES & LESSONS LEARNED: _____
_____
_____
_____

What are you grateful for today?   Stressed Angry Tired Sad Happy Excited
_____

REMEMBER! WAIT TO WRITE BELOW UNTIL THIS DAY NEXT YEAR!

DATE: _____ (S) (M) (T) (W) (T) (F) (S)

MEMORIES MADE: _____
_____
_____
_____
_____

TOUGH TIMES & LESSONS LEARNED: _____
_____
_____
_____

What are you grateful for today?   Stressed Angry Tired Sad Happy Excited
_____

Did you know? Carrots don't actually give you night vision, but they are good for your eyes! Carrots are rich in beta-carotene, which the body converts into vitamin A, which is important for healthy vision.

DATE: _____ (S) (M) (T) (W) (T) (F) (S)

MONDAY MANNERS:

> Unplug those headphones or ear buds around others. When you're around others, including roommates, friends, and even in class, take those things out of your ears. This is especially important when you're around your parents and grandparents! Save those for when you are alone. Take them out and socialize when you are with others. This is a small thing, but it shows respect and that you care and value shared time with others. Remember to keep earbuds away in social settings for a more engaged and considerate interaction.

MEMORIES MADE: _____

_____
_____
_____
_____
_____

TOUGH TIMES & LESSONS LEARNED: _____

_____
_____
_____
_____

What are you grateful for today?

Stressed | Angry | Tired | Sad | Happy | Excited

↙ REMEMBER! WAIT TO WRITE BELOW UNTIL THIS DAY NEXT YEAR!

DATE: _____ (S) (M) (T) (W) (T) (F) (S)

MEMORIES MADE: _____

_____
_____
_____
_____
_____

TOUGH TIMES & LESSONS LEARNED: _____

_____
_____
_____
_____

What are you grateful for today?

Stressed | Angry | Tired | Sad | Happy | Excited

Did you know? Eating blueberries can help improve your memory! Blueberries are packed with antioxidants that may protect brain cells and improve cognitive function.

DATE: _____ (S) (M) (T) (W) (T) (F) (S)

TUESDAY TIPS:

> Save your lecture notes and study materials for future reference. Just trust us on this. Whether it's a future class it may be useful for, or to use for your own health or family, class notes can come in handy. As wise mothers everywhere have said, "It's better to have it and not need it, than need it and not have it." The key is to label it well and keep them all together in a binder or electronically that you can access when you remember you need it all!

MEMORIES MADE: _____
_____
_____
_____
_____

TOUGH TIMES & LESSONS LEARNED: _____
_____
_____
_____
_____

What are you grateful for today?   Stressed Angry Tired Sad Happy Excited
_____

REMEMBER! WAIT TO WRITE BELOW UNTIL THIS DAY NEXT YEAR!

DATE: _____ (S) (M) (T) (W) (T) (F) (S)

MEMORIES MADE: _____
_____
_____
_____
_____

TOUGH TIMES & LESSONS LEARNED: _____
_____
_____
_____
_____

What are you grateful for today?   Stressed Angry Tired Sad Happy Excited
_____

Did you know? A group of flamingos is called a flamboyance! These social birds are known for their pink feathers and graceful movements. Go ahead. Share that with someone you know! Haha!

DATE: _____ (S) (M) (T) (W) (T) (F) (S)

WEDNESDAY (HUMP DAY!) HAPPY HACKS

> Enjoy and give attention to the present moment. Happy people are mindful of and savor the present. In fact, some of the happiest people on the planet are those who have learned to enjoy their day, including the present moment—who they are with, what they are doing, and the sights, sounds, and smells of people and things around them. Savor the present moment. It's really the only moment that you truly have. Your college days will go fast. Find joy in the moments in each day. What gets in the way of enjoying the moment? Some of the biggest happiness sponges are worry and fear. These emotions can hijack our joy and hinder our journey on our way to happiness and meaning. Slow down and learn to pay attention to the present moment.

MEMORIES MADE: _____
_____
_____
_____
_____
_____

TOUGH TIMES & LESSONS LEARNED: _____
_____
_____
_____
_____

What are you grateful for today?   Stressed Angry Tired Sad Happy Excited
_____

REMEMBER! WAIT TO WRITE BELOW UNTIL THIS DAY NEXT YEAR!

DATE: _____ (S) (M) (T) (W) (T) (F) (S)

MEMORIES MADE: _____
_____
_____
_____
_____
_____

TOUGH TIMES & LESSONS LEARNED: _____
_____
_____
_____
_____

What are you grateful for today?   Stressed Angry Tired Sad Happy Excited
_____

Did you know? The population of the Earth adds about 230,000 people every day!
That's like adding a whole city the size of Reno, Nevada every day.

DATE: _____   (S) (M) (T) (W) (T) (F) (S)

THURSDAY MYTHS:

> "
> Myth: "I'll become instant friends with everyone in my major."
>
> Reality: While you'll share common interests, friendships take time to develop. Bond over study groups and class projects, but don't force connections. It's like smoked brisket – it can't be rushed.
> "

MEMORIES MADE: _____
_____
_____
_____
_____

TOUGH TIMES & LESSONS LEARNED: _____
_____
_____
_____
_____

What are you grateful for today?
_____

Stressed | Angry | Tired | Sad | Happy | Excited

REMEMBER! WAIT TO WRITE BELOW UNTIL THIS DAY NEXT YEAR!

DATE: _____   (S) (M) (T) (W) (T) (F) (S)

MEMORIES MADE: _____
_____
_____
_____
_____

TOUGH TIMES & LESSONS LEARNED: _____
_____
_____
_____
_____

What are you grateful for today?
_____

Stressed | Angry | Tired | Sad | Happy | Excited

Chewing gum can improve your alertness and focus! Studies suggest that chewing gum can increase blood flow to the brain, leading to improved cognitive function.

DATE: _____ (S) (M) (T) (W) (T) (F) (S)

FRIDAY FILL IN THE BLANKS:

" An aspect of college life I didn't anticipate was ...
_____

and I've adapted by...
_____ "

MEMORIES MADE: _____
_____
_____
_____
_____
_____

TOUGH TIMES & LESSONS LEARNED: _____
_____
_____
_____
_____

What are you grateful for today?   Stressed Angry Tired Sad Happy Excited
_____

↳ REMEMBER! WAIT TO WRITE BELOW UNTIL THIS DAY NEXT YEAR!

DATE: _____ (S) (M) (T) (W) (T) (F) (S)

MEMORIES MADE: _____
_____
_____
_____
_____
_____

TOUGH TIMES & LESSONS LEARNED: _____
_____
_____
_____
_____

What are you grateful for today?   Stressed Angry Tired Sad Happy Excited
_____

Did you know? Some species of jellyfish can live forever! The Turritopsis dohrnii jellyfish has the ability to revert back to its polyp stage after reaching sexual maturity, essentially resetting its life cycle.

DATE: _____   S M T W T F S

SATURDAY TED TALKS:

> In his TED Talk, Krishna Sudhir dispels the myth of yoga as just stretching. He highlights its holistic impact on both body and brain. Physically, yoga builds strength, flexibility, and improves balance. Mentally, it reduces stress, boosts mood, and enhances focus. He explains how its unique combination of postures, breathing exercises, and meditation activates various brain regions, promoting calmness, clarity, and overall well-being. Whether you're seeking physical fitness or mental peace, yoga, Sudhir argues, offers a powerful path to a healthier, happier you.

MEMORIES MADE: _____
_____
_____
_____
_____
_____

TOUGH TIMES & LESSONS LEARNED: _____
_____
_____
_____
_____

What are you grateful for today?   Stressed Angry Tired Sad Happy Excited
_____

REMEMBER! WAIT TO WRITE BELOW UNTIL THIS DAY NEXT YEAR!

DATE: _____   S M T W T F S

MEMORIES MADE: _____
_____
_____
_____
_____
_____

TOUGH TIMES & LESSONS LEARNED: _____
_____
_____
_____
_____

What are you grateful for today?   Stressed Angry Tired Sad Happy Excited
_____

Did you know? Gold is edible! While not exactly a common food, gold is actually safe to consume and has been used in some cultures for medicinal purposes.

DATE: _____   S M T W T F S

SUNDAY STRESS BUSTERS:

> Soaking in a warm bath is a wonderful way to ease tension and find peace. For an even more relaxing experience, sprinkle in some Epsom salts, which can help loosen tight muscles. You can also add a few drops of essential oils like lavender or chamomile for a soothing aroma, or pour in some bath bubbles for a light-hearted touch. This combination works wonders for calming both your mind and body.

MEMORIES MADE: _____
_____
_____
_____
_____

TOUGH TIMES & LESSONS LEARNED:
_____
_____
_____
_____

What are you grateful for today?   Stressed Angry Tired Sad Happy Excited
_____

REMEMBER! WAIT TO WRITE BELOW UNTIL THIS DAY NEXT YEAR!

DATE: _____   S M T W T F S

MEMORIES MADE: _____
_____
_____
_____
_____

TOUGH TIMES & LESSONS LEARNED: _____
_____
_____
_____

What are you grateful for today?   Stressed Angry Tired Sad Happy Excited
_____

Did you know? The muscles in your eyes are the fastest in your body! These tiny muscles allow you to make rapid eye movements to track objects and scan your surroundings.

DATE: _____   (S) (M) (T) (W) (T) (F) (S)

MONDAY MANNERS:

> Take control of your education by speaking up in college. Don't have your parents call a professor for you. If you're confused, ask questions. If you think an answer is right but got marked wrong, talk to the professor during office hours—politely. Don't approach a professor at the end of the semester expecting them to give you special treatment or make changes. Approach them early on, especially if you have questions about a paper or test. You're smart and can handle important conversations on your own.

MEMORIES MADE: _____

_____
_____
_____
_____
_____

TOUGH TIMES & LESSONS LEARNED: _____

_____
_____
_____
_____

What are you grateful for today?   Stressed Angry Tired Sad Happy Excited

_____

> REMEMBER! WAIT TO WRITE BELOW UNTIL THIS DAY NEXT YEAR!

DATE: _____   (S) (M) (T) (W) (T) (F) (S)

MEMORIES MADE: _____

_____
_____
_____
_____
_____

TOUGH TIMES & LESSONS LEARNED: _____

_____
_____
_____
_____

What are you grateful for today?   Stressed Angry Tired Sad Happy Excited

_____

Did you know? Your brain uses more energy than any other organ in your body, even though it only makes up about 2% of your weight!

DATE: _____ (S) (M) (T) (W) (T) (F) (S)

TUESDAY TIPS:

> **"** Our toughest battle is against ourselves, caught between who we truly are and a version that seeks quick rewards. It's like having two selves: one that wants what's best in the long run and another that wants pleasure and what's easy right now. This clash is between our real self and our impulsive side. Overcoming this battle, choosing to be our true self instead of giving in to short-term desires, is crucial. It's about being genuine and making choices that are good for us in the long term. The best version of you is the still small voice inside. Pay attention to those inner nudges to rise higher and be better. That's the real you. **"**

MEMORIES MADE: _____

TOUGH TIMES & LESSONS LEARNED: _____

What are you grateful for today?
_____

Stressed | Angry | Tired | Sad | Happy | Excited

REMEMBER! WAIT TO WRITE BELOW UNTIL THIS DAY NEXT YEAR!

DATE: _____ (S) (M) (T) (W) (T) (F) (S)

MEMORIES MADE: _____

TOUGH TIMES & LESSONS LEARNED: _____

What are you grateful for today?
_____

Stressed | Angry | Tired | Sad | Happy | Excited

Cats have over 100 different vocalizations! While we might think of them as mostly meowers, cats can purr, chirp, trill, and even hiss to communicate their feelings.

DATE: _____ (S) (M) (T) (W) (T) (F) (S)

WEDNESDAY (HUMP DAY!) HAPPY HACKS:

> Write a letter to someone who is no longer alive. It may sound odd at first, but give this one a try. Is there someone you know who has died that you wished you could send a note of gratitude and appreciation? A grandparent? Relative? Friend? Ancestor? Even a pet? Try writing a detailed letter thanking him/her for the influence or difference they have made in your life. Write as much or as little as you want. If possible, find a quiet moment alone and sit on a chair or couch with an empty chair in front of you. Read the letter out loud as if the person is right there in front of you. Read slowly and pause to feel the emotions that come. Feel the gratitude in your bones. Keep the letter. Repeat the process with someone else. It can be powerful.

MEMORIES MADE: _____
_____
_____
_____
_____

TOUGH TIMES & LESSONS LEARNED: _____
_____
_____
_____
_____

What are you grateful for today?   Stressed Angry Tired Sad Happy Excited
_____

> REMEMBER! WAIT TO WRITE BELOW UNTIL THIS DAY NEXT YEAR!

DATE: _____ (S) (M) (T) (W) (T) (F) (S)

MEMORIES MADE: _____
_____
_____
_____
_____

TOUGH TIMES & LESSONS LEARNED: _____
_____
_____
_____
_____

What are you grateful for today?   Stressed Angry Tired Sad Happy Excited
_____

Did you know? Apples contain more fiber than a bowl of oatmeal!
Eat a few of those throughout the week to keep you regular! ;)

DATE: _____ (S) (M) (T) (W) (T) (F) (S)

THURSDAY MYTHS:

> Myth: "I won't miss family traditions while at college."
>
> Reality: Being away from home during holidays and special occasions can be tough. Create new traditions with friends or find ways to celebrate remotely. It's a bit like remixing a classic song – different but still enjoyable.

MEMORIES MADE: _____
_____
_____
_____
_____

TOUGH TIMES & LESSONS LEARNED: _____
_____
_____
_____
_____

What are you grateful for today?

Stressed | Angry | Tired | Sad | Happy | Excited
_____

REMEMBER! WAIT TO WRITE BELOW UNTIL THIS DAY NEXT YEAR!

DATE: _____ (S) (M) (T) (W) (T) (F) (S)

MEMORIES MADE: _____
_____
_____
_____
_____

TOUGH TIMES & LESSONS LEARNED: _____
_____
_____
_____
_____

What are you grateful for today?

Stressed | Angry | Tired | Sad | Happy | Excited
_____

Did you know? The phrase "go the whole 9 yards" has several possible origins, including the amount of fabric needed for a proper Scottish kilt or the length of ammunition belts in World War II fighter planes. It means to do something completely or thoroughly.

DATE: _____ (S) (M) (T) (W) (T) (F) (S)

FRIDAY FILL IN THE BLANKS:

> " A challenge I'm currently facing is...
> _____
>
> and I plan to overcome it by...
> _____ "

MEMORIES MADE: _____
_____
_____
_____
_____
_____

TOUGH TIMES & LESSONS LEARNED: _____
_____
_____
_____
_____

What are you grateful for today?   Stressed Angry Tired Sad Happy Excited
_____

REMEMBER! WAIT TO WRITE BELOW UNTIL THIS DAY NEXT YEAR!

DATE: _____ (S) (M) (T) (W) (T) (F) (S)

MEMORIES MADE: _____
_____
_____
_____
_____
_____

TOUGH TIMES & LESSONS LEARNED: _____
_____
_____
_____
_____

What are you grateful for today?   Stressed Angry Tired Sad Happy Excited
_____

Did you know? Engaging in self-talk isn't just a quirk; it can actually aid in organizing your thoughts, clarifying ideas, and solving problems more effectively. Just ease it up a little when you're with strangers! ;)

DATE: _____ (S) (M) (T) (W) (T) (F) (S)

SATURDAY TED TALKS:

> In her TED Talk, psychologist Susan David challenges our comfort with positivity and argues that true happiness lies in embracing and understanding all our emotions, not just the pleasant ones. She encourages emotional agility, the ability to move through emotions without getting stuck. By naming, understanding, and accepting our feelings, we gain control over them and avoid letting them control us. This emotional courage fosters resilience, authenticity, and deeper connections. So, ditch the emotional avoidance and embrace the full spectrum of your inner world to unlock true well-being!

MEMORIES MADE: _____
_____
_____
_____
_____

TOUGH TIMES & LESSONS LEARNED: _____
_____
_____
_____
_____

What are you grateful for today?

Stressed | Angry | Tired | Sad | Happy | Excited

REMEMBER! WAIT TO WRITE BELOW UNTIL THIS DAY NEXT YEAR!

DATE: _____ (S) (M) (T) (W) (T) (F) (S)

MEMORIES MADE: _____
_____
_____
_____
_____

TOUGH TIMES & LESSONS LEARNED: _____
_____
_____
_____
_____

What are you grateful for today?

Stressed | Angry | Tired | Sad | Happy | Excited

Did you know? Your ears can actually continue to grow slightly throughout your life, which is why some people's earlobes get longer as they age.

DATE: _____ (S) (M) (T) (W) (T) (F) (S)

SUNDAY STRESS BUSTERS:

> Incorporating regular periods of leisure reading into your routine can serve as a vital stress-reliever and mental health booster. Delving into non-academic material allows your mind to wander into realms of imagination and creativity, offering a sanctuary from the pressures of study and work. This practice not only stimulates your brain in diverse ways but also provides a valuable opportunity to unwind, recharge, and gain fresh perspectives, enriching your overall well-being and academic performance.

MEMORIES MADE: _____
_____
_____
_____
_____
_____

TOUGH TIMES & LESSONS LEARNED: _____
_____
_____
_____
_____

What are you grateful for today?
_____

Stressed Angry Tired Sad Happy Excited

REMEMBER! WAIT TO WRITE BELOW UNTIL THIS DAY NEXT YEAR!

DATE: _____ (S) (M) (T) (W) (T) (F) (S)

MEMORIES MADE: _____
_____
_____
_____
_____
_____

TOUGH TIMES & LESSONS LEARNED: _____
_____
_____
_____
_____

What are you grateful for today?
_____

Stressed Angry Tired Sad Happy Excited

Did you know? Humans are the only primates with white eyeballs, which some scientists believe may have helped with social interaction by allowing us to better see the direction of another person's gaze.

DATE: _____ (S) (M) (T) (W) (T) (F) (S)

MONDAY MANNERS:

> " Be a reliable friend. If you make plans, stick to them, even if a cooler option pops up. It's tricky but choosing to be a reliable friend matters. It's okay to check with friends to see if mixing the groups for the activity is okay, but bailing for something better hurts. Always treat others the way you'd want to be treated. Your friends will appreciate your loyalty and value you as a reliable and fun person and friend! "

MEMORIES MADE: _____
_____
_____
_____
_____

TOUGH TIMES & LESSONS LEARNED: _____
_____
_____
_____

What are you grateful for today?
_____

Stressed Angry Tired Sad Happy Excited

REMEMBER! WAIT TO WRITE BELOW UNTIL THIS DAY NEXT YEAR!

DATE: _____ (S) (M) (T) (W) (T) (F) (S)

MEMORIES MADE: _____
_____
_____
_____
_____

TOUGH TIMES & LESSONS LEARNED: _____
_____
_____
_____

What are you grateful for today?
_____

Stressed Angry Tired Sad Happy Excited

Did you know? Your belly button is a bustling ecosystem, hosting over 2,300 different species of bacteria, some of which are so unique they're found nowhere else on Earth!

DATE: _____ S M T W T F S

TUESDAY TIPS:

> Understand the college's academic integrity policy and adhere to it. Don't cheat. Just don't do it. Above all it's about honesty and integrity. Give 100% of your own honest effort. There are more ways to cheat and use AI such as Chat GPT and other websites in dishonest ways than ever before. Even when others choose to cut corners, be true and trustworthy throughout your life. Stay away from even the appearance of cheating. Commit to doing it the right way. Your Mom would agree with us. :)

MEMORIES MADE: _____
_____
_____
_____
_____
_____

TOUGH TIMES & LESSONS LEARNED: _____
_____
_____
_____
_____

What are you grateful for today?
_____

Stressed Angry Tired Sad Happy Excited

REMEMBER! WAIT TO WRITE BELOW UNTIL THIS DAY NEXT YEAR!

DATE: _____ S M T W T F S

MEMORIES MADE: _____
_____
_____
_____
_____
_____

TOUGH TIMES & LESSONS LEARNED: _____
_____
_____
_____
_____

What are you grateful for today?
_____

Stressed Angry Tired Sad Happy Excited

Did you know? Dark circles under your eyes are often caused by fatigue, allergies, or genetics. Getting enough sleep, staying hydrated, and managing allergies can all help reduce their appearance.

DATE: _____ (S) (M) (T) (W) (T) (F) (S)

WEDNESDAY (HUMP DAY!) HAPPY HACKS

> A simple happy hack is learning to be slow to judge and quick to love others. Our brains are wired to make quick judgements of others. We look for the negative and we're quick to find it. Learn to catch that thought of picking apart or judging others. There is awesome inside each of us. Every. Single. One. Learn to see past the person and peek inside their life story. Chances are the people we judge have struggles and challenges we aren't aware of. Love others. Don't judge them.

MEMORIES MADE: _____
_____
_____
_____
_____
_____

TOUGH TIMES & LESSONS LEARNED: _____
_____
_____
_____
_____

What are you grateful for today?
_____

Stressed | Angry | Tired | Sad | Happy | Excited

REMEMBER! WAIT TO WRITE BELOW UNTIL THIS DAY NEXT YEAR!

DATE: _____ (S) (M) (T) (W) (T) (F) (S)

MEMORIES MADE: _____
_____
_____
_____
_____
_____

TOUGH TIMES & LESSONS LEARNED: _____
_____
_____
_____
_____

What are you grateful for today?
_____

Stressed | Angry | Tired | Sad | Happy | Excited

Did you know? Your body temperature can actually drop slightly when you're feeling scared, as your body diverts blood flow away from your extremities and towards your core to prepare for a fight-or-flight response.

DATE: _____ (S) (M) (T) (W) (T) (F) (S)

THURSDAY MYTHS:

> Myth: "I'll travel a lot during college breaks."
>
> Reality: Traveling depends on your budget and schedule. Sometimes, breaks are for catching up on rest or work. It's like planning a road trip – sometimes you can go far, other times, it's just a short drive.

MEMORIES MADE: _____

_____

_____

_____

_____

TOUGH TIMES & LESSONS LEARNED: _____

_____

_____

_____

_____

What are you grateful for today?   Stressed Angry Tired Sad Happy Excited

_____

REMEMBER! WAIT TO WRITE BELOW UNTIL THIS DAY NEXT YEAR!

DATE: _____ (S) (M) (T) (W) (T) (F) (S)

MEMORIES MADE: _____

_____

_____

_____

_____

_____

TOUGH TIMES & LESSONS LEARNED: _____

_____

_____

_____

_____

What are you grateful for today?   Stressed Angry Tired Sad Happy Excited

_____

Did you know? Laughter is contagious! Hearing others laugh triggers the same parts of your brain as laughing yourself, helping spread the joy.

DATE: _____ (S) (M) (T) (W) (T) (F) (S)

FRIDAY FILL IN THE BLANKS:

> "
> The moment I felt most proud of myself in college was when...
> _____
>
> because...
> _____
> "

MEMORIES MADE: _____
_____
_____
_____
_____

TOUGH TIMES & LESSONS LEARNED: _____
_____
_____
_____

What are you grateful for today?
_____

Stressed · Angry · Tired · Sad · Happy · Excited

REMEMBER! WAIT TO WRITE BELOW UNTIL THIS DAY NEXT YEAR!

DATE: _____ (S) (M) (T) (W) (T) (F) (S)

MEMORIES MADE: _____
_____
_____
_____
_____

TOUGH TIMES & LESSONS LEARNED: _____
_____
_____
_____

What are you grateful for today?
_____

Stressed · Angry · Tired · Sad · Happy · Excited

Did you know? Newborns can cry real tears, but they don't produce tears of sadness until a few months old, likely because their tear ducts aren't fully developed yet.

DATE: _____   S M T W T F S

SATURDAY TED TALKS:

> Stuck in work mode after hours? Don't wage a losing battle with your thoughts! In his TED Talk, "How to turn off work thoughts during your free time," psychologist Guy Winch offers a different approach. Forget silencing your mind, which can backfire. Instead, create healthy boundaries. Leave your workspace or imagine a door closing on work. Schedule dedicated "worry time" to address work concerns, then let go during free time. Immerse yourself in hobbies or nature to be fully present. Connect and laugh with loved ones – humor is a powerful stressbuster. Finally, embrace imperfection. Don't try to control your thoughts; acknowledge them and refocus on enjoying your free time. Remember, true relaxation comes from disconnection.

MEMORIES MADE: _____
_____
_____
_____
_____

TOUGH TIMES & LESSONS LEARNED: _____
_____
_____
_____

What are you grateful for today?   Stressed Angry Tired Sad Happy Excited
_____

REMEMBER! WAIT TO WRITE BELOW UNTIL THIS DAY NEXT YEAR!

DATE: _____   S M T W T F S

MEMORIES MADE: _____
_____
_____
_____
_____

TOUGH TIMES & LESSONS LEARNED: _____
_____
_____
_____

What are you grateful for today?   Stressed Angry Tired Sad Happy Excited
_____

Did you know? Your tongue is the strongest muscle for its size, essential for talking, tasting, and swallowing, showcasing remarkable flexibility and endurance.

DATE: _____ (S) (M) (T) (W) (T) (F) (S)

SUNDAY STRESS BUSTERS:

> "Yoga is a great way to deal with stress. It includes doing different body positions, breathing in a controlled way, and either meditating or relaxing. This activity can help make you feel less stressed, lower your blood pressure, and keep your heart healthy. You can try joining a yoga class to be around others or do it at home whenever you like. Adding yoga to your everyday routine can be really good for your mind and body. Heck, even just a few stretches can help your body and brain feel better!"

MEMORIES MADE: _____
_____
_____
_____
_____

TOUGH TIMES & LESSONS LEARNED:
_____
_____
_____
_____

What are you grateful for today?   Stressed Angry Tired Sad Happy Excited
_____

↳ REMEMBER! WAIT TO WRITE BELOW UNTIL THIS DAY NEXT YEAR!

DATE: _____ (S) (M) (T) (W) (T) (F) (S)

MEMORIES MADE: _____
_____
_____
_____
_____
_____

TOUGH TIMES & LESSONS LEARNED: _____
_____
_____
_____

What are you grateful for today?   Stressed Angry Tired Sad Happy Excited
_____

Did you know? Your body language can actually influence your mood. Standing tall and confident can boost your feelings of self-esteem, while slouching can make you feel more down.

DATE: _____ (S) (M) (T) (W) (T) (F) (S)

MONDAY MANNERS:

> Be a buddy and share! If there's only one thing left, like the last breadstick or the final slice of pie, ask if someone else wants it before grabbing it. This rule works at home or when you're out with roommates or friends. Remember, it's good to think about others, not just yourself. Sometimes, it's okay to take the last bit, but it's always nice to be thoughtful and willing to share. Keep that battle between being a bit selfish and super generous in check, and choose to be considerate and share the last thing!

MEMORIES MADE: _____
_____
_____
_____
_____

TOUGH TIMES & LESSONS LEARNED: _____
_____
_____
_____

What are you grateful for today?

Stressed | Angry | Tired | Sad | Happy | Excited

REMEMBER! WAIT TO WRITE BELOW UNTIL THIS DAY NEXT YEAR!

DATE: _____ (S) (M) (T) (W) (T) (F) (S)

MEMORIES MADE: _____
_____
_____
_____
_____

TOUGH TIMES & LESSONS LEARNED: _____
_____
_____
_____

What are you grateful for today?

Stressed | Angry | Tired | Sad | Happy | Excited

Did you know? Your dreams can be influenced by what you eat before bed!
Spicy food or heavy meals can lead to more vivid or even bizarre dreams.

DATE: _____ S M T W T F S

TUESDAY TIPS:

> If you weren't afraid and couldn't fail, think of all the things you'd try! You might go after dreams you've always thought were too big, say yes to exciting chances, and try new things without worrying. This way of thinking could change your life, making it full of achievements and happiness. It could also encourage others to be brave and try new things, creating a world where everyone feels free to reach for their biggest goals. So ask yourself, "What would I do if fear wasn't a factor and failure wasn't possible?"

MEMORIES MADE: _____
_____
_____
_____
_____
_____

TOUGH TIMES & LESSONS LEARNED: _____
_____
_____
_____
_____
_____

What are you grateful for today?
_____

Stressed | Angry | Tired | Sad | Happy | Excited

REMEMBER! WAIT TO WRITE BELOW UNTIL THIS DAY NEXT YEAR!

DATE: _____ S M T W T F S

MEMORIES MADE: _____
_____
_____
_____
_____
_____

TOUGH TIMES & LESSONS LEARNED: _____
_____
_____
_____
_____

What are you grateful for today?
_____

Stressed | Angry | Tired | Sad | Happy | Excited

Did you know? We blink about 15-20 times per minute, but that rate plummets when we're reading or focused on a screen – so take breaks to keep your eyes lubricated when you get dialed in!

DATE: _____ (S) (M) (T) (W) (T) (F) (S)

WEDNESDAY (HUMP DAY!) HAPPY HACKS:

> Look forward to something coming up. Have you ever had a fun vacation or exciting adventure in the future that you love to think and talk about with others? Is there anything coming up right now that you are looking forward to? Think how happy you feel when you're looking forward to something, whether it's a holiday, a vacation, movie, or even the riveting last chapter of a book. Research shows that having something to look forward to can boost your mood, increase motivation, optimism, and patience, and decrease stress and irritability. Anticipation also creates discipline and delayed gratification, which teaches us that if we can be patient, a greater experience or reward is coming! This is especially true if you have some drudgery or difficult tasks that must be conquered before exciting events. Knowing that something good is coming your way pushes you to accomplish those tasks you may not necessarily want to do.

MEMORIES MADE: _____
_____
_____
_____
_____

TOUGH TIMES & LESSONS LEARNED: _____
_____
_____
_____

What are you grateful for today?   Stressed Angry Tired Sad Happy Excited
_____

REMEMBER! WAIT TO WRITE BELOW UNTIL THIS DAY NEXT YEAR!

DATE: _____ (S) (M) (T) (W) (T) (F) (S)

MEMORIES MADE: _____
_____
_____
_____
_____

TOUGH TIMES & LESSONS LEARNED: _____
_____
_____
_____

What are you grateful for today?   Stressed Angry Tired Sad Happy Excited
_____

Did you know? The human body can tell the difference between sweet and bitter on your tongue, but sour, salty, and umami are detected on your palate!

DATE: _____ S M T W T F S

THURSDAY MYTHS:

> Myth: "I won't have time for hobbies in college."
>
> Reality: Hobbies are essential for a balanced life. They provide a break from studies and can be a great way to meet people. It's like adding spices to a dish — they bring extra flavor.

MEMORIES MADE: _____
_____
_____
_____
_____

TOUGH TIMES & LESSONS LEARNED: _____
_____
_____
_____
_____

What are you grateful for today?

Stressed   Angry   Tired   Sad   Happy   Excited

REMEMBER! WAIT TO WRITE BELOW UNTIL THIS DAY NEXT YEAR!

DATE: _____ S M T W T F S

MEMORIES MADE: _____
_____
_____
_____
_____
_____

TOUGH TIMES & LESSONS LEARNED: _____
_____
_____
_____
_____

What are you grateful for today?

Stressed   Angry   Tired   Sad   Happy   Excited

Did you know? Your body contains enough calcium to build a small house frame!
This mineral is crucial for strong bones and teeth.

DATE: _____ (S) (M) (T) (W) (T) (F) (S)

FRIDAY FILL IN THE BLANKS:

> "
> A skill I've developed in college that I didn't expect to is...
> _____
>
> and it's useful because...
> _____
> "

MEMORIES MADE: _____
_____
_____
_____
_____

TOUGH TIMES & LESSONS LEARNED: _____
_____
_____
_____

What are you grateful for today?   Stressed Angry Tired Sad Happy Excited
_____

REMEMBER! WAIT TO WRITE BELOW UNTIL THIS DAY NEXT YEAR!

DATE: _____ (S) (M) (T) (W) (T) (F) (S)

MEMORIES MADE: _____
_____
_____
_____
_____

TOUGH TIMES & LESSONS LEARNED: _____
_____
_____
_____

What are you grateful for today?   Stressed Angry Tired Sad Happy Excited
_____

Did you know? Your body contains a network of trillions of nerve cells that transmit messages throughout your body at incredible speeds – some signals travel faster than 200 miles per hour!

DATE: _____ (S) (M) (T) (W) (T) (F) (S)

SATURDAY TED TALKS:

> " Forget endless scrolling! Psychologist Adam Alter, in his TED talk, reveals the dark side of screens. He argues they're designed to be addictive, stealing our time and hijacking our attention. This constant connectivity leads to decreased focus, less enjoyment of offline activities, and poorer sleep, ultimately impacting our happiness. He urges us to be mindful of our screen time, set boundaries, and reclaim control. Remember, real connection and present-moment experiences hold the key to true happiness, not the glow of our devices. So, put down the screen, engage with the world around you, and watch your happiness flourish! "

MEMORIES MADE: _____
_____
_____
_____
_____

TOUGH TIMES & LESSONS LEARNED: _____
_____
_____
_____
_____

What are you grateful for today?   Stressed Angry Tired Sad Happy Excited
_____

👉 REMEMBER! WAIT TO WRITE BELOW UNTIL THIS DAY NEXT YEAR!

DATE: _____ (S) (M) (T) (W) (T) (F) (S)

MEMORIES MADE: _____
_____
_____
_____
_____
_____

TOUGH TIMES & LESSONS LEARNED: _____
_____
_____
_____
_____

What are you grateful for today?   Stressed Angry Tired Sad Happy Excited
_____

Did you know? Our bodies can store memories in the proteins of our neurons!
This allows us to recall experiences from years ago in vivid detail.

DATE: _____   S M T W T F S

SUNDAY STRESS BUSTERS:

> Cultivating self-compassion involves treating yourself with the same kindness and understanding that you would offer a good friend, particularly in challenging moments. Recognize that facing stress is a natural aspect of the college journey, and it's entirely normal to have ups and downs. Remind yourself that perfection is unattainable and unnecessary for growth and learning. Embracing your imperfections and viewing setbacks as opportunities to develop resilience can significantly reduce stress and foster a healthier, more forgiving self-attitude.

MEMORIES MADE: _____
_____
_____
_____
_____
_____

TOUGH TIMES & LESSONS LEARNED: _____
_____
_____
_____
_____

What are you grateful for today?   Stressed Angry Tired Sad Happy Excited
_____

REMEMBER! WAIT TO WRITE BELOW UNTIL THIS DAY NEXT YEAR!

DATE: _____   S M T W T F S

MEMORIES MADE: _____
_____
_____
_____
_____
_____

TOUGH TIMES & LESSONS LEARNED: _____
_____
_____
_____
_____

What are you grateful for today?   Stressed Angry Tired Sad Happy Excited
_____

Did you know? The human brain is constantly rewiring itself! Throughout our lives, our brains form new neural connections and pathways based on our experiences.

DATE: _____ (S) (M) (T) (W) (T) (F) (S)

MONDAY MANNERS:

> "Watch your words! Saying "no offense" or "not to be rude" doesn't guarantee your words won't hurt. If you're thinking about using these phrases, maybe it's best not to say anything. Just because you hope someone won't be offended doesn't mean they won't be. If you need to say it, share with love in the right place and right time. Think twice before using those tricky phrases, and make sure what you're saying is important and can be shared with kindness!"

MEMORIES MADE: _____
_____
_____
_____
_____
_____

TOUGH TIMES & LESSONS LEARNED: _____
_____
_____
_____
_____

What are you grateful for today?   Stressed Angry Tired Sad Happy Excited
_____

REMEMBER! WAIT TO WRITE BELOW UNTIL THIS DAY NEXT YEAR!

DATE: _____ (S) (M) (T) (W) (T) (F) (S)

MEMORIES MADE: _____
_____
_____
_____
_____
_____

TOUGH TIMES & LESSONS LEARNED: _____
_____
_____
_____
_____

What are you grateful for today?   Stressed Angry Tired Sad Happy Excited
_____

Did you know? Humans are the only mammals that can cry tears of emotion.
This ability is thought to help us communicate distress and build social bonds.

DATE: _____ (S) (M) (T) (W) (T) (F) (S)

TUESDAY TIPS:

> "Embrace diversity and engage in conversations about important issues. We brought this one up earlier. This one is seriously a gamechanger. Don't fear differences in people or even difficult discussions with people. Learn how to speak your mind politely. But more importantly, be open to listening and learning from others, especially those who have different experiences. Remember, people do and say things for reasons that make sense to them. Strive to see the world from others' eyes - even if you still disagree. It's about understanding, embracing, and being kind."

MEMORIES MADE: _____
_____
_____
_____
_____
_____

TOUGH TIMES & LESSONS LEARNED: _____
_____
_____
_____
_____

What are you grateful for today?   Stressed Angry Tired Sad Happy Excited
_____

REMEMBER! WAIT TO WRITE BELOW UNTIL THIS DAY NEXT YEAR!

DATE: _____ (S) (M) (T) (W) (T) (F) (S)

MEMORIES MADE: _____
_____
_____
_____
_____
_____

TOUGH TIMES & LESSONS LEARNED: _____
_____
_____
_____
_____

What are you grateful for today?   Stressed Angry Tired Sad Happy Excited
_____

Did you know? The human body has a built-in compass! Tiny magnetic particles in your inner ear help you orient yourself and maintain balance.

DATE: _____   S M T W T F S

WEDNESDAY (HUMP DAY!) HAPPY HACKS

> Give some attention to "present" emotions. We experience all emotions in the present moment. But many of our emotions are anchored in the past or in the future. Notice the types of emotions that tend to be anchored in the past—emotions like anger, sadness, guilt, and regret. These emotions have their purpose, but don't set up camp in the past. "Future" emotions include worry, stress, fear, and anxiety. These are important emotions as well. But they tend to be things that haven't even happened yet. Don't stay there too long. Emotions felt and anchored in the present include joy, peace, excitement, love, and pleasure. These are awesome! The key is to be mindfully aware of your emotions and where you invest your emotional time because what you focus on grows. It's okay to be sad, mad or worried. But don't let these emotions overpower the joy or excitement of the moment.

MEMORIES MADE: _____
_____
_____
_____
_____

TOUGH TIMES & LESSONS LEARNED: _____
_____
_____
_____
_____

What are you grateful for today?   Stressed Angry Tired Sad Happy Excited
_____

> REMEMBER! WAIT TO WRITE BELOW UNTIL THIS DAY NEXT YEAR!

DATE: _____   S M T W T F S

MEMORIES MADE: _____
_____
_____
_____
_____

TOUGH TIMES & LESSONS LEARNED: _____
_____
_____
_____
_____

What are you grateful for today?   Stressed Angry Tired Sad Happy Excited
_____

Did you know? Your sense of taste weakens with age, but your sense of smell can actually improve! This is because the olfactory receptors in your nose continue to regenerate throughout life.

DATE: _____ (S) (M) (T) (W) (T) (F) (S)

THURSDAY MYTHS:

> Myth: "I need to be outgoing to make the most of college."
>
> Reality: Whether you're outgoing or reserved, college has something for everyone. Find activities that suit your personality. It's like choosing a book – not everyone likes the same genre. ("genre" what a silly word! Haha!)

MEMORIES MADE: _____
_____
_____
_____
_____

TOUGH TIMES & LESSONS LEARNED: _____
_____
_____
_____

What are you grateful for today?
_____

Stressed · Angry · Tired · Sad · Happy · Excited

REMEMBER! WAIT TO WRITE BELOW UNTIL THIS DAY NEXT YEAR!

DATE: _____ (S) (M) (T) (W) (T) (F) (S)

MEMORIES MADE: _____
_____
_____
_____
_____

TOUGH TIMES & LESSONS LEARNED: _____
_____
_____
_____

What are you grateful for today?
_____

Stressed · Angry · Tired · Sad · Happy · Excited

Did you know? You can actually train your gut bacteria! Eating a healthy diet rich in fiber and probiotics can promote the growth of good bacteria, which benefits your overall health and well-being.

DATE: _____ (S) (M) (T) (W) (T) (F) (S)

FRIDAY FILL IN THE BLANKS:

> When I think about my future after college, I feel ...
> _____
>
> because...
> _____

MEMORIES MADE: _____
_____
_____
_____
_____

TOUGH TIMES & LESSONS LEARNED: _____
_____
_____
_____

What are you grateful for today?   Stressed Angry Tired Sad Happy Excited
_____

REMEMBER! WAIT TO WRITE BELOW UNTIL THIS DAY NEXT YEAR!

DATE: _____ (S) (M) (T) (W) (T) (F) (S)

MEMORIES MADE: _____
_____
_____
_____
_____
_____

TOUGH TIMES & LESSONS LEARNED: _____
_____
_____
_____

What are you grateful for today?   Stressed Angry Tired Sad Happy Excited
_____

Did you know? The human body is constantly humming! This isn't a sound you can hear, but it's a low-frequency vibration caused by your muscles, organs, and blood flow.

DATE: _____   S M T W T F S

SATURDAY TED TALKS:

> Michael Norton busts the myth of "buying happiness" in his TED Talk. Forget material possessions! True joy, he argues, comes from experiences and relationships, not things. Spending on experiences we share with others and on gifts for others generates the most lasting happiness. He debunks common misconceptions like the "hedonic treadmill" where happiness quickly adapts to new purchases. Remember, investing in experiences and connections fosters genuine joy that money alone can't buy. So, prioritize experiences, share them with loved ones, and watch your happiness blossom!

MEMORIES MADE: _____
_____
_____
_____
_____

TOUGH TIMES & LESSONS LEARNED: _____
_____
_____
_____
_____

What are you grateful for today?   Stressed Angry Tired Sad Happy Excited
_____

REMEMBER! WAIT TO WRITE BELOW UNTIL THIS DAY NEXT YEAR!

DATE: _____   S M T W T F S

MEMORIES MADE: _____
_____
_____
_____
_____

TOUGH TIMES & LESSONS LEARNED: _____
_____
_____
_____
_____

What are you grateful for today?   Stressed Angry Tired Sad Happy Excited
_____

Did you know? We use less than 5% of our conscious awareness (not the same as our brain) to process the world around us. The rest is handled by our subconscious mind, which is constantly working behind the scenes.

DATE: _____ (S) (M) (T) (W) (T) (F) (S)

SUNDAY STRESS BUSTERS:

> "Getting involved in art, like drawing, painting, or making sculptures, is a good way to express yourself and deal with stress. Doing art lets you put your feelings and thoughts into your work, which can help let out stress. It's also a fun activity that can make you feel calm and happy. You don't have to be an expert at art to enjoy it; just creating something can give you a sense of peace and achievement."

MEMORIES MADE: _____
_____
_____
_____
_____

TOUGH TIMES & LESSONS LEARNED:
_____
_____
_____
_____

What are you grateful for today?
_____

Stressed Angry Tired Sad Happy Excited

REMEMBER! WAIT TO WRITE BELOW UNTIL THIS DAY NEXT YEAR!

DATE: _____ (S) (M) (T) (W) (T) (F) (S)

MEMORIES MADE: _____
_____
_____
_____
_____

TOUGH TIMES & LESSONS LEARNED: _____
_____
_____
_____
_____

What are you grateful for today?
_____

Stressed Angry Tired Sad Happy Excited

Did you know? Humans are hardwired for social connection. Our brains release feel-good chemicals like oxytocin when we interact with others, promoting bonding and cooperation.

DATE: _____ (S) (M) (T) (W) (T) (F) (S)

MONDAY MANNERS:

> Refuse to be average. Whether it's getting average grades, being an average cleaner, or being the average employee who just does the bare minimum, give your best at whatever you're doing. Writing a paper? Give it your best effort. Playing a sport? Give 100%. Working on a group project? Refuse to be average and go the extra mile by doing your best.

MEMORIES MADE: _____
_____
_____
_____
_____
_____

TOUGH TIMES & LESSONS LEARNED: _____
_____
_____
_____
_____

What are you grateful for today?
_____

Stressed Angry Tired Sad Happy Excited

REMEMBER! WAIT TO WRITE BELOW UNTIL THIS DAY NEXT YEAR!

DATE: _____ (S) (M) (T) (W) (T) (F) (S)

MEMORIES MADE: _____
_____
_____
_____
_____
_____

TOUGH TIMES & LESSONS LEARNED: _____
_____
_____
_____
_____

What are you grateful for today?
_____

Stressed Angry Tired Sad Happy Excited

Did you know? You have a unique laugh – just like your fingerprints, your laugh is influenced by your anatomy and even your mood!

DATE: _____ (S) (M) (T) (W) (T) (F) (S)

TUESDAY TIPS:

> Consider building a strong professional online presence on LinkedIn. Check out and become familiar with LinkedIn. It's full of professional people looking to connect in mutually beneficial ways. But keep it professional and don't share all your personal stuff on LinkedIn. Connections on LinkedIn can be super helpful in the future and may even lead to career opportunities. And we're just gonna say to watch what you post on other social media outlets. When you are interviewing for jobs, many bosses will look at your personal social media to get a better sense of who you are. Be wise my friends.

MEMORIES MADE: _____
_____
_____
_____
_____
_____

TOUGH TIMES & LESSONS LEARNED: _____
_____
_____
_____
_____

What are you grateful for today?   Stressed Angry Tired Sad Happy Excited
_____

REMEMBER! WAIT TO WRITE BELOW UNTIL THIS DAY NEXT YEAR!

DATE: _____ (S) (M) (T) (W) (T) (F) (S)

MEMORIES MADE: _____
_____
_____
_____
_____
_____

TOUGH TIMES & LESSONS LEARNED: _____
_____
_____
_____
_____

What are you grateful for today?   Stressed Angry Tired Sad Happy Excited
_____

Did you know? Earth's inner core is hotter than the surface of the Sun, reaching temperatures around 9,932 degrees Fahrenheit (5,505 degrees Celsius).

DATE: _____   S M T W T F S

WEDNESDAY (HUMP DAY!) HAPPY HACKS:

> Happiness is frequently found in the little things—we call it the "law of little things." Happy people find joy and meaning in the small and simple things in life. The song of a bird, rain drops and rainbows, a deep breath of fresh air, a warm cup of hot chocolate, the spike in adrenaline after working out. Little things are also the key to happy and healthy relationships. Expressions of gratitude, random acts of kindness, a text of appreciation to a family member. What "little" things bring you happiness and meaning? Slow down and find joy in the little things of life.

MEMORIES MADE: _____
_____
_____
_____
_____
_____

TOUGH TIMES & LESSONS LEARNED: _____
_____
_____
_____
_____

What are you grateful for today?   Stressed Angry Tired Sad Happy Excited
_____

REMEMBER! WAIT TO WRITE BELOW UNTIL THIS DAY NEXT YEAR!

DATE: _____   S M T W T F S

MEMORIES MADE: _____
_____
_____
_____
_____
_____

TOUGH TIMES & LESSONS LEARNED: _____
_____
_____
_____
_____

What are you grateful for today?   Stressed Angry Tired Sad Happy Excited
_____

Did you know? The pressure at the bottom of the Mariana Trench, the deepest point in the ocean, is about 8 tons per square inch - that's equivalent to the weight of an elephant standing on your thumb!

DATE:_____ (S) (M) (T) (W) (T) (F) (S)

THURSDAY MYTHS:

> Myth: "Grades don't matter as long as I get the degree."
>
> Reality: While a degree is important, grades can impact your opportunities for graduate school or competitive job markets. It's a balancing act — focusing on both the journey and the destination.

MEMORIES MADE: _____
_____
_____
_____
_____
_____

TOUGH TIMES & LESSONS LEARNED: _____
_____
_____
_____
_____

What are you grateful for today?   Stressed Angry Tired Sad Happy Excited
_____

REMEMBER! WAIT TO WRITE BELOW UNTIL THIS DAY NEXT YEAR!

DATE:_____ (S) (M) (T) (W) (T) (F) (S)

MEMORIES MADE: _____
_____
_____
_____
_____
_____

TOUGH TIMES & LESSONS LEARNED: _____
_____
_____
_____
_____

What are you grateful for today?   Stressed Angry Tired Sad Happy Excited
_____

Did you know? The placebo effect is a powerful phenomenon where a person's belief in a treatment can actually lead to positive results, even if the treatment itself is inert. The mind-body connection is fascinating!

DATE: _____ Ⓢ Ⓜ Ⓣ Ⓦ Ⓣ Ⓕ Ⓢ

FRIDAY FILL IN THE BLANKS:

> " The most significant way I've grown personally in college is…
> _____
>
> and it's important because…
> _____ "

MEMORIES MADE: _____
_____
_____
_____
_____

TOUGH TIMES & LESSONS LEARNED: _____
_____
_____
_____
_____

What are you grateful for today?   Stressed   Angry   Tired   Sad   Happy   Excited
_____

⬅ REMEMBER! WAIT TO WRITE BELOW UNTIL THIS DAY NEXT YEAR!

DATE: _____ Ⓢ Ⓜ Ⓣ Ⓦ Ⓣ Ⓕ Ⓢ

MEMORIES MADE: _____
_____
_____
_____
_____

TOUGH TIMES & LESSONS LEARNED: _____
_____
_____
_____

What are you grateful for today?   Stressed   Angry   Tired   Sad   Happy   Excited
_____

Did you know? Some plants can communicate with each other! Trees may release chemicals into the air to warn others of danger from insects or disease, showcasing a surprising level of plant intelligence.

DATE: _____ (S) (M) (T) (W) (T) (F) (S)

SATURDAY TED TALKS:

> Ron Gutman's TED Talk unveils the surprising power of smiling, revealing its profound impact on our health, well-being, and longevity. He presents research showing that smiling can reduce stress, boost our mood, and enhance relationships. Gutman suggests that smiles are contagious and can significantly influence our social interactions and personal success. He advocates for embracing the simple act of smiling as a powerful tool to improve our lives and the world around us.

MEMORIES MADE: _____
_____
_____
_____
_____

TOUGH TIMES & LESSONS LEARNED: _____
_____
_____
_____

What are you grateful for today?
_____

Stressed | Angry | Tired | Sad | Happy | Excited

> REMEMBER! WAIT TO WRITE BELOW UNTIL THIS DAY NEXT YEAR!

DATE: _____ (S) (M) (T) (W) (T) (F) (S)

MEMORIES MADE: _____
_____
_____
_____
_____

TOUGH TIMES & LESSONS LEARNED: _____
_____
_____
_____

What are you grateful for today?
_____

Stressed | Angry | Tired | Sad | Happy | Excited

Did you know? Elephants communicate using infrasound, low-frequency sound waves undetectable by the human ear. They can "talk" to each other over vast distances.

DATE: _____   (S) (M) (T) (W) (T) (F) (S)

SUNDAY STRESS BUSTERS:

> If stress starts to feel too heavy and begins to disrupt your everyday routines, it might be time to seek guidance from a mental health expert. Professionals in mental health, such as therapists or counselors, are equipped to provide not just support, but also practical techniques and coping strategies tailored to your unique situation. These services can become a cornerstone in learning how to navigate stress more effectively, ensuring it doesn't overpower your well-being and daily activities.

MEMORIES MADE: _____
_____
_____
_____
_____
_____

TOUGH TIMES & LESSONS LEARNED: _____
_____
_____
_____
_____

What are you grateful for today?   Stressed Angry Tired Sad Happy Excited
_____

REMEMBER! WAIT TO WRITE BELOW UNTIL THIS DAY NEXT YEAR!

DATE: _____   (S) (M) (T) (W) (T) (F) (S)

MEMORIES MADE: _____
_____
_____
_____
_____
_____

TOUGH TIMES & LESSONS LEARNED: _____
_____
_____
_____
_____

What are you grateful for today?   Stressed Angry Tired Sad Happy Excited
_____

Did you know? The population of the Earth breathes in about the weight of the Empire State Building in oxygen every single day!

DATE: _____ (S) (M) (T) (W) (T) (F) (S)

MONDAY MANNERS:

> "Practice patience. Do you get bugged easily? When roommates or others chew with their mouth open? Lick their fingers? Annoying laugh? Most all of us get bothered by little things. If you can bring it up with the person in a kind or humorous way and then chat about it, give it a try. If it's something they can't help (snoring!?), practice patience or get some earplugs. Chances are you will work and/or live with someone who bugs you. Learn patience and practice kindness. Remember people are more important than problems."

MEMORIES MADE: _____
_____
_____
_____
_____

TOUGH TIMES & LESSONS LEARNED: _____
_____
_____
_____
_____

What are you grateful for today?   Stressed Angry Tired Sad Happy Excited
_____

REMEMBER! WAIT TO WRITE BELOW UNTIL THIS DAY NEXT YEAR!

DATE: _____ (S) (M) (T) (W) (T) (F) (S)

MEMORIES MADE: _____
_____
_____
_____
_____

TOUGH TIMES & LESSONS LEARNED: _____
_____
_____
_____
_____

What are you grateful for today?   Stressed Angry Tired Sad Happy Excited
_____

Did you know? Sloths have incredibly slow digestive systems, taking up to a month for food to move through their entire digestive tract! This sluggish digestion is a consequence of their low-energy lifestyle.

DATE: _____ (S) (M) (T) (W) (T) (F) (S)

TUESDAY TIPS:
> Achieving your goals is less about technical know-how, which is only about 10%, and more about how you interact with others, making up over 90% of success. While liking, caring, and listening to people are important, the true essence lies in your own character. It all begins with who you are at your core. Your personal qualities, virtues, and values set the foundation for effective people skills, which, in turn, drive your ability to reach your objectives. Review your values and virtues that you (hopefully) completed in the beginning of this journal. Assess how you're doing. Are you living true to your core four?

MEMORIES MADE: _____
_____
_____
_____
_____
_____

TOUGH TIMES & LESSONS LEARNED: _____
_____
_____
_____
_____

What are you grateful for today?   Stressed Angry Tired Sad Happy Excited
_____

> REMEMBER! WAIT TO WRITE BELOW UNTIL THIS DAY NEXT YEAR!

DATE: _____ (S) (M) (T) (W) (T) (F) (S)

MEMORIES MADE: _____
_____
_____
_____
_____
_____

TOUGH TIMES & LESSONS LEARNED: _____
_____
_____
_____
_____

What are you grateful for today?   Stressed Angry Tired Sad Happy Excited
_____

Did you know? The human brain is constantly rewiring itself throughout our lives. This process, called neuroplasticity, allows us to learn new things, adapt to change, and even recover from brain injuries.

DATE: _____ (S) (M) (T) (W) (T) (F) (S)

WEDNESDAY (HUMP DAY!) HAPPY HACKS

> " Write another letter (yes, another letter). This time it's a gratitude email or letter to a former teacher in your life—anyone who has taught you well. It could be a parent, sibling, spiritual or religious leader, coach, mentor, employer, high school teacher. There are all kinds of teachers in your life. Write them a sincere thank you letter or email. Be as detailed as possible. Recall specific experiences and examples and express your gratitude. Repeat with another teacher in your life. You will feel better inside. We should never fail to thank those who have taught us well. "

MEMORIES MADE: _____
_____
_____
_____
_____

TOUGH TIMES & LESSONS LEARNED: _____
_____
_____
_____
_____

What are you grateful for today?
_____

Stressed | Angry | Tired | Sad | Happy | Excited

REMEMBER! WAIT TO WRITE BELOW UNTIL THIS DAY NEXT YEAR!

DATE: _____ (S) (M) (T) (W) (T) (F) (S)

MEMORIES MADE: _____
_____
_____
_____
_____

TOUGH TIMES & LESSONS LEARNED: _____
_____
_____
_____
_____

What are you grateful for today?
_____

Stressed | Angry | Tired | Sad | Happy | Excited

Did you know? The human brain is wired to find faces in random patterns.
This phenomenon, called pareidolia, is why we see faces in clouds, toast, or even car headlights.

DATE: _____ (S) (M) (T) (W) (T) (F) (S)

THURSDAY MYTHS:

> Myth: "I can only have fun if I drink or party."
>
> Reality: There are countless ways to enjoy college life without alcohol or parties. Explore clubs, outdoor activities, or cultural events. It's like a menu with many options — not everyone chooses the same dish.

MEMORIES MADE: _____
_____
_____
_____
_____

TOUGH TIMES & LESSONS LEARNED: _____
_____
_____
_____
_____

What are you grateful for today?   Stressed Angry Tired Sad Happy Excited
_____

> REMEMBER! WAIT TO WRITE BELOW UNTIL THIS DAY NEXT YEAR!

DATE: _____ (S) (M) (T) (W) (T) (F) (S)

MEMORIES MADE: _____
_____
_____
_____
_____

TOUGH TIMES & LESSONS LEARNED: _____
_____
_____
_____
_____

What are you grateful for today?   Stressed Angry Tired Sad Happy Excited
_____

Did you know? Hibernating bears recycle their own waste into protein during their winter slumber! This remarkable adaptation allows them to survive months without eating or going to the bathroom.

DATE: _____ (S) (M) (T) (W) (T) (F) (S)

FRIDAY FILL IN THE BLANKS:

> "
> An experience that took me out of my comfort zone was ...
> _____
>
> and I learned this from it...
> _____
> "

MEMORIES MADE: _____
_____
_____
_____
_____

TOUGH TIMES & LESSONS LEARNED: _____
_____
_____
_____
_____

What are you grateful for today?
_____

Stressed · Angry · Tired · Sad · Happy · Excited

REMEMBER! WAIT TO WRITE BELOW UNTIL THIS DAY NEXT YEAR!

DATE: _____ (S) (M) (T) (W) (T) (F) (S)

MEMORIES MADE: _____
_____
_____
_____
_____

TOUGH TIMES & LESSONS LEARNED: _____
_____
_____
_____
_____

What are you grateful for today?
_____

Stressed · Angry · Tired · Sad · Happy · Excited

Did you know? The human body contains enough sodium to fill a saltshaker! This essential mineral helps regulate fluids and nerve impulses in the body. Just don't be too salty! Haha! ;)

DATE: _____ (S) (M) (T) (W) (T) (F) (S)

SATURDAY TED TALKS:

> Shame thrives in silence, says Brené Brown in her TED Talk. Forget pretending it doesn't exist! She reveals shame's hidden costs: disconnection, self-doubt, and even addiction. The key to healing lies in understanding and talking about shame. By listening to shame stories with empathy and non-judgment, we create a safe space for understanding and healing. Sharing our own vulnerabilities and imperfections further breaks the silence and promotes connection. Remember, connection and empathy are the antidotes to shame. So, listen openly, share authentically, and watch shame lose its power over you!

MEMORIES MADE: _____
_____
_____
_____
_____

TOUGH TIMES & LESSONS LEARNED: _____
_____
_____
_____
_____

What are you grateful for today?   Stressed Angry Tired Sad Happy Excited
_____

REMEMBER! WAIT TO WRITE BELOW UNTIL THIS DAY NEXT YEAR!

DATE: _____ (S) (M) (T) (W) (T) (F) (S)

MEMORIES MADE: _____
_____
_____
_____
_____

TOUGH TIMES & LESSONS LEARNED: _____
_____
_____
_____
_____

What are you grateful for today?   Stressed Angry Tired Sad Happy Excited
_____

Did you know? Queen Elizabeth II technically owns all the unmarked swans in open water in England and Wales! This is a leftover law from medieval times when swans were considered a delicacy. I'm sure you wanted to know that!

DATE: _____ (S) (M) (T) (W) (T) (F) (S)

SUNDAY STRESS BUSTERS:

> " Keeping a positive outlook, especially when faced with tough situations, can be a powerful tool in managing stress. By choosing to see the glass half full, you equip yourself with a resilience that transforms stress into a manageable aspect of life. A positive mindset encourages you to view obstacles not as insurmountable problems, but as chances to grow and learn. This approach not only helps in coping with immediate stress but also in building long-term emotional strength and flexibility. "

MEMORIES MADE: _____
_____
_____
_____
_____

TOUGH TIMES & LESSONS LEARNED:
_____
_____
_____
_____

What are you grateful for today?
_____

Stressed Angry Tired Sad Happy Excited

REMEMBER! WAIT TO WRITE BELOW UNTIL THIS DAY NEXT YEAR!

DATE: _____ (S) (M) (T) (W) (T) (F) (S)

MEMORIES MADE: _____
_____
_____
_____
_____

TOUGH TIMES & LESSONS LEARNED: _____
_____
_____
_____
_____

What are you grateful for today?
_____

Stressed Angry Tired Sad Happy Excited

Did you know? The population of the Earth collectively throws away enough food every year to feed over 2 billion people! Food waste is a major global problem.

DATE: _____ (S) (M) (T) (W) (T) (F) (S)

MONDAY MANNERS:

> Improve self-awareness. Make time to regularly reflect on your thoughts, emotions, and actions. Before speaking your mind, pause and think about the situation and what you are about to do. Seek feedback from others and be open to others' suggestions. Journaling (in this!) can aid in understanding patterns and triggers. Cultivate a mindset of curiosity about yourself and your reactions. Clarify your core values and ensure your actions align with them. Developing self-awareness is an ongoing journey that involves introspection and a genuine desire for personal understanding.

MEMORIES MADE: _____
_____
_____
_____
_____

TOUGH TIMES & LESSONS LEARNED: _____
_____
_____
_____

What are you grateful for today?
_____

Stressed Angry Tired Sad Happy Excited

REMEMBER! WAIT TO WRITE BELOW UNTIL THIS DAY NEXT YEAR!

DATE: _____ (S) (M) (T) (W) (T) (F) (S)

MEMORIES MADE: _____
_____
_____
_____
_____

TOUGH TIMES & LESSONS LEARNED: _____
_____
_____
_____

What are you grateful for today?
_____

Stressed Angry Tired Sad Happy Excited

Did you know? The human body contains a population of bacteria that outweighs our own body weight by about 1 to 1! These gut microbes play a crucial role in digestion, immunity, and even mood.

DATE: _____ (S) (M) (T) (W) (T) (F) (S)

TUESDAY TIPS:

> " The idea that you're the sum of the five people closest to you suggests that the traits, habits, and attitudes of your nearest friends and family significantly influence your own. This means that the people you spend the most time with shape your behavior, thoughts, and even your success. Surrounding yourself with positive, supportive, and ambitious individuals can uplift you and help you grow, whereas being around negative influences might hold you back. Choose your circle wisely, as they deeply impact who you become. Seek out the people who bring out the best in you, not the stress in you. "

MEMORIES MADE: _____
_____
_____
_____
_____
_____

TOUGH TIMES & LESSONS LEARNED: _____
_____
_____
_____
_____

What are you grateful for today?
_____

Stressed | Angry | Tired | Sad | Happy | Excited

REMEMBER! WAIT TO WRITE BELOW UNTIL THIS DAY NEXT YEAR!

DATE: _____ (S) (M) (T) (W) (T) (F) (S)

MEMORIES MADE: _____
_____
_____
_____
_____
_____

TOUGH TIMES & LESSONS LEARNED: _____
_____
_____
_____
_____

What are you grateful for today?
_____

Stressed | Angry | Tired | Sad | Happy | Excited

Did you know? The population of the Earth collectively chews about 600,000 tons of gum every year! That's a lot of bubble-blowing potential.

DATE: _____ (S) (M) (T) (W) (T) (F) (S)

WEDNESDAY (HUMP DAY!) HAPPY HACKS:

> Be aware of cruise control. In life there are times when we get stuck on "cruise control" when each day feels the same and we just "go with the flow" because it doesn't take much effort. Most of us probably take the same roads and route to get home. It would take more effort and brain power to take a new or unfamiliar route. The same principles hold true with creating new habits and trying new things in our lives. They may be unfamiliar; they may take more effort. As you try new things in your life, be aware of the voice inside that says, "that takes too much effort." Instead, celebrate small wins. When you try something, celebrate it! It can create an upward spiral and lead to other small changes and improvements. Remember, we're aiming for progress, not perfection. What aspect of your life is on cruise control, but you would like to be in "active control?"

MEMORIES MADE: _____
_____
_____
_____
_____

TOUGH TIMES & LESSONS LEARNED: _____
_____
_____
_____

What are you grateful for today?   Stressed Angry Tired Sad Happy Excited
_____

REMEMBER! WAIT TO WRITE BELOW UNTIL THIS DAY NEXT YEAR!

DATE: _____ (S) (M) (T) (W) (T) (F) (S)

MEMORIES MADE: _____
_____
_____
_____
_____

TOUGH TIMES & LESSONS LEARNED: _____
_____
_____
_____

What are you grateful for today?   Stressed Angry Tired Sad Happy Excited
_____

Did you know? Octopuses have three hearts! Two hearts pump blood to their gills, while a third heart circulates blood throughout the rest of their body.

DATE: _____ (S) (M) (T) (W) (T) (F) (S)

THURSDAY MYTHS:

> Myth: "I'll be completely independent in college."
>
> Reality: While college offers more independence, you'll still rely on others in some ways, whether it's financial support, advice, or emotional guidance. It's like learning to drive – you may be behind the wheel, but sometimes you need a co-pilot.

MEMORIES MADE: _____
_____
_____
_____
_____
_____

TOUGH TIMES & LESSONS LEARNED: _____
_____
_____
_____
_____

What are you grateful for today?
_____

Stressed | Angry | Tired | Sad | Happy | Excited

↳ REMEMBER! WAIT TO WRITE BELOW UNTIL THIS DAY NEXT YEAR!

DATE: _____ (S) (M) (T) (W) (T) (F) (S)

MEMORIES MADE: _____
_____
_____
_____
_____
_____

TOUGH TIMES & LESSONS LEARNED: _____
_____
_____
_____
_____

What are you grateful for today?
_____

Stressed | Angry | Tired | Sad | Happy | Excited

Did you know? The population of the Earth collectively spends 1 billion hours watching cat videos online every month! What the what!?? Who knew??

DATE: _____ (S) (M) (T) (W) (T) (F) (S)

FRIDAY FILL IN THE BLANKS:

> " A tradition or event at my college that I love is...
> _____
>
> because it...
> _____ "

MEMORIES MADE: _____
_____
_____
_____
_____
_____

TOUGH TIMES & LESSONS LEARNED: _____
_____
_____
_____
_____

What are you grateful for today?   Stressed Angry Tired Sad Happy Excited
_____

REMEMBER! WAIT TO WRITE BELOW UNTIL THIS DAY NEXT YEAR!

DATE: _____ (S) (M) (T) (W) (T) (F) (S)

MEMORIES MADE: _____
_____
_____
_____
_____
_____

TOUGH TIMES & LESSONS LEARNED: _____
_____
_____
_____
_____

What are you grateful for today?   Stressed Angry Tired Sad Happy Excited
_____

Did you know? The human knee is the largest and most complex joint in the body.
It allows for a wide range of motion, but also makes it vulnerable to injury. Thanks knees!

DATE: _____ (S) (M) (T) (W) (T) (F) (S)

SATURDAY TED TALKS:

> In her TED Talk, Tina Seelig argues "luck" isn't a cosmic dice roll, but rather something you cultivate. Forget passively waiting for good fortune! She suggests three "little risks" to increase your "luck": 1. Be open to appreciation: Notice and express gratitude for the good things already in your life, attracting more positivity. 2. Reframe "crazy" ideas: Don't shy away from unconventional thoughts, they might hold hidden opportunities. View them as possibilities, not impossibilities. 3. Actively connect and share: Build relationships and share your ideas generously. You never know who might be the missing piece of your "lucky" puzzle. Remember, luck favors the prepared and connected, not the passive bystanders. Embrace these small risks, open yourself to possibilities, and watch your "luck" bloom!

MEMORIES MADE: _____
_____
_____
_____
_____

TOUGH TIMES & LESSONS LEARNED: _____
_____
_____
_____
_____

What are you grateful for today?   Stressed Angry Tired Sad Happy Excited
_____

⬇ REMEMBER! WAIT TO WRITE BELOW UNTIL THIS DAY NEXT YEAR!

DATE: _____ (S) (M) (T) (W) (T) (F) (S)

MEMORIES MADE: _____
_____
_____
_____
_____

TOUGH TIMES & LESSONS LEARNED: _____
_____
_____
_____

What are you grateful for today?   Stressed Angry Tired Sad Happy Excited
_____

Did you know? The population of the entire world could fit inside the state of Texas, with plenty of room to spare! This highlights the vastness of our planet and the uneven distribution of human population.

DATE: _____   (S) (M) (T) (W) (T) (F) (S)

SUNDAY STRESS BUSTERS:

> Learn how to manage stress and cope with academic pressure. You're gonna feel it! It's going to be intense at times. You're going to have days where you are busy studying all day and still don't get it all done. There are tons of ways to manage stress in healthy ways – just keep reading the tips in this journal! One of the best ways to manage intense stress is to close your eyes and take several slow deep breaths. You might even try the "Power of 3s." Ask yourself whether what you are stressing about will really matter in 3 days, 3 months, or even 3 years from now.

MEMORIES MADE: _____
_____
_____
_____
_____

TOUGH TIMES & LESSONS LEARNED: _____
_____
_____
_____

What are you grateful for today?   Stressed Angry Tired Sad Happy Excited
_____

REMEMBER! WAIT TO WRITE BELOW UNTIL THIS DAY NEXT YEAR!

DATE: _____   (S) (M) (T) (W) (T) (F) (S)

MEMORIES MADE: _____
_____
_____
_____
_____

TOUGH TIMES & LESSONS LEARNED: _____
_____
_____
_____

What are you grateful for today?   Stressed Angry Tired Sad Happy Excited
_____

Did you know? The population of the Earth collectively speaks over 6,500 different languages! This incredible diversity of communication reflects the rich cultural tapestry of humanity.

DATE: _____ (S) (M) (T) (W) (T) (F) (S)

MONDAY MANNERS:

> "Don't get sucked into gossip. Speaking negatively about others is hurtful. Avoid spreading rumors or opinions, even if it feels fun and entertaining. It's often not your business. Shut down gossip with phrases like, "I think he's nice" or "I've had others talk about me and it feels awful." Plus, people who gossip are hard to trust and earn bad reputations. If you've experienced gossip's pain, you know its consequences. One-sided stories and targeting are painful. Spending time on negativity only creates problems in the end. Be the one to stop the cycle; choose kindness over gossip."

MEMORIES MADE: _____

_____
_____
_____
_____
_____

TOUGH TIMES & LESSONS LEARNED: _____

_____
_____
_____
_____

What are you grateful for today?

Stressed Angry Tired Sad Happy Excited

_____

REMEMBER! WAIT TO WRITE BELOW UNTIL THIS DAY NEXT YEAR!

DATE: _____ (S) (M) (T) (W) (T) (F) (S)

MEMORIES MADE: _____

_____
_____
_____
_____
_____

TOUGH TIMES & LESSONS LEARNED: _____

_____
_____
_____
_____

What are you grateful for today?

Stressed Angry Tired Sad Happy Excited

_____

Did you know? That brain freeze you get from icy treats comes from the rapid blood vessel constriction in the roof of your mouth! This tricks your brain into thinking your head is freezing!

DATE: _____   (S) (M) (T) (W) (T) (F) (S)

TUESDAY TIPS:

> Keep an open mind and remain adaptable to change. It's called humility. The sooner you learn it the better off you'll be in life and in your relationships. Be open minded. Be flexible. The ability to adapt and change is a great life skill. Things are not always going to go your way. And that's okay. Go with what happens, not what you thought or wanted to happen. There's always lessons to learn. Change sometimes seems unfair. And sometimes it is. But change is going to happen throughout your life. Learn how to respond rather than react!

MEMORIES MADE: _____
_____
_____
_____
_____
_____

TOUGH TIMES & LESSONS LEARNED: _____
_____
_____
_____
_____

What are you grateful for today?
_____

Stressed Angry Tired Sad Happy Excited

REMEMBER! WAIT TO WRITE BELOW UNTIL THIS DAY NEXT YEAR!

DATE: _____   (S) (M) (T) (W) (T) (F) (S)

MEMORIES MADE: _____
_____
_____
_____
_____
_____

TOUGH TIMES & LESSONS LEARNED: _____
_____
_____
_____
_____

What are you grateful for today?
_____

Stressed Angry Tired Sad Happy Excited

Did you know? Strong emotional stress can actually mimic a heart attack! This temporary weakening of the heart muscle, caused by emotional distress, is called Takotsubo cardiomyopathy. It can cause chest pain and shortness of breath. Take some deep breaths!

DATE: _____ S M T W T F S

WEDNESDAY (HUMP DAY!) HAPPY HACKS

> The "Fun 15" refers to a concept introduced by Michael Babyak and his colleagues in their research on the effects of exercise on depression. The idea is based on a study that found as little as 15 minutes of physical activity a day can significantly improve mood and have antidepressant effects. This concept promotes the idea that engaging in short, enjoyable physical activities—hence the "fun" in "Fun 15"—can be an effective strategy for boosting mental health and well-being. Aim for 15 minutes of "fun" exercise to battle the blues!

MEMORIES MADE: _____
_____
_____
_____
_____
_____

TOUGH TIMES & LESSONS LEARNED: _____
_____
_____
_____
_____

What are you grateful for today?

Stressed Angry Tired Sad Happy Excited

REMEMBER! WAIT TO WRITE BELOW UNTIL THIS DAY NEXT YEAR!

DATE: _____ S M T W T F S

MEMORIES MADE: _____
_____
_____
_____
_____
_____

TOUGH TIMES & LESSONS LEARNED: _____
_____
_____
_____
_____

What are you grateful for today?

Stressed Angry Tired Sad Happy Excited

Did you know? Feeling hot and bothered isn't just about temperature!
Anxiety and anger can trigger the body to release heat, making you feel flushed.

DATE: _____ (S) (M) (T) (W) (T) (F) (S)

THURSDAY MYTHS:

> Myth: "College relationships are not serious."
>
> Reality: Relationships in college can be as meaningful as at any other stage of life. They offer opportunities for growth and learning about yourself and others. It's like any relationship – what you put into it determines what you get out of it.

MEMORIES MADE: _____
_____
_____
_____
_____

TOUGH TIMES & LESSONS LEARNED: _____
_____
_____
_____
_____

What are you grateful for today?
_____

Stressed | Angry | Tired | Sad | Happy | Excited

↳ REMEMBER! WAIT TO WRITE BELOW UNTIL THIS DAY NEXT YEAR!

DATE: _____ (S) (M) (T) (W) (T) (F) (S)

MEMORIES MADE: _____
_____
_____
_____
_____

TOUGH TIMES & LESSONS LEARNED: _____
_____
_____
_____
_____

What are you grateful for today?
_____

Stressed | Angry | Tired | Sad | Happy | Excited

Did you know? While most people dream in color, some dream exclusively in black and white. This doesn't necessarily indicate any underlying condition.

DATE: _____ S M T W T F S

FRIDAY FILL IN THE BLANKS:

> "
> A realization I had about myself recently is...
> _____
>
> and it's significant because...
> _____
> "

MEMORIES MADE: _____
_____
_____
_____
_____

TOUGH TIMES & LESSONS LEARNED: _____
_____
_____
_____
_____

What are you grateful for today?   Stressed Angry Tired Sad Happy Excited
_____

REMEMBER! WAIT TO WRITE BELOW UNTIL THIS DAY NEXT YEAR!

DATE: _____ S M T W T F S

MEMORIES MADE: _____
_____
_____
_____
_____

TOUGH TIMES & LESSONS LEARNED: _____
_____
_____
_____
_____

What are you grateful for today?   Stressed Angry Tired Sad Happy Excited
_____

Did you know? Humans have a natural "fight-or-flight" response triggered by the amygdala, a part of the brain responsible for emotions like fear and aggression.

DATE: _____ (S) (M) (T) (W) (T) (F) (S)

SATURDAY TED TALKS:

> Larry Smith doesn't sugarcoat success in his TED Talk. Forget expecting a "great career" to magically happen! He calls out excuses and self-doubt as the true saboteurs. We fear rejection, struggle with "if only" thoughts, and settle for mediocrity. The antidote? Embrace challenges, silence the "unless" voice, and take bold action. Pursue your passions, even if they seem impractical. Embrace failure as a learning opportunity, not a dead end. Remember, a great career isn't handed over, it's earned through courage, hard work, and refusing to let excuses hold you back. So, get out of your own way and start building the career you truly desire!

MEMORIES MADE: _____
_____
_____
_____
_____

TOUGH TIMES & LESSONS LEARNED: _____
_____
_____
_____

What are you grateful for today?
_____

Stressed | Angry | Tired | Sad | Happy | Excited

REMEMBER! WAIT TO WRITE BELOW UNTIL THIS DAY NEXT YEAR!

DATE: _____ (S) (M) (T) (W) (T) (F) (S)

MEMORIES MADE: _____
_____
_____
_____
_____
_____

TOUGH TIMES & LESSONS LEARNED: _____
_____
_____
_____

What are you grateful for today?
_____

Stressed | Angry | Tired | Sad | Happy | Excited

Did you know? Your brainwaves actually change depending on your emotional state!
Meditation practices, for example, can promote relaxation by influencing brainwave patterns.

DATE: _____ (S) (M) (T) (W) (T) (F) (S)

SUNDAY STRESS BUSTERS:

> Be aware of the "warning lights" in your life. Most vehicles have warning lights that come on to alert us of something. These are meant to alert us to something that needs attention, and some are more urgent than others. If we don't pay attention to the warning lights that come on, ignore them, or even cover them up and hope they will go away, it could lead to more serious problems and challenges down the road. If we relate these warning lights to our own lives, we can see that some of life's challenges can be overwhelming, and if we ignore them or hope they just go away, it could really be problematic. For example, lack of sleep may be solved by taking a nap or going to bed earlier, while losing a job can feel overwhelming and add all kinds of stress. It's important to pay attention to the warning lights in your life and try to prevent problems by keeping up on maintenance and repairs, or keeping your body and mind healthy so you can respond better to challenges that arise.

MEMORIES MADE: _____
_____
_____
_____
_____
_____

TOUGH TIMES & LESSONS LEARNED:
_____
_____
_____
_____

What are you grateful for today?
_____

Stressed Angry Tired Sad Happy Excited

REMEMBER! WAIT TO WRITE BELOW UNTIL THIS DAY NEXT YEAR!

DATE: _____ (S) (M) (T) (W) (T) (F) (S)

MEMORIES MADE: _____
_____
_____
_____
_____
_____

TOUGH TIMES & LESSONS LEARNED: _____
_____
_____
_____
_____

What are you grateful for today?
_____

Stressed Angry Tired Sad Happy Excited

Did you know? This is a citrusy paradox! Lemons float due to their air pockets, while limes sink because they're denser (more dense??).

DATE: _____ (S) (M) (T) (W) (T) (F) (S)

MONDAY MANNERS:

> Respect your professors! They invest a ton of time preparing lectures, assignments and activities. If you interrupt or cause issues, it's super distracting. Contribute to a positive learning environment by listening, participating, and avoiding distractions—including your phone (just put it away and take out your earbuds). Encourage others to do the same. Professors are people with feelings. They notice when you aren't listening and they thrive when students are cooperative and respectful. And be sure to thank them on your wait out—they rarely hear that. Be part of the solution, not the problem.

MEMORIES MADE: _____
_____
_____
_____
_____

TOUGH TIMES & LESSONS LEARNED: _____
_____
_____
_____
_____

What are you grateful for today?   Stressed Angry Tired Sad Happy Excited
_____

> REMEMBER! WAIT TO WRITE BELOW UNTIL THIS DAY NEXT YEAR!

DATE: _____ (S) (M) (T) (W) (T) (F) (S)

MEMORIES MADE: _____
_____
_____
_____
_____

TOUGH TIMES & LESSONS LEARNED: _____
_____
_____
_____
_____

What are you grateful for today?   Stressed Angry Tired Sad Happy Excited
_____

Did you know? Ever wondered how long it would take to fall to the Earth's core?
That dizzying drop would take about 19 minutes.

DATE: _____ (S) (M) (T) (W) (T) (F) (S)

TUESDAY TIPS:

> "The idea that "You are what you read" highlights how deeply books can influence us. When you're absorbed in a story, you might not only relate to the main character but also start mirroring their traits and behaviors. This connection shows the strong impact reading can have on our thoughts and actions. By exploring a variety of books, we expose ourselves to new perspectives and ideas, which can shape our understanding of the world and contribute to our personal development. Be wise in what you read!"

MEMORIES MADE: _____
_____
_____
_____
_____

TOUGH TIMES & LESSONS LEARNED: _____
_____
_____
_____
_____

What are you grateful for today?
_____

Stressed | Angry | Tired | Sad | Happy | Excited

REMEMBER! WAIT TO WRITE BELOW UNTIL THIS DAY NEXT YEAR!

DATE: _____ (S) (M) (T) (W) (T) (F) (S)

MEMORIES MADE: _____
_____
_____
_____
_____

TOUGH TIMES & LESSONS LEARNED: _____
_____
_____
_____
_____

What are you grateful for today?
_____

Stressed | Angry | Tired | Sad | Happy | Excited

Did you know? That funky symbol you use on social media? The hashtag (#) actually has a proper name - the octothorpe. Get it right, people! ;)

DATE: _____ (S) (M) (T) (W) (T) (F) (S)

WEDNESDAY (HUMP DAY!) HAPPY HACKS:

> Stop chasing happiness. Hopefully you have learned some things that bring you happiness, joy, and meaning. One mistake some people make is chasing or pursuing happiness as the end goal. There is a thrill that comes with a party, a kiss, or eating your favorite food. But continually chasing the next party or the next new phone won't last long. It turns out that how we pursue happiness makes a big difference. Some have compared pursuing or chasing happiness to trying to catch a butterfly with your hands. The harder we try to reach out and grasp it, the more likely it is to flutter away. In fact, some research shows that the more people try to be happy, the less happy they are. Instead of chasing happiness, lose yourself in kindness, gratitude and helping others and then pause for the feeling of peace and joy that often follows.

MEMORIES MADE: _____
_____
_____
_____
_____
_____

TOUGH TIMES & LESSONS LEARNED: _____
_____
_____
_____
_____

What are you grateful for today?
_____

Stressed Angry Tired Sad Happy Excited

REMEMBER! WAIT TO WRITE BELOW UNTIL THIS DAY NEXT YEAR!

DATE: _____ (S) (M) (T) (W) (T) (F) (S)

MEMORIES MADE: _____
_____
_____
_____
_____
_____

TOUGH TIMES & LESSONS LEARNED: _____
_____
_____
_____
_____

What are you grateful for today?
_____

Stressed Angry Tired Sad Happy Excited

Did you know? Those tiny pockets in your jeans? They weren't meant for loose change! Originally, they were designed to hold pocket watches.

DATE: _____ (S) (M) (T) (W) (T) (F) (S)

THURSDAY MYTHS:

> Myth: "I have to figure out everything by myself."
>
> Reality: Seeking advice from peers, mentors, or counselors is wise. They can offer valuable insights and guidance. It's like using a map - sometimes it's the best way to navigate new territory.

MEMORIES MADE: _____
_____
_____
_____
_____
_____

TOUGH TIMES & LESSONS LEARNED: _____
_____
_____
_____
_____

What are you grateful for today?
_____

Stressed | Angry | Tired | Sad | Happy | Excited

REMEMBER! WAIT TO WRITE BELOW UNTIL THIS DAY NEXT YEAR!

DATE: _____ (S) (M) (T) (W) (T) (F) (S)

MEMORIES MADE: _____
_____
_____
_____
_____
_____

TOUGH TIMES & LESSONS LEARNED: _____
_____
_____
_____
_____

What are you grateful for today?
_____

Stressed | Angry | Tired | Sad | Happy | Excited

Did you know? This might surprise you, but there's not a single number before 1,000 that contains the letter A!

DATE: _____ (S) (M) (T) (W) (T) (F) (S)

FRIDAY FILL IN THE BLANKS:

> " The most relaxing way I unwind from college stress is...
> _____
>
> and it helps me by...
> _____ "

MEMORIES MADE: _____
_____
_____
_____
_____

TOUGH TIMES & LESSONS LEARNED: _____
_____
_____
_____

What are you grateful for today?   Stressed Angry Tired Sad Happy Excited
_____

↙ REMEMBER! WAIT TO WRITE BELOW UNTIL THIS DAY NEXT YEAR!

DATE: _____ (S) (M) (T) (W) (T) (F) (S)

MEMORIES MADE: _____
_____
_____
_____
_____

TOUGH TIMES & LESSONS LEARNED: _____
_____
_____
_____

What are you grateful for today?   Stressed Angry Tired Sad Happy Excited
_____

The longest time someone has spent holding their breath underwater is 24 minutes and 37 seconds!
Please don't try to break this record! ;)

DATE: _____ (S) (M) (T) (W) (T) (F) (S)

SATURDAY TED TALKS:

> Forget dwelling on negativity! Martin Seligman, in his TED Talk, ushers in the era of positive psychology. Beyond fixing problems, it focuses on building strengths, happiness, and well-being. He highlights interventions like gratitude practices, savoring positive experiences, and fostering optimism. These approaches don't just feel good, they boost resilience, creativity, and even physical health. Remember, happiness isn't just a byproduct, it's a skill that can be nurtured. So, embrace the positive psychology movement and unlock your full potential!

MEMORIES MADE: _____
_____
_____
_____
_____
_____

TOUGH TIMES & LESSONS LEARNED: _____
_____
_____
_____
_____

What are you grateful for today?

Stressed | Angry | Tired | Sad | Happy | Excited

REMEMBER! WAIT TO WRITE BELOW UNTIL THIS DAY NEXT YEAR!

DATE: _____ (S) (M) (T) (W) (T) (F) (S)

MEMORIES MADE: _____
_____
_____
_____
_____
_____

TOUGH TIMES & LESSONS LEARNED: _____
_____
_____
_____
_____

What are you grateful for today?

Stressed | Angry | Tired | Sad | Happy | Excited

A chicken once lived for 18 months without its head. It's true! Google it! His name was Mike the headless chicken! A blood clot kept him from bleeding out!

DATE: _____ S M T W T F S

SUNDAY STRESS BUSTERS:

> Joining study groups can significantly ease academic pressures by providing a supportive learning environment where tasks are shared, making the workload more manageable. Working alongside peers allows for the exchange of ideas and strategies, fostering a collaborative spirit that can transform studying from a solitary chore into a more engaging and enjoyable activity. This sense of community not only aids in academic achievement but also reduces feelings of isolation, making the process less stressful and more productive.

MEMORIES MADE: _____
_____
_____
_____
_____

TOUGH TIMES & LESSONS LEARNED: _____
_____
_____
_____

What are you grateful for today?
_____

Stressed   Angry   Tired   Sad   Happy   Excited

REMEMBER! WAIT TO WRITE BELOW UNTIL THIS DAY NEXT YEAR!

DATE: _____ S M T W T F S

MEMORIES MADE: _____
_____
_____
_____
_____

TOUGH TIMES & LESSONS LEARNED: _____
_____
_____
_____

What are you grateful for today?
_____

Stressed   Angry   Tired   Sad   Happy   Excited

Did you know? Most of the facts in this journal are made up? Haha, just kidding. Most are verified true! Here's one for ya: Platypuses sweat milk. Fact or fiction?

SUDOKU CHALLENGE!

	4	
7		
1		

	2	
6		8
		4

8	6	5
7		2

	1	8
		5

7	4	
2		9
	8	6

6		
1	5	

9		1
8	7	3

5		
8		2
	6	

		6
		7
	2	

WORD SCRAMBLE! (COLLEGE EDITION)

1. PSCLHARSHIO _____
2. AANLFNIIC IDA _____
3. MRJAO _____
4. ENEDISRT ALHL _____
5. IBALYRR _____
6. EXBSKTOTO _____
7. PLAAITONCPI _____
8. DEEREG _____
9. ATPVRIE _____
10. AOBRCSLEH _____
11. MAESRTS _____
12. TACNPEEACC _____

DATE: _____ (S) (M) (T) (W) (T) (F) (S)

MONDAY MANNERS:

> "Be respectful of all questions. Never mock what people say with remarks like "You don't know that?" or "How can you not get it?" If someone asks, it means they genuinely want to know. Be kind and respond politely in a kind tone or listen patiently. People learn things at different rates; your prior knowledge doesn't mean others had the same chance. Let them learn without feeling foolish. Everyone faces moments of not knowing, so foster a respectful environment for all."

MEMORIES MADE: _____
_____
_____
_____
_____

TOUGH TIMES & LESSONS LEARNED: _____
_____
_____
_____

What are you grateful for today?
_____

Stressed | Angry | Tired | Sad | Happy | Excited

REMEMBER! WAIT TO WRITE BELOW UNTIL THIS DAY NEXT YEAR!

DATE: _____ (S) (M) (T) (W) (T) (F) (S)

MEMORIES MADE: _____
_____
_____
_____
_____

TOUGH TIMES & LESSONS LEARNED: _____
_____
_____
_____

What are you grateful for today?
_____

Stressed | Angry | Tired | Sad | Happy | Excited

Did you know? Your fingerprints are formed in the womb, and no two people (not even identical twins) have the same ones!

DATE: _____ (S) (M) (T) (W) (T) (F) (S)

TUESDAY TIPS:

> Avoid the path of least resistance. Courses are not just about doing well and getting good grades or finishing with a high GPA. It's not something you just get through, hoping to magically change by graduation. College is an awesome time for personal growth and development. Just doing the minimum is like having a fancy car without an engine; it might look good, but it's missing what really matters inside. Learn to love learning.

MEMORIES MADE: _____
_____
_____
_____
_____

TOUGH TIMES & LESSONS LEARNED: _____
_____
_____
_____
_____

What are you grateful for today? Stressed Angry Tired Sad Happy Excited
_____

REMEMBER! WAIT TO WRITE BELOW UNTIL THIS DAY NEXT YEAR!

DATE: _____ (S) (M) (T) (W) (T) (F) (S)

MEMORIES MADE: _____
_____
_____
_____
_____

TOUGH TIMES & LESSONS LEARNED: _____
_____
_____
_____
_____

What are you grateful for today? Stressed Angry Tired Sad Happy Excited
_____

Did you know? The human body constantly sheds skin cells! You lose about 30,000-40,000 dead skin cells every minute, which is why regularly washing and exfoliating is important.

DATE: _____ (S) (M) (T) (W) (T) (F) (S)

WEDNESDAY (HUMP DAY!) HAPPY HACKS:

> Search for meaning. Happiness and meaning are often related, but not always. Most mothers don't find pregnancy and giving birth a fun and enjoyable experience, but it can bring significant meaning. Same thing with a marathon runner or a cyclist or giving service – there may be bursts of happiness and joy along the way, but parts of the journey itself may not be enjoyable, but it can be meaningful. Some research suggests that happiness has more to do with having your needs satisfied, getting what you want, and feeling good, whereas meaning is more related to purpose, using our strengths, and turning outward and upward for a higher cause. What brings meaning in your life?

MEMORIES MADE: _____
_____
_____
_____
_____
_____

TOUGH TIMES & LESSONS LEARNED: _____
_____
_____
_____

What are you grateful for today?   Stressed Angry Tired Sad Happy Excited
_____

REMEMBER! WAIT TO WRITE BELOW UNTIL THIS DAY NEXT YEAR!

DATE: _____ (S) (M) (T) (W) (T) (F) (S)

MEMORIES MADE: _____
_____
_____
_____
_____
_____

TOUGH TIMES & LESSONS LEARNED: _____
_____
_____
_____

What are you grateful for today?   Stressed Angry Tired Sad Happy Excited
_____

Did you know? "Burn the midnight oil" stems from the time period before electricity when people used oil lamps for light. Working late into the night meant burning oil, hence "burning the midnight oil" to signify working late or hard.

DATE: _____ (S) (M) (T) (W) (T) (F) (S)

THURSDAY MYTHS:

> Myth: "If you go outside with wet hair on a cold day, you'll catch a cold."
>
> Reality: Colds are caused by viruses, which you can't get just from being outside in the cold. You may feel sick if you're outside all day in the cold or rain — runny nose, chills, fatigue — but it's not because of a virus. It's because you can experience the same symptoms when you are chilled as when you are sick.

MEMORIES MADE: _____
_____
_____
_____
_____
_____

TOUGH TIMES & LESSONS LEARNED: _____
_____
_____
_____
_____

What are you grateful for today?
_____

Stressed Angry Tired Sad Happy Excited

REMEMBER! WAIT TO WRITE BELOW UNTIL THIS DAY NEXT YEAR!

DATE: _____ (S) (M) (T) (W) (T) (F) (S)

MEMORIES MADE: _____
_____
_____
_____
_____
_____

TOUGH TIMES & LESSONS LEARNED: _____
_____
_____
_____
_____

What are you grateful for today?
_____

Stressed Angry Tired Sad Happy Excited

Did you know? The term "crocodile tears" comes from an ancient belief that crocodiles weep while consuming their prey, a notion that dates back to medieval times and was thought to imply insincerity in human emotions.

DATE: _____ S M T W T F S

FRIDAY FILL IN THE BLANKS:

" My favorite brand(s) of clothing is...
_____

and my favorite item(s) is...
_____ "

MEMORIES MADE: _____
_____
_____
_____
_____
_____

TOUGH TIMES & LESSONS LEARNED: _____
_____
_____
_____
_____

What are you grateful for today?   Stressed Angry Tired Sad Happy Excited
_____

REMEMBER! WAIT TO WRITE BELOW UNTIL THIS DAY NEXT YEAR!

DATE: _____ S M T W T F S

MEMORIES MADE: _____
_____
_____
_____
_____
_____

TOUGH TIMES & LESSONS LEARNED: _____
_____
_____
_____
_____

What are you grateful for today?   Stressed Angry Tired Sad Happy Excited
_____

Did you know? "Close but no cigar" is a phrase that originated from old fairground games in the US, where cigars were often prizes. Coming close to winning but not winning meant you didn't get the cigar.

DATE: _____ (S) (M) (T) (W) (T) (F) (S)

SATURDAY TED TALKS:

> Our minds naturally wander, impacting focus and well-being. But fear not! Amishi Jha, in her TED Talk, offers hope for taming your "wandering mind." Ditch brute force strategies like mental combat. Instead, cultivate "paying attention to your attention." Simple techniques like mindfulness practices, focusing on the present moment, and scheduling designated worry time help reign in wandering thoughts. Remember, taming your mind isn't about silencing it, but gently guiding it towards focus and present-moment awareness. Implement these strategies and reclaim your mental space for greater clarity and well-being!

MEMORIES MADE: _____
_____
_____
_____
_____
_____

TOUGH TIMES & LESSONS LEARNED: _____
_____
_____
_____
_____

What are you grateful for today?
_____

Stressed Angry Tired Sad Happy Excited

REMEMBER! WAIT TO WRITE BELOW UNTIL THIS DAY NEXT YEAR!

DATE: _____ (S) (M) (T) (W) (T) (F) (S)

MEMORIES MADE: _____
_____
_____
_____
_____
_____

TOUGH TIMES & LESSONS LEARNED: _____
_____
_____
_____
_____

What are you grateful for today?
_____

Stressed Angry Tired Sad Happy Excited

Did you know? "Saved by the bell" is popularly believed to be from an old custom of attaching bells to coffins to allow the "dead" to alert those above if they were still alive, there's no historical evidence to support this. The phrase more likely comes from boxing, where a boxer is saved from being counted out by the bell signaling the end of a round.

DATE: _____ (S) (M) (T) (W) (T) (F) (S)

SUNDAY STRESS BUSTERS:

> " Maintaining a positive outlook, especially during tough times, is crucial for emotional well-being and resilience. Striving to stay optimistic, even when faced with difficulties, can profoundly impact your ability to manage stress and navigate obstacles. Adopting a positive mindset not only aids in coping with immediate challenges but also transforms potential setbacks into valuable learning experiences and opportunities for personal growth, fostering an environment where obstacles are seen as stepping stones rather than roadblocks. "

MEMORIES MADE: _____
_____
_____
_____
_____
_____

TOUGH TIMES & LESSONS LEARNED: _____
_____
_____
_____
_____

What are you grateful for today?   Stressed Angry Tired Sad Happy Excited
_____

REMEMBER! WAIT TO WRITE BELOW UNTIL THIS DAY NEXT YEAR!

DATE: _____ (S) (M) (T) (W) (T) (F) (S)

MEMORIES MADE: _____
_____
_____
_____
_____
_____

TOUGH TIMES & LESSONS LEARNED: _____
_____
_____
_____
_____

What are you grateful for today?   Stressed Angry Tired Sad Happy Excited
_____

Did you know? The phrase "penny for your thoughts" dates back to the 16th century when a "penny" was a significant amount, suggesting that the speaker is willing to pay to know what someone is thinking.

DATE: _____ (S) (M) (T) (W) (T) (F) (S)

MONDAY MANNERS:

> Nail that first impression. Whether it's a job interview, meeting new friends, or greeting a blind date, your first impression matters. Nail a positive first impression by confidently introducing yourself. Shake hands firmly, smile, make eye contact, and introduce yourself. A strong initial impression is crucial for being taken seriously. Master the art of self-introduction with confidence, even if it feels awkward initially. This simple skill, perfected through practice, significantly impacts how others perceive you.

MEMORIES MADE: _____
_____
_____
_____
_____
_____

TOUGH TIMES & LESSONS LEARNED: _____
_____
_____
_____
_____

What are you grateful for today?   Stressed Angry Tired Sad Happy Excited
_____

REMEMBER! WAIT TO WRITE BELOW UNTIL THIS DAY NEXT YEAR!

DATE: _____ (S) (M) (T) (W) (T) (F) (S)

MEMORIES MADE: _____
_____
_____
_____
_____
_____

TOUGH TIMES & LESSONS LEARNED: _____
_____
_____
_____
_____

What are you grateful for today?   Stressed Angry Tired Sad Happy Excited
_____

Did you know? The adrenal glands change size throughout life; they are largest when we are infants and shrink as we age.

DATE: _____ (S) (M) (T) (W) (T) (F) (S)

TUESDAY TIPS:

> A previous thought discussed not needing a study-abroad experience. But some should consider studying abroad for a unique experience. While this isn't for everyone, we recommend you at least go explore the options out there. Chances are you likely won't have these types of opportunities to study and learn in other countries and cultures. And for bonus points, talk to some students who have studied abroad and you'll think twice about packing your bags for a crazy awesome adventure. Seriously!

MEMORIES MADE: _____
_____
_____
_____
_____
_____

TOUGH TIMES & LESSONS LEARNED: _____
_____
_____
_____
_____

What are you grateful for today?
_____

Stressed | Angry | Tired | Sad | Happy | Excited

REMEMBER! WAIT TO WRITE BELOW UNTIL THIS DAY NEXT YEAR!

DATE: _____ (S) (M) (T) (W) (T) (F) (S)

MEMORIES MADE: _____
_____
_____
_____
_____
_____

TOUGH TIMES & LESSONS LEARNED: _____
_____
_____
_____
_____

What are you grateful for today?
_____

Stressed | Angry | Tired | Sad | Happy | Excited

Did you know? Stretching before bed can improve sleep quality by relaxing muscles and relieving tension, making it a beneficial routine for better sleep.

DATE: _____ (S) (M) (T) (W) (T) (F) (S)

WEDNESDAY (HUMP DAY!) HAPPY HACKS

> " When things don't go your way, don't act like a child. Unhelpful responses to stress and struggles in life include turning to responses and reactions we had as young children. They includes words that start with the letters A, B, C, D, and E. Under stress, the "child brain" resorts to Avoiding, Blaming, Criticizing and Complaining, Defending and Demanding, and making Excuses. Catch yourself if you fall back into managing stress with any of these childish behaviors. Catch it. Check it. Change it with better choices. "

MEMORIES MADE: _____
_____
_____
_____
_____

TOUGH TIMES & LESSONS LEARNED: _____
_____
_____
_____
_____

What are you grateful for today?

Stressed | Angry | Tired | Sad | Happy | Excited

REMEMBER! WAIT TO WRITE BELOW UNTIL THIS DAY NEXT YEAR!

DATE: _____ (S) (M) (T) (W) (T) (F) (S)

MEMORIES MADE: _____
_____
_____
_____
_____

TOUGH TIMES & LESSONS LEARNED: _____
_____
_____
_____
_____

What are you grateful for today?

Stressed | Angry | Tired | Sad | Happy | Excited

Did you know? Your body produces about 2 million red blood cells every second to replace the ones lost.

DATE: _____ (S) (M) (T) (W) (T) (F) (S)

THURSDAY MYTHS:

> Myth: "The friends I make in the first year will be my friends throughout college."
>
> Reality: Friendships evolve. The friends you make in your first year might not be the same ones you graduate with, and that's okay. It's a journey, and people come and go, adding to your experience.

MEMORIES MADE: _____
_____
_____
_____
_____
_____

TOUGH TIMES & LESSONS LEARNED: _____
_____
_____
_____

What are you grateful for today?   Stressed   Angry   Tired   Sad   Happy   Excited
_____

REMEMBER! WAIT TO WRITE BELOW UNTIL THIS DAY NEXT YEAR!

DATE: _____ (S) (M) (T) (W) (T) (F) (S)

MEMORIES MADE: _____
_____
_____
_____
_____
_____

TOUGH TIMES & LESSONS LEARNED: _____
_____
_____
_____

What are you grateful for today?   Stressed   Angry   Tired   Sad   Happy   Excited
_____

Did you know? Random acts of kindness, such as helping a classmate or volunteering, not only benefit others but also increase your own happiness and life satisfaction.

DATE: _____ (S) (M) (T) (W) (T) (F) (S)

FRIDAY FILL IN THE BLANKS:

> "The most memorable vacation I took was to...
> _____
>
> and the best part was...
> _____"

MEMORIES MADE: _____
_____
_____
_____
_____

TOUGH TIMES & LESSONS LEARNED: _____
_____
_____
_____
_____

What are you grateful for today?   (>_<) (>_<) (zzz) (:-() (:-)) (;-))
_____   Stressed Angry Tired Sad Happy Excited

⬇ REMEMBER! WAIT TO WRITE BELOW UNTIL THIS DAY NEXT YEAR!

DATE: _____ (S) (M) (T) (W) (T) (F) (S)

MEMORIES MADE: _____
_____
_____
_____
_____

TOUGH TIMES & LESSONS LEARNED: _____
_____
_____
_____
_____

What are you grateful for today?   (>_<) (>_<) (zzz) (:-() (:-)) (;-))
_____   Stressed Angry Tired Sad Happy Excited

Did you know? A human's little finger (pinky) contributes over 50% of the hand's strength, emphasizing its importance despite its size.

DATE: _____ (S) (M) (T) (W) (T) (F) (S)

SATURDAY TED TALKS:

> Forget chasing external factors for happiness! Cognitive researcher Nancy Etcoff, in her TED Talk, reveals surprising truths. Happiness, she argues, isn't just about achieving goals or having good circumstances. It's also influenced by internal factors like smiling (which actually impacts your brain chemistry) and positive thinking, which can be trained. So, ditch the chase, embrace genuine smiles, and cultivate a hopeful outlook. The key to happiness may lie within your own mind and body!

MEMORIES MADE: _____
_____
_____
_____
_____

TOUGH TIMES & LESSONS LEARNED: _____
_____
_____
_____

What are you grateful for today?

Stressed | Angry | Tired | Sad | Happy | Excited

REMEMBER! WAIT TO WRITE BELOW UNTIL THIS DAY NEXT YEAR!

DATE: _____ (S) (M) (T) (W) (T) (F) (S)

MEMORIES MADE: _____
_____
_____
_____
_____

TOUGH TIMES & LESSONS LEARNED: _____
_____
_____
_____

What are you grateful for today?

Stressed | Angry | Tired | Sad | Happy | Excited

Did you know? Taking a warm bath with essential oils like lavender or chamomile can be a relaxing and rejuvenating self-care ritual. Soak away your worries!

DATE: _____ (S) (M) (T) (W) (T) (F) (S)

SUNDAY STRESS BUSTERS:

> Doing things you love, like hobbies or fun activities, is a great way to relax and take your mind off stress. It could be anything you enjoy, like painting, playing a sport, or any other hobby. These activities give you a nice break from schoolwork and help you feel happier and less stressed. Spending time on your hobbies isn't just fun; it's also really good for your health and happiness. It's like giving your brain a mini-vacation from all the hard work.

MEMORIES MADE: _____
_____
_____
_____
_____
_____

TOUGH TIMES & LESSONS LEARNED: _____
_____
_____
_____
_____

What are you grateful for today?   Stressed Angry Tired Sad Happy Excited
_____

REMEMBER! WAIT TO WRITE BELOW UNTIL THIS DAY NEXT YEAR!

DATE: _____ (S) (M) (T) (W) (T) (F) (S)

MEMORIES MADE: _____
_____
_____
_____
_____
_____
_____

TOUGH TIMES & LESSONS LEARNED: _____
_____
_____
_____
_____

What are you grateful for today?   Stressed Angry Tired Sad Happy Excited
_____

Did you know? Cramming for exams is actually counterproductive! Spacing out your studying and getting enough sleep enhances memory retention and cognitive performance.
Prioritize quality over quantity.

DATE: _____ (S) (M) (T) (W) (T) (F) (S)

MONDAY MANNERS:

> Say it with confidence. When talking with others, be sure to use basic communication manners such as looking people in the eye, talking clearly and loudly enough for people to hear and understand. This is especially true if you make a comment, or you are called on in a class. Speak up and make eye contact. The same tips hold true in loud or distracting environments. If someone asks you to repeat something, don't roll your eyes and get annoyed. Just repeat what you said a bit louder and more clearly.

MEMORIES MADE: _____
_____
_____
_____
_____

TOUGH TIMES & LESSONS LEARNED: _____
_____
_____
_____

What are you grateful for today?   Stressed Angry Tired Sad Happy Excited
_____

REMEMBER! WAIT TO WRITE BELOW UNTIL THIS DAY NEXT YEAR!

DATE: _____ (S) (M) (T) (W) (T) (F) (S)

MEMORIES MADE: _____
_____
_____
_____
_____

TOUGH TIMES & LESSONS LEARNED: _____
_____
_____
_____

What are you grateful for today?   Stressed Angry Tired Sad Happy Excited
_____

Did you know? Your heart beats over 3 billion times in your lifetime - that's enough to fill an Olympic-sized swimming pool with blood! Keep that ticker pumping!

DATE: _____ (S) (M) (T) (W) (T) (F) (S)

TUESDAY TIPS:

> "Practice good online safety and privacy habits. Okay, you might be thinking, "duh, I get it. I'm not dumb." But college-age students are prime candidates for online scams and credit card companies. Be smart online. Especially with dating apps. Make sure your location is not available and be slow to give out your cell or email. Make sure your trust is slowly earned and be extra cautious out there!"

MEMORIES MADE: _____
_____
_____
_____
_____
_____

TOUGH TIMES & LESSONS LEARNED: _____
_____
_____
_____
_____

What are you grateful for today?   Stressed Angry Tired Sad Happy Excited
_____

REMEMBER! WAIT TO WRITE BELOW UNTIL THIS DAY NEXT YEAR!

DATE: _____ (S) (M) (T) (W) (T) (F) (S)

MEMORIES MADE: _____
_____
_____
_____
_____
_____

TOUGH TIMES & LESSONS LEARNED: _____
_____
_____
_____
_____

What are you grateful for today?   Stressed Angry Tired Sad Happy Excited
_____

Did you know? Human lips have a reddish color due to the high concentration of tiny capillaries just below the skin. Pucker up!

DATE: _____ Ⓢ Ⓜ Ⓣ Ⓦ Ⓣ Ⓕ Ⓢ

WEDNESDAY (HUMP DAY!) HAPPY HACKS:

> Try smiling more. Some call it the 10:5 rule. When you are 10 feet from another person, smile. When you are within 5 feet of each other, greet the person with a "hello" and ask how they are doing. It's simple (notice simple and smile have most of the same letters? Cool huh?) and it's powerful. Just don't give people the creepy smile. Nobody likes a creeper. ;)

MEMORIES MADE: _____
_____
_____
_____
_____
_____

TOUGH TIMES & LESSONS LEARNED: _____
_____
_____
_____
_____

What are you grateful for today?   Stressed Angry Tired Sad Happy Excited
_____

REMEMBER! WAIT TO WRITE BELOW UNTIL THIS DAY NEXT YEAR!

DATE: _____ Ⓢ Ⓜ Ⓣ Ⓦ Ⓣ Ⓕ Ⓢ

MEMORIES MADE: _____
_____
_____
_____
_____
_____

TOUGH TIMES & LESSONS LEARNED: _____
_____
_____
_____
_____

What are you grateful for today?   Stressed Angry Tired Sad Happy Excited
_____

Did you know? Regular physical activity greatly reduces the risk of developing type 2 diabetes, emphasizing the importance of exercise in maintaining overall health.

DATE: _____ (S) (M) (T) (W) (T) (F) (S)

THURSDAY MYTHS:

> Myth: "All-nighters are an effective way to get work done."
>
> Reality: Regular sleep is crucial for academic performance and health. All-nighters can disrupt your sleep pattern and negatively affect your cognitive abilities. It's like running a marathon on no sleep — not the best strategy for success.

MEMORIES MADE: _____
_____
_____
_____
_____
_____

TOUGH TIMES & LESSONS LEARNED: _____
_____
_____
_____
_____

What are you grateful for today?   Stressed Angry Tired Sad Happy Excited
_____

REMEMBER! WAIT TO WRITE BELOW UNTIL THIS DAY NEXT YEAR!

DATE: _____ (S) (M) (T) (W) (T) (F) (S)

MEMORIES MADE: _____
_____
_____
_____
_____
_____

TOUGH TIMES & LESSONS LEARNED: _____
_____
_____
_____
_____

What are you grateful for today?   Stressed Angry Tired Sad Happy Excited
_____

Did you know? Limiting sugary drinks and processed foods not only helps with weight management but also reduces inflammation and improves overall health. Ditch the sugar for a brighter future!

DATE: _____   (S) (M) (T) (W) (T) (F) (S)

FRIDAY FILL IN THE BLANKS:

" I can't start my day without...
_____

it's essential because...
_____ "

MEMORIES MADE: _____
_____
_____
_____
_____
_____

TOUGH TIMES & LESSONS LEARNED: _____
_____
_____
_____
_____

What are you grateful for today?   Stressed Angry Tired Sad Happy Excited
_____

> REMEMBER! WAIT TO WRITE BELOW UNTIL THIS DAY NEXT YEAR!

DATE: _____   (S) (M) (T) (W) (T) (F) (S)

MEMORIES MADE: _____
_____
_____
_____
_____
_____

TOUGH TIMES & LESSONS LEARNED: _____
_____
_____
_____
_____

What are you grateful for today?   Stressed Angry Tired Sad Happy Excited
_____

Did you know? Creating a budget and tracking your spending empowers you to make informed financial decisions and reach your financial goals. Take control of your finances!

DATE: _____ (S) (M) (T) (W) (T) (F) (S)

SATURDAY TED TALKS:

> In his TED talk "How to Break Bad Habits," Judson Brewer discusses a simple method for breaking bad habits: mindfulness. He explains that being curious about the feelings and sensations we experience when we're craving can help us step back and understand our habits better. This awareness allows us to break the cycle of behavior by becoming less interested in the habit and its supposed rewards. Brewer emphasizes that by paying attention to our actions and learning to ride out the urge without reacting, we can replace old habits with new, more positive ones.

MEMORIES MADE: _____
_____
_____
_____
_____

TOUGH TIMES & LESSONS LEARNED: _____
_____
_____
_____
_____

What are you grateful for today?

Stressed · Angry · Tired · Sad · Happy · Excited

REMEMBER! WAIT TO WRITE BELOW UNTIL THIS DAY NEXT YEAR!

DATE: _____ (S) (M) (T) (W) (T) (F) (S)

MEMORIES MADE: _____
_____
_____
_____
_____

TOUGH TIMES & LESSONS LEARNED: _____
_____
_____
_____
_____

What are you grateful for today?

Stressed · Angry · Tired · Sad · Happy · Excited

Did you know? Taking breaks and engaging in mindfulness meditation can improve focus, reduce stress, and enhance overall learning. Breathe your way to better grades!

DATE: _____ (S) (M) (T) (W) (T) (F) (S)

SUNDAY STRESS BUSTERS:

> Keeping a social life is key, even when school gets busy. Hanging out with friends, going to events, or joining clubs can help you relax and have fun. It's good to mix studying with meeting people and doing things you enjoy. This balance keeps you happy and helps you handle stress better. Making time for friends and fun activities makes your school life more enjoyable and can even help you do better in your studies by keeping you refreshed.

MEMORIES MADE: _____
_____
_____
_____
_____

TOUGH TIMES & LESSONS LEARNED: _____
_____
_____
_____

What are you grateful for today?
_____

Stressed | Angry | Tired | Sad | Happy | Excited

REMEMBER! WAIT TO WRITE BELOW UNTIL THIS DAY NEXT YEAR!

DATE: _____ (S) (M) (T) (W) (T) (F) (S)

MEMORIES MADE: _____
_____
_____
_____
_____

TOUGH TIMES & LESSONS LEARNED: _____
_____
_____
_____

What are you grateful for today?
_____

Stressed | Angry | Tired | Sad | Happy | Excited

Did you know? The human brain can process information in as little as 13 milliseconds!
We're lightning-fast thought machines.

DATE: _____ (S) (M) (T) (W) (T) (F) (S)

EXTRA PAGES FOR WHEN YOU NEED A LITTLE MORE ROOM TO WRITE!

What are you grateful for today?

_____

Stressed Angry Tired Sad Happy Excited

Embrace new experiences for growth. YOLO! (you only live once). As a college student, it's prime time to try different things (but use your noggin and be safe!!), discover talents, and explore interests. Accept being a beginner and learn from the experience. You have ample time to practice new pursuits. Embrace mistakes as crucial for growth. Don't feel pressured to have all your interests, goals, and even your major sorted out. Find what you love through experience, so be brave and try new things. Set a goal to attempt something new this year— you might discover a passion!

DATE: _____ (S) (M) (T) (W) (T) (F) (S)

EXTRA PAGES FOR WHEN YOU NEED A LITTLE MORE ROOM TO WRITE!

What are you grateful for today?

_____

Stressed Angry Tired Sad Happy Excited

Celebrate others' successes genuinely. When something good happens to someone, share in their joy without downplaying it or attributing it to luck. Avoid comparing or feeling entitled. Let them shine and relish the moment. Emotional maturity involves being genuinely happy for others. Instead of being jealous, turn it into admiration and motivation. Choosing to be happy for others, especially early in life, sets you ahead. Celebrating their victories can bring you joy and demonstrates internal confidence, which is attractive! If envy arises, use it as a signal to focus on your own ambitions.

DATE: _____ (S) (M) (T) (W) (T) (F) (S)

EXTRA PAGES FOR WHEN YOU NEED A LITTLE MORE ROOM TO WRITE!

What are you grateful for today?

Stressed | Angry | Tired | Sad | Happy | Excited

Practice mindfulness. Mindfulness means paying attention to what's happening right now, including your thoughts, feelings, and what's around you, without judging anything. It's connected to happiness because it lowers stress and worry. When you focus on the present, you don't get stuck thinking about past problems or future fears. Mindfulness helps you enjoy small things more and makes you feel better about life. It also helps you deal with tough emotions more easily. Doing mindfulness activities like meditation or just paying attention while walking on campus can make you more positive and happier overall.

DATE: _____ (S) (M) (T) (W) (T) (F) (S)

EXTRA PAGES FOR WHEN YOU NEED A LITTLE MORE ROOM TO WRITE!

_____
_____
_____
_____
_____
_____
_____
_____
_____
_____
_____
_____
_____
_____
_____
_____
_____
_____
_____
_____
_____
_____
_____
_____
_____
_____
_____
_____
_____
_____
_____
_____
_____
_____
_____
_____
_____
_____
_____
_____
_____
_____

What are you grateful for today?   Stressed Angry Tired Sad Happy Excited
_____

Make sure you're doing your laundry regularly ;) Don't let your clothes pile up in big heaps and then take up the washer and dryer for the day. And get those clothes dried soon to prevent mildew and stink! If you forget, add a bit of vinegar or baking soda to the load and rewash it all before drying. Don't overlook washing sheets and pillowcases to prevent skin issues—and it's gross. Clean clothes and sheets are crucial for better hygiene habits now and in the future. These regular routines will lead to better lifelong habits.

DATE: _____ S M T W T F S

EXTRA PAGES FOR WHEN YOU NEED A LITTLE MORE ROOM TO WRITE!

_____

What are you grateful for today?   Stressed   Angry   Tired   Sad   Happy   Excited
_____

Be aware of the vibe in the room. When in a group, consider the current situation and the feelings of those present. For example, avoid discussing a fun upcoming trip knowing you're your friend wasn't invited. Read the room by recognizing emotions—don't bring up that you just aced a test when your roommate bombed a paper. Before speaking, think about how your words will sound and be received. Practice this awareness, and it will improve. You're more likely to make and keep friends as you master this skill!

DATE: _____ (S) (M) (T) (W) (T) (F) (S)

EXTRA PAGES FOR WHEN YOU NEED A LITTLE MORE ROOM TO WRITE!

What are you grateful for today?

Stressed Angry Tired Sad Happy Excited

Practice bathroom etiquette. Respect others by considering those nearby or who will use the bathroom later—especially if you have roommates and share the bathroom! Use the fan, wipe the seat, close the lid, flush, and wash and dry your hands before leaving. Also, wipe down the sink, spray air freshener if available, and inform someone if supplies are low. Everyone uses a toilet, but maintaining cleanliness and courtesy is crucial. Good bathroom manners matter, especially in others' apartments and living spaces!

Made in United States
Troutdale, OR
05/30/2024